IN
PURSUIT
OF
DISOBEDIENT
WOMEN

IN PURSUIT OF DISOBEDIENT WOMEN

A Memoir of Love, Rebellion, and Family, Far Away

DIONNE SEARCEY

BALLANTINE BOOKS
NEW YORK

Published in the United States by Ballantine Books,
an imprint of Random House, a division of
Penguin Random House LLC, New York.

BALLANTINE and the HOUSE colophon are registered trademarks
of Penguin Random House LLC.

Hardback ISBN 9780399179853
Ebook ISBN 9780399179860

Printed in Canada on acid-free paper

randomhousebooks.com

9 8 7 6 5 4 3 2 1

First Edition

Book design by Diane Hobbing

For Todd, Luther, Zola and Maude

And for Shehu. Na gode.

CONTENTS

AUTHOR'S NOTE

Much of the dialogue and descriptions in this book come straight from my notebook. Some of it was reconstructed to the best of my recollection. Memories are not perfect but I have tried to remain as true to incidents as possible. A few events are presented out of chronological order. In a very few places, names were changed.

WEST AND CENTRAL AFRICA

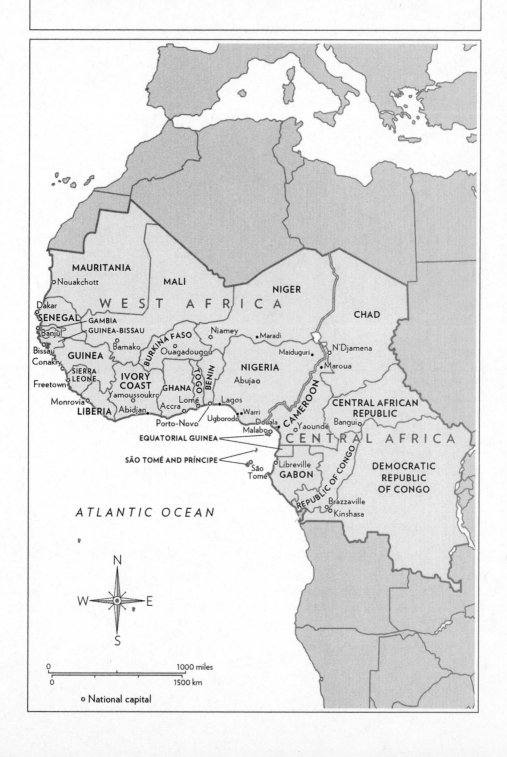

MAURITANIA

Nouakchott

MALI

NIGER

CHAD

W E S T   A F R I C A

Dakar
SENEGAL
GAMBIA
Banjul
GUINEA-BISSAU
Bissau
GUINEA
Conakry
SIERRA
LEONE
Freetown
Monrovia
LIBERIA

Bamako
BURKINA FASO
Ouagadougou
IVORY
COAST
Yamoussoukro
Abidjan

Niamey
Maradi

Maiduguri
N'Djamena

NIGERIA
Abuja
Maroua

GHANA
TOGO
BENIN
Lomé
Accra
Lagos
Warri
Porto-Novo
Ugborodo
Douala
Malabo

CAMEROON
Yaoundé
Bangui

CENTRAL AFRICAN
REPUBLIC

EQUATORIAL GUINEA

SÃO TOMÉ AND PRÍNCIPE

São
Tomé
Libreville
GABON
REPUBLIC OF CONGO
Brazzaville
Kinshasa

C E N T R A L   A F R I C A

DEMOCRATIC
REPUBLIC
OF CONGO

ATLANTIC OCEAN

N
W   E
S

0   1000 miles
0   1500 km

◦ National capital

IN
PURSUIT
OF
DISOBEDIENT
WOMEN

PROLOGUE

THE HOTEL LOOKED like all the other big hotels around here. It was trying hard to be five-star but was no match for the elements. One too many rainy seasons had dulled and dented its mirrored exterior. The heat seeped in from outside, overwhelming the airconditioning. The lobby's mahogany-looking floors were actually cheap linoleum that had buckled in the humidity. Mold crept along the edges of the walls.

It was early 2016, but the music blaring out of the speakers was a mix of Elton John and Billy Joel and Sting, an easy-listening soundtrack apparently meant to soothe the harsh realities behind the lobby's glass doors.

I had been living in the region for only a few weeks when I shipped out for one of my first assignments as West Africa bureau chief for *The New York Times.*

Fifteen hours of airplane and car rides later, I arrived in the muggy southern tip of Nigeria, deep in the country's oil-rich Niger Delta, tucked right in the geographic middle of the continent's armpit.

My plan was to talk to residents about the damage a group of militants had done as they blew up oil pipelines in a country that relied on oil proceeds to pay for almost everything in its budget.

I was waiting to see Peter, a local journalist who was my "fixer"—the savvy, street smart, on-the-ground operator who arranges interviews and guides international reporters through and, importantly, out of unfamiliar areas.

In his prime Peter had led other reporters across some of Nigeria's roughest spots. Now he was almost 60 and nearing the end of his journalism career. He wore striped golf shirts that didn't quite cover his potbelly. His thick, black-rimmed glasses magnified his eyes. The first time I worked with him, he had to be roused from his bed half drunk and nearly missed an assignment. New to the job, I didn't know anyone else more qualified. I hired him to take me to the Delta.

The Niger Delta is a dangerous corner of the world in a dangerous corner of the world, where militants were making a sport of taking foreigners for ransom. I didn't want to be one of those people who worried about getting kidnapped just because they wandered into new places without understanding them. But around here, that fear seemed legitimate. The local papers were reporting new kidnappings every month.

Peter might have caved to the occasional bender but he knew the region well. I was pretty certain he wasn't going to get me kidnapped—at least not intentionally.

In the city of Warri at the hotel check-in desk, foreign refinery workers from Chevron, Shell and other big oil companies were checking out. Their lives were calculated to be at risk and their corporate overlords were bringing them home.

The people blowing up the oil pipelines were the newest generation of militants who in the past decade had been prowling the Delta's web of mangrove-lined creeks armed with dynamite. The government for years had honored a deal that paid them to stop, but a new president was threatening to cut off the payments. Attacks were ramping up.

Before I could even set down my bags in my hotel room, Peter called my cell.

"There's someone here to meet us," he said. "Come to the lobby."

I didn't realize we had a "meeting" scheduled. I grabbed my notebook and rushed to the lobby, where a Celine Dion song was blaring from the speakers now. I spotted Peter and another round-bellied man wearing a beret, who motioned for me to sit down in a corner near the bar. Peter introduced us.

The man, Victor, was from a place called Ugborodo, one of the communities deep in the Delta's miles of skinny, vein-like waterways that curl around specks of islands before spilling into the Atlantic. Ugborodo was across the water from a giant, gleaming Chevron natural gas terminal—a miles-long space station monstrosity that was itself a modern city, complete with its own air-conditioned apartments and airstrip.

Victor began telling me of his village's misery. Their biggest concern wasn't the terrorists. Years of careless oil company drilling and transport had time and again spilled Exxon Valdez–sized amounts of oil into the water. No one properly cleaned it up. People were so poor they were forced to dine on the fish they pulled from polluted swamps. Most everyone in his community was unemployed, yet the oil and gas companies imported workers from abroad. Those corporations were earning billions at the expense of Victor's people. They lived in tin shacks with no electricity and shared a single, shabby outhouse propped up in the middle of a murky lagoon.

This is going to be an important story, I thought. Maybe Peter wasn't so bad after all.

The lobby music was overpowering the conversation. I leaned closer to catch each of Victor's eloquent, pained words, trying to ignore the Sting song now blaring in my ear.

"The president can't turn his back on the Niger Delta. This region lays the golden egg for the rest of the country."

You could say I lost my faith in the people on TV, Sting sang.

"Our land is polluted. Agriculture no longer thrives," Victor said.

You could say I'd lost my belief in our politicians, they all seemed like game show hosts to me, Sting wailed.

I turned around to look for a bartender to lower the volume of the stupid music.

"Dionne!" Peter shouted. Probably for the third time.

I snapped my head toward him. A dozen men in grubby jeans and tight T-shirts were standing in front of me.

The man closest to me was dressed in all black, tall and bald with mirrored sunglasses dangling from his collar. His biceps bulged out of his T-shirt. He wasn't smiling.

My mind raced. Peter had sold me out. These were the kidnappers I had been hearing about.

But before I could really worry, my phone beeped with a calendar alert I had set for myself a few weeks back. Out of instinct, I looked down.

"Kids need to wear green to school today for Earth Day celebration."

I swiped away the alert, along with the notion that my husband would ever remember to dress the kids in green to save the planet—let alone remember, while I was being held for the next few months in a damp, dark kidnappers' hideout, which of our kids hates watermelon-flavored anything, which one likes to go to bed with the hallway light on and which one needs her stuffed tiger to fall asleep.

I looked up at Peter. He looked at me. I did the only thing I could think to do. I stood and introduced myself. And one by one, the men all shook my hand.

They were Victor's friends. And they were here to talk, not kidnap me.

But they were, in fact, terrorists. Or at least they used to be until a couple years ago when they struck an amnesty deal with the government to lay down their explosives in exchange for cash. Their own pipeline-busting days were behind them, they assured me.

I spent the next few hours talking with them about explosives, best practices for backyard oil refining and the topic they were most interested in, the bombastic and unlikely candidate for American president back then, Donald Trump.

The men laid out the case for how jilted their region had been, not just by the oil companies but by their own government. Leaders for years had skimmed oil revenues to buy armored Hummers and opulent mega-mansions in the capital city while everyone in the Delta lived in sweltering, small metal shacks on islands where oil flares glared on the horizon, as though they were blowing a fiery raspberry at their misery.

To tell their story, I knew I had to see the community they were describing.

"Can you take me there tomorrow morning?" I asked.

"Yes," answered an enthusiastic Victor. "But it's a three-hour ride through the creeks in a small speedboat."

That's a long time to spend out in the remote, oil-soaked mangroves with a group of ex-militants when other not-so-ex militants are roaming around. Especially for an American journalist who might as well have dollar bills stapled to her forehead.

Victor must have read my mind. "We know the area. It will be safe," he assured me. I believed him.

But Mike, the guy in the sunglasses, was agitated, waving his arms and mumbling something to the others, who were getting just as squirmy.

"It's *OK*," I said, reassuring him that I wasn't worried about my safety. "I believe Victor, and I trust you guys. It'll be fine." Did they think I was chicken? I knew this job required more guts than shouting questions at a press conference.

"It's not you we're worried about," Mike said.

They were afraid that if the military spotted them out in the middle of nowhere with a foreigner, let alone a foreign woman, soldiers would assume I was a hostage. They'd be arrested, accused of kidnapping me, and were quite certain no one would believe anything to the contrary.

So I spent the next half hour convincing this band of retired terrorists that *I* was safe to hang with. We eventually came up with a plan we were confident would keep everyone out of trouble.

The next morning I put on my long-sleeved shirt, a pair of jeans that covered my ankles, leather boots, and I headed to the lobby. I had decided this would be my standard mosquito-repelling, non-offending work outfit in a region rife with malaria and conservative Christians and Muslims. Nigeria's Delta wasn't known for being uptight, but we were heading far, far away from any major anything, and my years of reporting had taught me that offending the locals isn't the best way to get them to open up. Like when I showed up at a mosque without a headscarf and the imam refused to talk to me until I wrapped my Banana Republic cardigan around my head.

When I arrived at the lobby the young American photographer the *Times* had assigned to me was already there, dressed in a strappy black tank top, Lululemon capri pants and a wispy scarf around her neck. I looked like a hillbilly lumberjack in comparison.

I started to scold her for her choice of outfit but heard myself sounding like a mom. So I stopped. I needed to get used to working with millennials. Most every foreign journalist I had met so far seemed to be a decade or two younger than me.

"Why did you wait until now to take a job like this?" she and all the others had wanted to know.

"Midlife crisis," I always told them.

As we arrived at the dock I thought about the truth. I had dreamed of reporting abroad when I was younger. But I always had been either too inexperienced for a newspaper to consider sending me to a far-flung posting or lacked the confidence to know how to convince the editors otherwise. I could have winged it as a freelancer but I didn't have a trust fund to support my career. I was worried about going overseas on my own without the financial backing of a company that paid for everything from plane tickets to ballpoint pens. Then, once I had built the confidence and experience, newspapers were losing money and cutting back on international coverage. Anyhow, by then I was in a relationship, then I had kids, and then—

The twin-engine motorboat pulled up outside the closest thing the city of Warri had to a yacht club, an old concrete building with floors that in some spots were just rubble and walls where curls of faded blue paint hung in patches. A worker emerged to unlock a rusty chain-link gate, allowing us to walk out on the dock of rotting planks. We carefully stepped down a slippery set of moss-covered stairs to the speedboat.

Amid a cloud of blue engine smoke, we were off. Soon the port of Warri, once a base for the booming slave trade, disappeared and gave way to a swampy wilderness.

The boat weaved in and out of the network of creeks, cutting through oily rainbows that stretched along the surface of the water. The channels were lined by one of the most extensive mangrove forests in West Africa. The roots, coated in spilled crude, looked as if they'd been dipped in chocolate.

We sped by a massive oil tank farm and row after row of storage tanks. Giant barges floated next to wooden canoes piloted by little kids using their hands to dip fishing lines into the water.

Hours later we arrived at Ugborodo, Victor's hometown. The narrow island community was just one of the dozens of small towns floating in an area that had become a giant oil refinery cesspool; the gas flares and shimmering terminals towering in the distance were like Oz set against the thicket of mangroves and zinc shacks.

It was late morning when the boat docked in Ugborodo but already the place was rocking. Loud music was playing from a ramshackle bar next to where we docked. The bars here had a reputation for hosting oil workers who only bother to make it across the narrow creek to visit the prostitutes hanging out there. Being a hooker was one of the best jobs in town.

Victor guided us through the narrow island community, which couldn't have been more than three or four miles long. It was crisscrossed by pipelines, which every few hundred feet jutted out of swamps like the neck of the Loch Ness monster. We walked by stacks of decaying, empty oil barrels used to collect rainwater and a table where an old woman was hawking a couple dozen spears of okra and a handful of tomatoes. Weeds poked around a heap of rolled-up construction material that had been delivered to stop the massive shore erosion that the residents blamed on oil company activity. No one had ever returned to install it. In the meantime, Ugborodo was sinking.

I stood on the town's lone paved road, which bisected the island. Rain began to fall, plopping into the inky swamps. Homes and shops were nothing more than tacked together rusty sheets of metal. Trash was piled everywhere. People huddled under awnings along the road for shelter.

I needed to start filling my notebook. It wasn't hard. With my freckles and reddish hair, I was an obvious outsider. To them I must have looked like a modern-day Lucille Ball with more unruly curls. I walked along and people came from their houses to check me out. As soon as they learned I was a journalist, the stories flowed. They were eager to tell me how the government, as part of its amnesty program, had trained them in engineering and pipefitting. But the oil companies would hire them only for temporary work, a few weeks at a time. And lately even that had dried up.

The rain started coming down harder. As I made my way to the middle of the long, narrow island I came to a large concrete home, gleaming white with a pointy tiled roof. The blue glass windows, tinted to keep out the sun, were framed in baby blue paint. An ornate silver railing twisted along the front porch, which was made of swirly brown-and-white marble. A dark green Jaguar was parked in front.

Victor walked on ahead as I stood with my mouth open, looking at the home, a stunning monument to luxury alongside the surrounding shacks. How did that car even get on the island? Through the sheets of rain I saw a group of people approaching.

They came into focus: a swaggering young man under a flowery umbrella that was being carried for him by a teenager who was trotting alongside him, getting soaked. Several other young men trailed them.

The guy staying dry was the owner of the home, the de facto mayor of Ugborodo. The others were his entourage. Victor had told me the government distributes its payments first to community leaders just like this owner, local bosses who keep a tight grip over their turf in exchange for a big cut of the money before it's paid out to the militants. None of it trickles down to the community.

"How can you live like this when everyone else is so poor here?" I asked, loud enough so his umbrella holder, and the rest of my group could hear.

He smirked. So did the other young men.

"Doesn't it bother you that you're living like this when these people have nothing?"

More smirking.

"Where did you get the money to buy this house?"

He muttered something about his family being involved in a successful international business and walked onto his porch, where more groupies awaited.

I turned to a member of his entourage hanging back in the road.

"Does this bother you?" I asked, pointing at the house. "Look at how the rest of you are living."

"God created everyone differently," the man said to me and walked away.

It was getting late in the afternoon but Victor was insisting I meet the town elders as a show of respect. We trudged to the opposite end of the island, where a group of old men were waiting for us. One of them handed me a business card that read "Ambassador of Peace."

We sat around the room while the elders repeated everything we'd heard all day. The community needed a high school, a health clinic, steady electricity, potable water and indoor plumbing.

Out of nowhere the Ambassador of Peace started yelling. He was pointing at me. I hadn't said a word.

Victor motioned at my legs. "Women don't do that here."

As the Ambassador of Peace was rambling, I had crossed my legs, proper-lady style. But by doing that, I, in my lumberjack outfit, sitting next to sexy tank top woman, had somehow managed to offend every old man in the room.

I uncrossed my legs and the men calmed down. Really, they had no choice. They were desperate to have their stories told. Yet their pleas seemed tired. They'd been making them for years to oil executives and government officials, and little had changed.

"*The New York Times* is here to save us!" the Ambassador of Peace announced to the elders.

"I'll do my best to make sure your voices are heard," I told them.

How could I convey in newsprint what these people were experiencing at the hands of government, oil corporations and their own leaders, all of whom were profiting off their misery?

It was easier for a group of men to pick up a stick of dynamite, but for the people of the Delta, the violence had changed nothing.

CHAPTER 1

Bridge Too Far

THE GLOSSY SEA lions were swimming laps and barking into the evening sky as Todd rushed past them. My husband's office at the Bronx Zoo was next to their turquoise, rocky enclosure but he barely paid attention to them anymore. He was too focused on getting home to us.

He heaved open the dented car door and specks of orange rust landed on his suit jacket. He wiped them away and folded his lanky, 6-foot-3-inch frame into our humiliating minivan, chugging onto the wretched freeway that serves up a mix of terror, anger and hospital-grade stress in every trip: the Brooklyn-Queens Expressway.

His other alternative was the subway, a grueling two-hour ride to our house in Brooklyn, *if* the trains were running on time. He couldn't manage that kind of commute when he wanted to spend time with our kids.

Out on the BQE, he dodged the taxis meandering across lanes as though there were none and patches of asphalt so rough they turned hubcaps into projectiles. Traffic piled up, and my normally reasonable husband loosened his outlet mall Ferragamo tie, dialed my number and spewed in a tone of voice that conveyed a quiet, seething rage, "I won't be home until after 7. Again."

We were living in New York, the greatest city in the world, and Todd spent most of his free time staring at brake lights.

So I suppose his idea made sense.

That evening after everyone was tucked in, Todd cracked open a beer and laid out his argument. Our three little kids could play on grass instead of the blacktop at their crowded, big-city school. We could go for walks in the woods instead of weaving through concrete-lined commercial strips. We could have backyard barbecues at the neighbors' instead of out on the fire escape with the mini Weber grill.

But when he said the words *I want to move to the suburbs,* I froze.

I loved the energy of the city, and of our part of Brooklyn in particular. The too-loud restaurants and bars. Prospect Park at dawn on a snowy day. Summer bike rides to the Red Hook public pool with the Salvadoran pupusas and milky horchata served up across the street. The sparkling Christmas trees centered in the picture windows of giant brownstones we'd never be able to afford. The crusty old barber who shaved the stubs of Todd's soft brown curls when they started to spring from his head. The mere fact that it wasn't Manhattan, which had become overrun with Wall Street bros and chain stores. Plus, all our friends were in Brooklyn— former colleagues from jobs we'd left behind, neighborhood fixtures who called out to us from their diner or their Laundromat, dog park pals from the days when the only thing we had to take care of was a frisky Labrador.

Though if I was honest, that version of Brooklyn already had disappeared for us not that long ago, after we had a son still in diapers then suddenly were outnumbered with—surprise!—identical twins born 18 months later.

And lately the husband I used to know seemed like a distant memory too. The bubbly, brown-eyed guy with patchy stubble who practically skipped in the door every night to see me? He stormed inside in a fury after spending 45 minutes in a desperate hunt for a legal parking space on the street.

IT HAD BEEN barely a year since I landed a position at what I had always considered the best newspaper in the world.

My job as an economics reporter for the *Times* was to chronicle the growing gap between the rich and the poor in America. I was writing about the aftershocks of the Great Recession—how the nation had split into two: the wealthiest 1 percent of people and the rest of us. The middle class was evaporating.

The transformation was especially hard on women, economists were saying. I wrote about how more than six decades after women left their kitchens for job sites, many now were dropping out of the workforce during their peak earning years, overcome by the demands of childcare. At the same time, in towns with shuttered factories and out-of-work husbands, I interviewed women who were taking on new roles as breadwinners, upending family power dynamics and causing marital friction.

In both scenarios, whether they were giving up or taking control, the women I interviewed said they felt like they were losing.

"I'm just really tired when I get home," one mom who was the family breadwinner told me as she stood in her little boy's bedroom, where the floor was littered with Thomas the Tank Engine train cars and piles of dirty clothes.

My mom was a single parent who gave up her full-time job as an English teacher to raise three kids after my dad died in a car accident when I was in kindergarten. She found solace—and an escape from us, I imagine—in our small Nebraska town's evangelical church, where she was organist, Sunday school teacher and later the secretary.

When I was a teenager, all my classmates earned extra cash in the summer "detasseling"—working in the fields to strip the tops of corn plants by hand, a tedious process that helped farmers control pollination. It involved grueling hours in the summer sun in tall cornfields that ringed my hometown. My mom refused to let me do it.

"Where will you go to the bathroom?" she asked, ignoring the fact that women have been not just peeing but giving birth in fields around the world for generations.

I was supposed to stay out of trouble and go to a Christian college to get what my mom called my M-R-S degree. She wanted me to find a nice minister-in-training and spend my days as a stay-at-home preacher's wife, serving my husband, my kids and the Lord. It worked for my sister.

I tried Christian college for a semester, until the Rolling Stones came to town and I sneaked out of my dormitory after curfew to see the show. I got busted, ratted out by a girl on my dorm floor. It was the Steel Wheels tour, but the way everyone reacted you'd think I had been part of the melee at Altamont. Administrators talked about hard labor and forcing me to clean the dormitory roof. They considered suspension or even expulsion. I saved them the trouble of deciding by dropping out and enrolling at the University of Nebraska.

There, instead of Jesus, I found journalism.

FOR THE TIMES, I traveled now and then for work—to Boston, to Reno, to Seattle; quick mid-week trips that I scheduled around my husband's extensive travel abroad, during which he met with government officials, donors and employees he managed. He was an executive at a conservation nonprofit based at the Bronx Zoo that was trying to save forests and wildlife habitats around the globe.

Todd's trips took him inside yurts in upper Mongolia or traipsing across a Patagonian peat moss bog. On my trips, I stayed at the airport Marriott in Dallas. He piled on the frequent flier miles. I racked up plastic tokens at Chuck E. Cheese's, where I retreated with the kids while he was away. It was the only place in the city with a manned gate that gave me a fighting chance as I chased after the three of them.

I had read articles about women who came home from their

jobs to shoulder all the work around the house. Economists called it "the second shift." Those women were giving their husbands a free pass. I wasn't going to do that. Todd had a PhD from Princeton. He could figure out how to change a diaper. And he did.

We had a haphazard parenting arrangement that aimed for a 50-50 share of the responsibilities. We took turns doing the dishes, cooking, washing the clothes, waking with a sick kid, buying groceries and making sure the bills were paid.

I was lucky. I had married up. I had amazing kids. I had a dream job and a husband who helped out at home. But we still couldn't get the balance right.

As new parents, it didn't take long for us to become locked in competition with each other—over who got the most sleep, who went out with friends, who made dinner, who got to go for a run, who was "allowed" to stay late at work.

The fallout from our dual-career household was brutal. Our New York life had devolved into a huge, rat-raced rut. The sense of adventure had been drained from our togetherness. It was school, soccer practice, baseball practice, homework, playdates, birthday parties, squabble over whose turn it was to do what and, of course, work, work, work. On warm summer evenings as we sheltered in place to adhere to the kids' bedtimes, the noise from the bands playing in the outdoor amphitheater in the distance drifted in through our open windows like some kind of haunting of our past life.

We always had said we would only stay in New York City a few years before heading elsewhere, but there we were, fourteen years later, with Todd aching for a bigger space to kick balls in the backyard to try to re-create his own happy suburban childhood.

We had gotten a loan from my in-laws, the only way we could afford a down payment on a house in Brooklyn. Its patch of a backyard featured a tree-sized lavender wisteria vine as a centerpiece.

I had hoped this little backyard would curb Todd's suburban

yearnings. It wasn't big enough for ball games, but I envisioned afternoons of playing in the sandbox with the kids. Maybe we'd get a grill, even, have some friends over, grow some tomatoes.

Instead, feral cats pooped in the sandbox. Everything we planted died. Our seedlings couldn't poke through the thousands of pieces of broken glass that churned up from the soil. Piles of dust blew under the front door when the street sweeper passed. We soon realized the wisteria that seemed so beautiful had crawled into the neighbor's giant trees, wound around large branches and was slowly yanking them toward our yard. They might come crashing down at any moment. We blew a couple thousand dollars on a tree specialist to disentangle the whole thing while I had nightmares the wisteria was strangling us.

We were so overwhelmed we had never even taken a family vacation. Our holidays were spent with our relatives. At least they could feed the kids breakfast while we slept in. Our date nights, when we managed them, ended either in arguments or exhaustion after staying up past 10 P.M.

Like many working mothers, I was paranoid that if I took off too much time to care for my kids, my career would stall. I was convinced that in American corporate culture a worn-out, grouchy employee in the office is better than one who doesn't show up.

Part of me felt sorry for the moms who stayed home. On the subway, I got to read a book with sentences that didn't rhyme. In the newsroom, I read the paper without someone tearing it to shreds over demands for more Cheerios. I went to the bathroom by myself at the office, without anyone sobbing and pounding at the door.

For my husband, moving to the suburbs meant deliverance from our crazy city life. He thought it could be a relief valve for our co-parenting madness. But all I imagined was more of the same, plus another kind of crazy: fighting for a seat on Metro North and a parking space at the mall.

———

I NEEDED TO take action to get us out of this gloom. Journalism had saved me from becoming a preacher's wife. Maybe journalism could rescue my family life. *The Times* was one of the only newspapers in the country that still operated a number of bureaus across the country and even the world. That could be our ticket out of the city—or better, to an even bigger opportunity.

Why not? Todd and I had hit it off when we met abroad, and we loved to travel together in the years before we had kids, forgoing nice furniture and fancy restaurants so we could afford adventurous travel overseas.

So maybe we should shift our setting out of the country. I thought an international move might remind us of why we liked each other enough to have a family in the first place.

My motivation was selfish, too. The majority of my reporting for the past decade had been carried out over the phone, from my cubicle in a glassy office tower high above the honking traffic of Midtown Manhattan. I had become a newsroom rat. I knew which elevator bank offered the fastest route to the company cafeteria, which stairwell spit me out closest to the subway station, which vending machines were stocked with Doritos.

Journalism was supposed to be about bearing witness. The only thing I was witnessing were new buds sprouting in my co-worker's desktop terrarium. The plants inside were alive. They were even healthy. But theirs was an artificial existence trapped in a protective bubble. I didn't want that kind of life anymore.

Breaking out would be good for Todd, too. He loved his job but he literally worked inside a zoo.

I raised the idea of moving abroad for the *Times* with Todd in an email, the way most meaningful conversations happen between two working parents.

I'm not sure he took me seriously. How many times had we

mused about getting out of the city? But, at 44 years old, I had logged enough journalism experience at other newspapers— covering politics, crime, corruption and corporations, even a couple short war tours in Iraq—that I knew the editors at the *Times* had to at least give me a bit of consideration.

The international desk had a few job openings. India. Exciting, I thought, but I worried about the pollution everyone complains about in big cities there. Japan. Interesting, but wouldn't it be too expensive? Afghanistan. That might be too dangerous. And, curiously, a regional beast of a beat that sprawled across some two-dozen nations in West and Central Africa that offered a mix of every kind of reporting. The job required writing about parts of the world that most Americans don't even know exist. I looked at a map of the region. I couldn't pronounce the names of some of the cities. I'd need to brush up on Nouakchott, Yaoundé, N'Djamena and Ouagadougou, a capital city so unfamiliar to Americans that the *Times* offers a handy pronunciation guide in parentheses every time it appears in print: "wah-gah-DOO-goo."

One of the editors, a dedicated dad, talked to me about the responsibilities of the beat.

"Your trips are going to be long. It's not easy getting from one place to another," he said. "But when you aren't traveling, you manage your own time."

I pushed ahead with the idea. I was well into discussions exploring overseas postings with editors—even though it had been weeks and I still hadn't received any meaningful response from Todd. This was one of the few times in our relationship we had ever had to make a major life decision. We had always let our careers guide us through everything, as though we were along for the ride.

"Can you give me some sign of life about this West Africa thing?" I emailed him.

"I am not being quiet. I think we should investigate," he wrote back with a detached logic that was typical for him. "Let's find out the details. Will they pay for housing and school? How dangerous is the capital city? Is there any green space? The paper probably is getting a lot of applicants."

I kept going with the process at the *Times*, meeting with layers of editors. Things moved so fast that I sometimes forgot to update Todd about just *how* quickly this was all coming together.

In reality, my timing happened to be perfect. Overseas jobs offered the opportunity to shape American policy or the opinions of readers about nations they may never go to themselves. They changed things in faraway places for the better. But they also could be dangerous. The killing of a handful of Western journalists by extremists had scared off some recruits. The paper didn't want rookies to fill their overseas bureaus. And hiring more experienced reporters was a strategy that worked best in the days when husbands were breadwinners married to stay-at-home moms who tagged along where their spouses' jobs led them. It was harder for dual-career families to pack up and move abroad. For the West Africa position in particular, people weren't lining up for a post that involved working in countries that had both terrorist activity and some of the worst rankings for quality of life on the entire planet.

Even more, the West Africa job required French language skills. In America, where the Latino population is booming, where our biggest wars are being fought in Arabic-speaking lands and where China is emerging as an economic threat, what go-getter American can speak passable French these days? *Moi,* for one. I soared above the competition.

The *Times,* like most American newspapers, almost makes a sport out of hiring novices to new beats, believing that a fresh set of eyes can see things in a new, important light. The paper's opera writer came to the beat after covering state politics. One reporter who had roamed Japan with a Geiger counter during a nuclear disaster moved on to cover the growing market for yoga pants as everyday wear. One of our arts reporters was now focused on stories about overhauling the tax code. The Atlanta bureau chief who had covered the racially tinged execution of a Georgia inmate was writing about wood-aged cheese for the Dining section.

I made my case as a fast learner to the powers-that-be at the *Times*, and voilà, I had a job offer.

After years of newsroom hopping across America, armed with credentials that included years' worth of Sunday school perfect-attendance pins and a bachelor's degree from a state known for its corn, it must have been clear to them that I'd been a foreign correspondent my whole adult life.

"You're a natural," one of the international editors told me.

I called my husband and told him I'd been offered the job.

"That's terrific," he said, holed up in his office at work so no one would hear him. "So what should we do?"

"Well, I can't say no now," I explained. "Not after I've lobbied for the job."

We hadn't spent hours wrangling with the idea. But what was there to discuss? It was a huge leap. Maybe I shoved Todd off the ledge a little, but he knew it was a good job for me and the chance for new experiences for the family. The suburbs would always be there. He was game to push the pause button on his career and give this new life a try.

"I think it's exciting," he said, "and there will never be a perfect time to do it. Let's say yes."

WE HAD A lot of paperwork to sign before we could consider how to tell the kids we were moving. There was the work contract; the extra life insurance policies; the emergency evacuation insurance; the bulletproof vest measurements. I signed up for a hostile environments training course. I studied the instruction manual for a GPS tracker that would emit a ping to help the paper find me anywhere in the world. I filled out forms with proof-of-life questions that only I would know in case I got kidnapped and my captors were to call the office and start making demands. If they offered my maternal grandmother's middle name, then my employers could trust that they really had me in their clutches.

The whole process took weeks. It seemed like a cruel secret to keep from the kids, but they were also too young—my son, Luther, was in fourth grade and his twin sisters, Maude and Zola, were in second grade—not to wait until all was settled.

In the meantime, I used my motherly powers of manipulation to plant ideas in their minds.

"Wouldn't it be so fun to go to a school with a swimming pool?" I hinted when I dropped them off at the cramped asphalt playground at their elementary school.

"I wish we lived by the beach," I fake-whined as I helped zip up their puffy winter coats.

Our new home was going to be in Dakar, the capital of Senegal, a peaceful, politically stable democracy untouched by the militant groups that operate elsewhere in the region. The country was a popular vacation spot for French retirees. It had a lot of Muslims. Farmers there grew peanuts.

I wasn't one of those people who always had a fascination or adoration for this part of the world, so I didn't know much more. I started reading a suitcase full of books to help fill in the seismic gaps in my knowledge.

Authors portrayed a region where governments pass laws without public scrutiny. Foreign entities influence elections, they wrote, and politicians decry media reports as fake. Presidents fail to condemn murders and violence carried out against minority groups, and they treat women like second-class citizens. All the while state television lurks in the background, propping up narcissistic presidents. It was hard to imagine what life would be like in a place like this.

Some of our friends and relatives told us they would never consider moving their kids abroad, let alone to West Africa. But Todd's approach to our new setting was practical. Bad things that happen anywhere in the world are statistical anomalies, he would say, and then not worry about anything. While I wasn't paranoid, I did worry. I was concerned about the what-ifs but tried my best to follow Todd's lead.

One night at the dinner table, we decided to tell the kids about our big move. I followed up the announcement by whipping out my laptop to show them a website with photos of their new international school.

Maude and Zola squealed when they saw the pool on campus. Luther burst into tears and ran into his room, slamming the door behind him. I was devastated. Todd quietly trailed him. He sat down beside Luther, who had shoved his face into his pillow stamped with little blue and red toy cars. I heard their muffled voices through the door. Luther didn't want to move far away. He loved his school. He didn't want to leave his friends.

"You'll make so many new friends in Dakar," Todd told him. "And we can come back and visit Brooklyn."

Luther's outburst lasted mere minutes. His curiosity got the best of him and soon enough he was downstairs vying for a look at his new school's swimming pool.

THE NEXT MORNING, I weaved through the mosh pit of early-morning Manhattan commuters and pushed through the heavy glass doors of the *Times*. The only sound was the crackle of the security guard's radio echoing off the white oak floors. I had arrived early to pack up my desk for the big move.

I stopped to search for my ID badge in front of the lobby's modern art display—snippets of sentences yanked at random from the pages of the day's newspaper. The words flashed in digital blue lettering across little alarm-clock-sized rectangles that covered one wall.

"The right to investigate Mrs. Clinton's email." "A small Syrian boy whose body washed up." "The killing of Mr. Brown and the unrest that followed." "Mr. Trump's reality show antics."

I reached inside my bag, fishing through pens, notebooks,

iPhone, Metro pass, crumpled school field-trip permission slip, stray Lego blocks. The badge was stuck to the back of an empty juice box.

I pressed it against the bar code reader, and the steel arm of the security gate flipped open.

Inside the newsroom, fluorescent lights cast a blue sheen over the empty chairs. I sunk into my desk and flicked on my computer.

I heard shuffling. I peeked over my screen. A tuft of white hair was zigzagging through the maze of cubicles. I knew right away who it was: Arthur Ochs Sulzberger, Jr., the publisher of the paper who had inherited the *Times* throne from generations before him. When he wasn't windsurfing or tearing up the Catskills highway on his motorcycle, he was known to roam the halls of the newsroom.

It's awfully early for him to be around, I thought to myself as I shoved photos of my kids in a moving box.

"Hello there," I heard a voice say.

I looked up. Arthur Sulzberger was standing right over me. He had been zigzagging the aisles in search of *me*.

Hovering over me like a proud dad, he delivered a charming farewell on behalf of himself and the newspaper. He wished me luck on my new assignment as the paper's West Africa bureau chief.

His words were touching, and I was humbled that he took the time to seek me out. I thanked him for giving me the opportunity to represent the *Times* abroad and the support to send me thousands of miles away. He started to walk away, but turned back.

"If you come to a bridge too far," he said, as the smile vanished from his face, "don't take it."

He left.

I wasn't quite sure what he meant. It sounded important, and ominous.

I wanted to shove his remarks aside as melodramatic—the mere ramblings of a wealthy newspaper owner who had repeated the same speech to dozens of other correspondents he had sent into the field. He probably didn't even think about what he was saying anymore. Or maybe he said that because he knew I was a mom? I didn't think so, but he was right that I needed to be careful.

I sat at my desk and repeated in my head the stream of consciousness lecture that I always gave myself when I was about to head into a dangerous situation for my job.

You know dozens of reporters who have been in dodgy circumstances and made it out just fine. Some of the best reporting is done around the edges of conflicts and disasters, far away from imminent danger. You don't need to stand in the middle of flying bullets to tell a story. Nothing is ever as bad as it seems from the outside. Think of all of the regular people who spend their whole lives in dodgy places.

Most of the time that all makes me feel better. But this time was different. I was taking my family with me.

We were catapulting out of the mayhem of New York, for that I was thankful. But plopping down into what, exactly?

I looked outside the window of my climate-controlled office and stared at the cars stuck in traffic below. Just like other women, I wanted a fulfilling career and a vibrant family life. In many ways, I already had all that. Had I already reached a bridge too far?

CHAPTER 2

Welcome to Dakar

"THERE HAS BEEN a marked increase of incidents of violent attacks using knifes or machetes during robberies. . . . Public protests, demonstrations, and strikes occur regularly and at times lead to violence. . . . There exists a real, growing threat of regional terrorism."

The 2016 U.S. State Department warning for Dakar sounded ominous. But looking around, this place didn't seem bad at all.

Bright puffs of purple and orange bougainvillea spilled over cracked concrete walls and lined the sandy streets of Dakar. Tall, rocky bluffs hovered over the sparkling aquamarine sea. Shepherds walked down the road with herds of goats for their weekly washing in the surf. The beaches were lined with animals getting baths in between swimmers and fishermen.

Women on the street looked like walking mermaids in their fitted dresses that flared at the bottom. Nescafé vendors poured hot water into powdered coffee in long streams from high above their heads. People sold baguettes stuffed with lentils, beef, mayo and French fries, tucked inside old election ballots as wrappers.

Practically everyone here followed Sufi-ism, a mystical, almost hippie form of Islam with its talk of peace and love. As we wandered the city, people beckoned for us to share their meals around a giant aluminum platter, or to stop for a gritty, chicory-flavored coffee called café Touba. It was an expression of the Senegalese culture ruled by a set of values known as *Teranga*, a word that describes a particular concept of hospitality.

Words in the most commonly spoken language, Wolof, seemed to bounce as they were exhaled, a bubbly rhythm of oos and ohs. People greeted one another with how-are-you in three languages.

"*Al-salamu alaykum*" the first greeting often kicks off, in Arabic, which nearly everyone had learned a bit of in this mostly Muslim city.

"*Wa alaykumu al-salam,*" comes the reply.

"*Nanga def?*" is next, in Wolof.

"*Mangi fi,*" is the response.

"*Ça va?*" in French.

"*Ça va bien, merci,*" wraps it all up, although in October the greetings expand to inquiries about how everyone was holding up in the punishing, unbearable heat.

Dakar was in mid-dry season when we arrived, with harmattan clouds of powdery sand blowing in from the Sahara to coat the palm fronds and mango tree leaves, making them blend in with the unpainted concrete buildings and sandy streets. The whole place was the same color of beige. Even the feathers of red, sparrow-sized fire finches were dulled from the dust.

The city's atmosphere was somehow so arid it chapped my lips and dried the ink in my ballpoint pens, yet so muggy that people warned about the metal guts of electronics rotting.

Our kids were transfixed by everything. The rickety wooden pirogues painted in swirls of yellow and blue and green, piloted by fishermen who offered to take them out on their boats. The fat, awkward baobabs that were so different from any kind of tree they'd seen in Prospect Park. The horse carts that rumbled down the street—Dakar's version of a pickup truck. The colorful *car rapide* minibuses with tassels dangling from the side mirrors and plastered with portraits of holy men as though they were rock stars. Fare collectors hung out the open, swinging back doors. On one, a monkey mascot rode on the roof.

Away from the traffic, Dakar's soundtrack was a melody of dozens of new birdcalls—hornbills and raptors and wild parrots and neon yellow weavers among them—so loud it sounded like some kind of exotic arboretum. Some days, even the trash glistened. One pile strewn across a hillside included miles of unspooled black videocassette tape. In the morning sun it looked like tinsel.

Here, time is measured in rainy seasons and Ramadans. And everything seemed to have its own occasion. In butterfly season, tiny white creatures descended, lining trees and yards and patio furniture in what looked from a distance like snow. Jellyfish season turned up in purple and blue see-through blobs with long rope-like tentacles that made it nearly impossible to swim without getting stung. Red algae season coated the water in acrid-smelling plants. Mutant alien grasshopper season brought giant, harmless bugs that sounded like they were screaming when they rubbed their wings together.

A ROW OF towering palm trees lined the street in front of our new home, a house so big it was called a villa and was situated behind a tall wall. At the edge of the neighborhood, the ocean glistened. The *Times* bureau was inside our house, on the ground floor, so the place came with a staff—a security guard, a housekeeper, a gardener and an office manager, who lined up to greet us outside. The company car was parked out front. The newspaper had determined there were certain luxuries that made its bureau chiefs more efficient. They were right, of course, but it seemed over the top. The bureau even had a job opening for a chauffeur.

Wandering through the worn-out, cavernous, colonial-era house-slash-office on that first day, I found the remnants of *Times* bureau chiefs past. Dusty flak jackets and warped armored helmets were stuffed into closets dating from long-ago coups and rebel uprisings. Nearly worthless coins from 25 countries were stacked in a big metal box on top of a shelf filled with weathered books on the struggles of the continent. An old, sun-faded campaign poster with Pidgin English slogans clung to one wall. Tacked to another were headshots of journalists who had been killed for exposing corruption in the region.

The intimidation of how little I knew about this place and how to do this job started to sink in. The people who had left all this behind after holding the job before me all were wildly successful now, with Pulitzer Prizes, top-ranking editor titles and bestselling academic books to their names.

Would I be the one failure? What did failure even look like? Getting kidnapped, or worse, killed, was too awful to dwell on. What if I did no better than write 500-word stories buried in the paper, which no one would ever read? That would be a disservice to the region and most likely career-ending. I sat down to unpack my boxes and a crumpled note fell out from a stack of papers. It was a kid's blocky handwriting, scribbled on the back of an old prescription. It looked familiar but I don't think I had ever paused to consider its message.

"Zola lost a tooth," it read. "You should have been here."

By the time Maude, my younger daughter by one C-section minute, had written this, the kids all were in elementary school and must have lost altogether more than a dozen teeth. But to them, each individual tooth that came out with the bite of an apple or a tug of little fingers was still epic. To her, the loss of her twin's tooth was a big event. I must have been away on a work trip and missed it.

The note stirred a touch of resentment. Am I supposed to be there for every lost tooth? But also it made me sad. The kids were getting bigger, and tooth fairy visits soon would be a thing of the past. How many other milestone moments was I going to miss? I taped the note to my wall as a reminder to not get too carried away by this job.

Yet I had a big job to do. I was idealistic enough to think my work could be a force for good here. And now I was the one responsible for putting food on the table.

IN OUR NEW neighborhood, guards stood outside the monster-sized villas. We walked along streets that were potholed but paved, a rarity in this city of sand, on the way to the kids' new, walled-off, private international school, a mix of locals and foreigners. An armed soldier stood at the school entry. A queue of dark SUVs piled up outside the school; one by one, each driver got out and opened the door for their young charges nestled in the backseat.

Across the road an unfriendly old woman with a sprinkling of teeth was hawking vegetables beside a man who had spread out six pairs of knock-off Chuck Taylors for sale. Child beggars passed, carrying plastic collection cans that looked like old Cool Whip containers.

I stood in the middle of the road between both scenes and it hit me that in our first days in Dakar we had been clinging to the nice parts of town, retreating to the palm trees and security guard and all the strange luxuries that were a part of our new life. Meanwhile, outside our villa wall, an enormous population of people clung to the rock bottom rung of the economy, crammed into one-room apartments, sleeping on nothing more than plastic mats. Others slept in the sand, spending their days on the side of a freeway, selling boxes of tissues to passing cars.

Everyday life in this part of the world played out amid a backdrop of economic, political and social gaps on steroids, in countries that hadn't had a new leader since Jimmy Carter was in office, in economies overflowing with oil yet so broken they import gasoline. Regular people live inside mud walls at the base of the same hill where government ministers mount their gold-encrusted palaces. Elites here drive their Mercedes, and get stuck in traffic behind nomads guiding their three cows to market. Tourists go glamping and toast the sunset atop dunes in the very same desert where migrants were dying from thirst on a desperate trek to Europe.

I knew all that, of course, but being dropped into the middle of it was jarring. Back in Brooklyn, it had been easy to forget my privilege amid the designer handbags and designer donuts, the $6 coffees and multimillion-dollar apartments. Here, in an instant we had become superrich people who worked from home and sent our kids to private school. Our wealth, our privilege, our elitism, whatever I wanted to call it, was on full display 24/7, whenever the metal door of our home clanged shut behind us and we stepped into the company SUV.

The inequalities seen in much of West Africa seemed like a dystopian vision of the fears that were gripping America, prompting politicians to run campaigns to bring back the golden age of the middle class, to rebuild the American dream, to make America great again.

They were targeting places like my Nebraska hometown, population 1,600, where the middle class once thrived but now seemed to have vanished.

When I was growing up, my maple-tree-lined neighborhood was a diorama of the larger American middle class, populated by a hardware store owner, a pharmacy owner, a utility company worker, a bank teller and a few factory workers.

America's economic shock waves changed everything. Walmart moved in 20 miles up the highway, and soon after the drugstore and hardware store closed. Enron collapsed and the utility worker lost his life savings. Online retail wiped out the factory that made store shelving. The one remaining factory in the area, American Tool, closed down and moved to China. The only growth industries were a nursing home and funeral home—until even the nursing home became a victim of corporate downsizing and closed.

The middle-class workers on my street died off. In their place came the families with part-time jobs and Powerball tickets and refrigerators full of government cheese.

IN DAKAR, OUR new neighborhood offered a real mix. Retired government ministers and even the president owned homes there. A street salesman took naps on our corner after peddling bunches of colorful brooms that he hoisted on his shoulder and marched around town. Men walked by the house holding cages crammed with birds. A small herd of runaway cows with long horns that tapered into ice picks sometimes escorted our threesome home from school. We had a little park that was nothing more than dirt and a few broken concrete benches. A tiny store sold tapalapa, a dense baguette created to fill the stomach for an entire day when finances are strained. Stray cats outside the corner mosque produced regular piles of kittens. The kids begged us to take one home.

No way, I told them. Not until we figure this place out.

I couldn't explain why, but everything seemed to throw me off—even the scrawny kittens mewling at us innocently in the street—as if we were always about to make that one wrong move.

There was no apparent reason I felt strange. Yes, there were trash piles but there were also neighbors out sweeping the streets in front of homes every morning and a volunteer group that organized regular beach cleanups. People on the road and at the markets were friendly. Traffic wasn't that much worse than what we'd experienced on a bad day on the BQE in New York. The neighborhood mosque was packed on Fridays the same way my hometown church parking lot overflowed on Sundays. Almost everything had a correlate from life back home. Even the guards posted outside villas in our neighborhood hollered hearty hellos. But what were they guarding anyway? Why were they necessary?

One afternoon, I braved my first solo driving trip into Dakar's busy downtown to look for the city's version of IKEA. I got lost amid the half-finished office towers and clogged streets and wound up going the wrong way on a one-way street. Frustrated, I rolled down my window to ask a man walking along the street for directions. He rounded my car, opened the passenger door and hopped in.

"What are you doing?" I said, startled, looking at the stranger in my passenger seat.

"I'm guiding you," he said.

The man directed me through traffic straight to my destination—and then hopped out and went on his way before I had a chance to properly thank him. Gmaps and Waze were unreliable in Dakar, and many people couldn't afford a smartphone anyway. So people navigated by asking directions. Personal escorting was a common act of kindness that strangers offered to lost drivers. I was embarrassed for being nervous.

"Why do I feel so uncomfortable here sometimes?" I asked Todd one morning after we dropped the kids at school. He confessed to having the same feeling.

"In America, I can tell if I turn a corner and something seems . . . off," he said. "But here, it's like my Spidey sense is out of whack. I just don't know what to expect."

We both were responding to being in a deeply unfamiliar setting—but also to being in a society that Hollywood portrays as a continent-wide war zone full of machete-wielding militiamen and witch doctors, leaving the impression a lion lurks around every corner, making you feel you always must be on guard. The paranoid State Department travel warnings didn't help matters.

The warning we read before arriving in Dakar was issued after a string of late-night muggings. Some Western diplomats had been banned from strolling along the corniche, the loveliest stretch of ocean-side road in the city. They lived in gated communities, their diplomatic pouches stuffed with shipments from Amazon.com so they rarely had to go to local shops.

Some foreigners dabbled in Dakar, sampling African society through buying African art made by French people and joining

African drumming circles led by other expats. We gave up on bringing America to Dakar after the Instant Pot we brought in our checked bags blew up the transformer and started a kitchen fire in our house.

Working for the *Times,* I set my own rules. How would I even trust guidance from my editors sitting inside their office building in Midtown Manhattan? I was happy to be free from restrictions that would keep me from interacting with one of the very places I was supposed to be writing about. Instead of avoiding the no-go corniche road, I joined the locals and went for daily runs.

"Courage! Courage!" men shouted as I jogged past. "Exercise is good! Bravo!"

"Faster, faster!" some hollered.

At first I was put off by the commentary and ignored it. It wasn't exactly a catcall but it seemed condescending. It was, after all, only the men who hollered this . . . advice, I guess you could call it.

I still wasn't sure how I fit in here, not only as a foreigner, but as a woman. This was a city where a neighborhood with twin hills was named The Boobs, *Mamelles* in French. But I had nothing to lose by engaging with this odd cheering section.

"Happy running!" hollered a gardener tending his mini baobabs.

"Happy working!" I shouted back. He smiled and punched his fist in the air.

I began to pass a familiar cast of characters along my running route: the soldiers guarding a base who always encouraged me to speed up; the two old men who sat in plastic lawn chairs yelling to me from under the shade of flowering vines so thick I never saw their faces; the money collector balancing on the back bumper of an overcrowded *car rapide* who high-fived me when he passed; the homeless man who slept under a bench and raised his head to nod at me; and his homeless dog that chased me like I was a passing car and then stopped to wait for a pat on the head.

"Join us!" a group of police recruits shouted as they whizzed by.

I was way too slow to keep up with their pace. Drivers paused to let me across busy streets, signaling that I could pass with a hearty thumbs-up.

Growing up, I had all kinds of misplaced notions about my new home continent, if I thought about it at all. I wasn't different from a lot of Americans.

The only time I recall Africa ever coming up in my youth was when the elementary physical education teacher bought a set of tinikling sticks, bamboo poles that we used for jumping and agility games that we were told were popular in Africa. In fact, they're used in a Filipino folk dance.

Not much had changed since then.

"How are you?" a high school friend wrote my first week on the job. "How is life in South America?"

"I'm in Africa," I replied. "West Africa."

"Are there even schools over there?" a relative asked.

"Yes, there are schools and universities," I patiently replied.

"How's Darfur?" wrote even a colleague at the *Times*.

"I'm in Dakar. On the other side of the continent."

My mission, I decided as I walked around the city, was to help Americans relate to this place, to make the other people who, like me, had spent most of their lives not giving more than a passing thought to the region or the continent, even, to sit up and pay attention.

"Don't be a tourist," one editor advised, counseling me to let the stories guide my coverage, not my desire to cover as much ground as possible.

"Rely on descriptions," another editor offered, explaining that by slipping in details about what people are eating or wearing I can broaden understanding of the culture.

"Start an Instagram account," another suggested. "No one even knows what that place looks like."

I did. But after my photo of palm trees and a pink lake outside of Dakar got four "likes" I decided that wasn't going to be enough.

The quickest path toward getting the attention this part of the world deserved was to land a story on the front page, that elusive slice of real estate occupied by five or six of the most important stories of the day. Sure, a lot of people read the paper online now. But politicians and powerful people still take their cues from what the *Times* decides to publish on the front page—as do the humans and robots that place stories front and center on our website. I had cracked the front page once or twice on the economy beat. But I wasn't sure how I'd land there with stories about a part of the world that most people hardly knew anything about.

THERE WAS NO way I could do my job without the help of local journalists. My predecessor had assembled a group of them in each country in my region to assist the *Times*. They made introductions, offered context, sometimes arranged interviews and were compensated and credited with bylines in the paper if they helped with reporting. I decided to hire someone to help me do all that and hold down the journalism fort in Dakar while I traveled. But my bureau didn't have a budget line for a second reporter. We only had an opening for a chauffeur.

A photographer friend had put me in touch with a young Sierra Leonean journalist, Jaime Yaya Barry, who had helped the *Times* cover the world's worst Ebola outbreak, which had ravaged three West African countries. Maybe I could throw him some work from time to time, my friend suggested.

Jaime had helped me when I flew to Guinea a few months earlier as a test run for the job, to write about the end of the Ebola outbreak that was winding down after two long years. Thousands of people had died grueling deaths as the disease consumed entire families and even neighborhoods. Back when the outbreak began, Jaime had been working for a tourism agency in Sierra Leone, one of the countries where the disease had spread. When the tourists all fled he became a fixer, helping our reporters navigate the disease-ridden landscape in his country.

I had finished my reporting and was stuck in Guinea's capital city, Conakry, for a couple days before I could get a flight home and was hoping to find an extra story while I waited. I flipped through the local papers and poked around Google News to look for ideas. The only story that popped up when I typed in "Guinea" was one about 65 guinea pigs rescued from a Pennsylvania home.

I called Jaime.

"Do you have any ideas for stories in Conakry?" I said, feeling a bit sheepish that I was so new to the region that I didn't have my own long list to tap.

"How about the boys who sell old money for new money?"

"Huh?"

Jaime directed me to a group of young men—former war refugees he knew from Sierra Leone—who made a living working under a highway overpass by charging people fees for trading their sweaty, wrinkled currency bills for crisp new ones the young men stockpiled. The men cleverly were tapping a niche market: Guineans liked their money fresh and clean for giving as gifts at weddings or other celebrations. Buying the bills from the men under the overpass was quicker than standing in long lines at the bank.

I spent the afternoon with the group of money changers. On a typical day they earned maybe $13 and were often chased off by police, who beat them and confiscated their inventory. It wasn't a great way to make a living. Under the shade of a concrete overhang, we talked about other job options. There weren't many; 60 percent of young people in Guinea were unemployed. A few of the men said they planned to become famous soccer stars. Any day now, a scout from Manchester United would pass and discover them. They were certain of it.

"I might start a job as a wheelbarrow pusher," one of the men quietly said to me.

What a clever way to make a buck, I thought to myself as I packed up to leave town. Someone always needed something hauled, and not very many people could afford cars, or even a taxi ride. Customers could hire him and his wheelbarrow for small jobs, hauling debris or small furniture. Maybe the money changer guys could even start a proper business, like a U-Haul for these small handcarts.

I mentioned the money changer's idea to Jaime. He sighed—and patiently explained that so many people had the same idea that those men stood as much of a chance of becoming famous on the soccer pitch as they did earning a viable living in the wheelbarrow business.

Then I noticed it, all across Conakry as I rode to the airport, and later in every new city, in every country. Hundreds of men with the same idea, pushing empty wheelbarrows down highways and sandy roads.

Jaime knew the money-changing business, the wheelbarrow business and was teeming with ideas about sports, art, subcultures and beyond. He had lived in four countries and traveled to a half-dozen more. And like most West Africans, he spoke numerous languages—eleven, to be exact. He would make an excellent partner for me in Dakar.

My editor suggested I try to bring Jaime to the paper through the chauffeur opening.

"When he's not driving, he can report," my editor said.

But there was one problem with hiring Jaime as the bureau's chauffeur: he didn't have a driver's license. I hired him anyway. I could train him to drive—how hard can that be? Jaime readily accepted my job offer and made plans to move to Dakar.

MEANWHILE, TODD, IN his own new role as lead parent, was trying to make friends with the stay-at-home moms. The expat community was teeming with them. Tall, thin, Stepford Wife types from all over the world—the kinds of women who don't work but who showed up to morning drop-off at school in skinny jeans or sundresses, wearing lipstick and mascara and navigating the broken choppy asphalt street in tall platform sandals. For that feat alone I admired them. I tripped in clunky Birkenstocks that I thought would be so sturdy.

These moms had sacrificed their careers to follow their husbands overseas, where they were designated the humiliating title of "trailing spouses." Dakar was a regional hub for many NGOs and corporations. Their husbands spent much of their time traveling for work. The wives spent their days bouncing between yoga classes, backyard art and jewelry sales at homes of other expats, day drinking at seaside restaurants and finding charities worthy of their attention. A few who couldn't figure out what to do with their lives became certified as "life coaches," instructing other women, for a fee, on what to do with theirs. They had created an official women's social club to keep themselves busy. The no-boys-allowed rule left Todd out.

"Be an ambassador for your family," a stay-at-home mom friend had counseled Todd before we moved. "Stick around to socialize. It will help with arranging playdates and other outings that will benefit the kids in making new friends."

Todd tried. He lingered before and after school to chat up the moms. At first they seemed amused at having a man try out this new role. But their tone changed when he suggested the various ways that they could all help one another out. He was trying to lay the groundwork for a backup network to help facilitate his work life. He had planned on quitting his job when we moved here. But before we could think through the toll that might take on his ego, his bosses asked him to stay. They negotiated reduced responsibilities and a lower salary. He would stay tethered to his career, albeit from afar.

But more than that, Todd was raised Unitarian. He believed in community and like-minded people creating a support network. Maybe they could host our kids if he and I ever happened to be out of the country at the same time? He would be happy to reciprocate if they were ever in the same position, or just needed a kid-free break.

Soon afterward, a couple of the stay-at-home moms invited me out to lunch, and I slipped away from work to join them. We settled into a table near the water and launched into the conversation common among all mothers—school, kids and husbands. But the topic turned specifically to *my* husband.

"He keeps asking us for help," one of the women griped.

"He's so needy," the other woman chimed in.

I'd been to dozens of similar outings with new girlfriends in the past where we engaged in healthy venting about our own husbands. But I'd never experienced *other* women complaining about *my* husband. Was this a lunch or an intervention? Then I realized: they weren't used to dads being childcare providers. Potential counterattacks swirled through my head. Their husbands had probably never changed a diaper, made dinner or booked a dentist appointment, I thought. But I kept my mouth shut and grinned through the rest of the meal.

Still, I worried Todd was going to be the odd one out here, in devastating ways if that continued for the long term. Our kids' school had always offered instant parent friends. He was a social person. I would be away a lot. How would he find a community?

CHAPTER 3

Va Te Faire Foutre

THE HOUSEWIVES' INTERVENTION made it clear that we weren't like other expat families here. At the same time, we seemed different from the local families, too, especially when it came to our parenting.

In Brooklyn, we lived in a world where helicopter parenting was the norm. Our kids weren't allowed to ride their bikes down the street or stay home alone for any stretch of time. They ate organic baby carrots. They sat in booster seats in the car and wore closed-toed sandals with nonslip treads. Every bit of snot was wiped away by one of us, every set of dirty hands washed.

Here, toddlers sat on the laps of parents in the front seats of vehicles and rode on the backs of motorbikes, clinging to their father's waist. Helmetless kids pedaled bicycles down four-lane roadways, two to a bike. Runny-nosed children played barefoot in the dirt. Organic vegetables did not exist. In their place were onions and peppers watered with sewage-tainted runoff, fertilized sometimes with petroleum, rumor had it, and then, to counter all that, rinsed with a splash of bleach before it was doused with palm oil or boiled in high-sodium bouillon-cube broth.

We soon decided we'd been paranoid back in Brooklyn. What had we been thinking? We bought our kids flip-flops. We let them skateboard on the broken streets without their elbow pads and helmets. They took turns sitting in the front seat of the car. We put them on camels and watched them disappear over the dunes with a guide who spoke no English. We let them swim in the sometimes polluted ocean, avoiding plastic bags and other debris, even when the red algae bloomed. We signed them up for surf lessons in water where they had to avoid kicks from obstinate horses being bathed by their owners. We abandoned the malaria medicine our pediatrician had prescribed. Long sleeves, candles, bed nets and spray were more than enough to keep us safe. We felt silly we had ever bought in to all the Western paranoia.

The kids played in tidal pools while they waited for their grilled fish or onion-smothered yassa chicken plates at seaside restaurants. They could see the ocean from our roof, where they bounced balls or rode their scooters. The house was big enough for a ping-pong table and a basketball hoop on the patio and skateboarding in the living room. They ate breakfast outside most days and drank from fresh coconuts sold on the street. They washed their sandy feet in the French bidet, perfect for spraying off grains between little toes. They sang along with the call to prayer from the neighborhood mosque, murmuring *"Allaaaaaaaaahu Akbar"*—God is great—in the same deep voice as the imam.

One day, while my son was rolling around in the sand at the beach, another expat mom nudged me.

"You really shouldn't let him do that."

"Oh, we don't mind if he gets dirty," I said. "It's part of being a kid."

"He might get mangoworms."

Wait, what?

The dreaded mangoworm: it was the nightmare of all expats. I had read warnings about them in the travel guidebooks. The stories were passed on to newcomers. It seemed too gross to be true. Certain kinds of flies here lay eggs in sand, in grass, on clothes hung out to dry. When your body has prolonged contact with those eggs the little flies find their way to embed in your skin, creating a boil that, when popped, hatches a baby.

Those babies, of course, are maggots.

I looked at Luther frolicking in the sand like a happy wet puppy.

"Get up!" I yelled, pulling him from the sand.

Sure enough, a couple weeks later, a boil emerged on Luther's waistline. Unwilling to accept reality, I called a doctor who I hoped would tell me it was a pimple or a rash.

In Dakar, if you can afford it or if you are lucky enough to have health insurance, doctors make house calls. Soon, Dr. Boubacar, a lanky, soft-spoken Senegalese physician in a white coat, showed up at our house clutching his black medical bag. He approached Luther, a normally stoic boy who was rattled about his new role as parasitic host. He started squealing in anticipation. Todd had to sit on the kid to keep him still. Dr. Boubacar squeezed the bubble, wiped away the critter that emerged, doused the skin with antibiotic, and that was that. I could have done it myself. Mangoworms turned out to be no more harmful—or stressful—than a big zit. It was practically a West African rite of passage.

In times like these it seemed helpful to think of a Western equivalent. It didn't take long to come up with one: ticks. What would a Senegalese mom think if I told her about the tick invasion upstate New York was undergoing? Kids and pets couldn't play in the backyard without worries about a tick latching to them. Mangoworms were gross but Lyme disease is an actual health hazard.

All this letting go of my Western helicopter parenting was far from straightforward. It was countered with flashes of worst-case scenarios, creating a constant mental tug-of-war. The what-ifs were ever present and always seemed more intense than what I knew from back home. *What if we get food poisoning from the sandwiches sold on the street? What if the kids' head cold is malaria? What if a dog bites one of us and we can't find rabies vaccine?*

One European mom tsk-tsked us when we expressed the smallest of concerns. But on the other side were American moms who kept their kids on anti-malarial medication for years, following the advice of doctors who had never set foot on the continent. The Senegalese moms sensibly strapped their babies on their backs and went on with their lives.

Luther walked to his international school alone most days. His route took him on a shortcut through an apartment building hallway where one day he heard soft cries coming from a hole in the concrete wall. He poked his head into the void. It was a tiny kitten. He reached inside and scratched its chin.

Every day he passed the kitten, retreating home to tell me new stories from the hole, trying to convince me to let him bring the kitty home.

"Mom, today there was a bowl of rice in the hole," he said.

"See? Someone is feeding it," I told him. "It's fine in there."

The kitten followed him along his walk, retreating back to its hole when Luther reached a busy street. Every day it was waiting for him.

One morning we awakened to find rainy season in full force. The downpour left lake-sized puddles all across the city with its poor drainage system. Luther grabbed his umbrella and headed out for school. When he arrived at the hole, it was empty. He reached the apartment complex courtyard and spotted the kitten— facedown in a giant puddle. It had drowned.

When I picked up the kids from school that afternoon Luther whispered the story as we crossed the same courtyard. It killed me that my little boy had been alone when he came upon that grim scene in the puddle.

As he was talking, we approached two men chatting and tearing at a baguette. We got closer and I realized they were dropping breadcrumbs to a small tiger-striped kitten meowing for more. It wasn't far from the hallway hole, and it looked about the same size as the other kitten. It even had the same coloring. It was probably from the same litter as the dead kitten.

"Is that your cat?" I asked the men.

"No, it's a stray," one said.

"Grab that kitty," I told my son. "We're taking him home."

The kitten was covered in fleas, filled with parasites and gave us all ringworm. I even found a mangoworm on his paw. I proudly squeezed it out myself. But we loved him, worms and all.

We had been in Dakar for months and had begun to accept and embrace this new life and new culture we'd entered. We never completely shut off our sense of high alert, but we were settling in, learning to enjoy the quirks and not get overwhelmed by the struggles.

HAVING AGREED TO come on board, Jaime, with his dark-rimmed Buddy Holly glasses, soul patch and short afro, arrived in Dakar armed with a glossy new driver's license from Sierra Leone. I didn't even want to ask how he'd managed to acquire it with little driving experience. He assured me he had been behind the wheel enough to know what he was doing. I took him out on a Sunday morning for a test ride.

Jaime climbed into the driver's seat. The cabin filled with the overpowering scent of what to me smelled like stale bug spray. It was the cologne of choice for many West African young men. The beads on his stack of bracelets clanged against the steering wheel as he checked the mirrors and started the car. He tapped the gas, then the brakes, then the gas. We lurched along in fits and starts. I had a new appreciation for how anxious my mom must have been teaching me to drive on the gravel road out by the cemetery in our hometown. I tried to stay calm.

"Hands at 10 o'clock and 2 o'clock," I said, trying to think of advice from my high school drivers' education teacher. I'd never taught anyone to drive before. I didn't know what to say.

Behind the wheel of the company car with his new boss, Jaime was too nervous to respond. He sped ahead, going too fast over the potholes in our neighborhood. Both our heads jerked forward.

"Watch where you're going," I said, stating the obvious.

I directed him onto the four-lane corniche, whose wide, smooth lanes I knew would be empty on a Sunday and offer a buffer in case he weaved. Jaime turned onto the road. He steered the car for a few minutes without a problem as we wound down the pavement, passing several roundabouts and heading toward the American embassy. He seemed to have trouble lining up the wheels to go where he wanted them to go. He panicked.

"Turn the steering wheel!" I yelled.

He ran the car up on a curb, right in front of the embassy and its security officers posted everywhere. A policeman approached our car. Jaime handed his Sierra Leonean license to the officer, apologizing over and over.

The officer let us go on our way. I decided Jaime should stick to reporting.

Thankfully he was a better reporter than driver. Early on, he suggested he write a feature story about the religious significance of the Sunday bathing of the sheep in the ocean.

"You mean bathing of the *goats*," I corrected him. After all, I had watched this ritual myself with the kids.

"No," he said, "I'm talking about sheep."

"Wait. Are you telling me those animals on the beach aren't goats?"

"No," he said, laughing. "They're sheep."

I had fallen for a common Western expat mistake: mixing up sheep and goats. To the uninitiated, the difference is slight. The coats of West African sheep were adapted for the hot climate. They didn't have bulky, furry wool; they had short, close-cropped hair. Other than their rounded noses, flappy ears and drooping tails, they looked like goats to my American eye.

Jaime didn't make me feel dumb for my mistake. He just corrected me. It presented an opening for me to ask him everything I didn't understand about our new setting. Together, we created a crucial safe space for cultural exchange, judgment free.

"What are those little red birds the men carry around in cages?"
I asked.

"They call them 'pithis,' and if you pay the guy he'll set it free, to
wash away your sin," he said.

"Why does every car have a horse hair pony tail tied to their
bumper?"

"For good luck," he said.

"What are those sticks people always have in their mouths?"

"They use them for toothbrushes."

In turn, he grilled me about Americans—specifically, about
white people.

"What does it feel like to be in the sun without cream?" he
asked.

"Bad sunburns hurt like hell for white people," I told him. "Like
burning your hand on the stove."

"Why don't white people like spicy food?"

"Some white people do," I assured him.

While Jaime settled in, I flew off to file more stories from other
places on the continent—the capital of Gabon, where a presidential campaign was under way; rural Niger, where people fleeing
war were camping out along a half-finished highway, the only
place they felt safe because it was patrolled by the military. I saw a
ruthless dictator from Chad throw a temper tantrum after a court
convicted him of war crimes. I went to refugee camps, presidential
palaces and boozy embassy parties. I stood outside a sidewalk café
in Burkina Faso, looking at a half-eaten pizza and a spilled bottle of
wine, the remnants of a diner's last meal before terrorists stormed.

My leg-crossing incident with the Ambassador of Peace in the
Niger Delta wasn't my only awkward reporting moment.

I lost my train of thought during a filmed interview with the
president of Senegal when aides crawled on their bellies out of
the camera frame to reposition a stuffed white lion the president
had insisted be centered in the background. In Mali, I played third
wheel as the interior minister flirted with my translator. A warlord

in the Central African Republic mocked my mediocre French. On a road trip in Gabon, I peed in a field, I thought out of sight, and wound up in the background of my colleague's photo of a village chief. In the capital of Ghana, I mistakenly sat in a seat reserved for the president. More than once I tripped over a VIP's fancy boubou—a shiny, poufy tunic with numerous folds of fabric, worn by men—on my way to shake his hand.

I was a reporter with two decades of experience yet I always seemed to wind up in these Bridget Jones-y situations. It was ridiculous. I reminded myself that each country was a brand-new episode. Embarrassment was going to be part of the experience. And so were the accompanying insults about my outsider status.

"Just look at her profile picture," one Nigerian reader tweeted in response to a story I'd written about Nigerian politics.

The reader was furious after the paper's Twitter robots had tweeted out a photo of the president of Ghana that was automatically attached to my story focusing on the Nigerian president. My article included a few paragraphs on the Ghanaian president, and for some reason the automated system had seized on his name and published a photo of the leader of Ghana with the tweet. It made me look like I didn't know the difference between Ghana and Nigeria—it was embarrassing. Twitter piled on. I stayed silent.

The haters of course had a point. It came from a long history of being misrepresented in the Western press and mass media.

Dialogue in many American films and TV shows often refer to anywhere around here as merely "Africa," dismissing away myriad countries, cultures and topographies.

Western reporters were criticized for focusing on wars, on disease, on famine, on voodoo or wild beasts, perpetuating stereotypes of savagery. That seemed exaggerated until I came across one story that included a passage about Africans who believe eating giraffe can cure AIDS. Africa + exotic animal + awful disease. It was a perfect storm of stereotypes. The African Onion, were there such a thing, couldn't have outdone it.

Scholars have argued that kind of reporting leads to the per-petuation of a belief that tragedy in Africa, a place presented as so "backward" seeming, is inevitable and not newsworthy.

Colonialism in this part of the world added another layer of skepticism about the Western gaze. The horrors inflicted by white Europeans who poured in, slaughtered millions, imposed new rul-ers and cultures, plundered resources, exported slaves and stole art exhibited in Paris and London museums is rightfully hard to move beyond. Especially when traces of the colonial mindset still exist.

It was alive and well one evening at my next-door neighbor's back patio in Dakar where, at a get-to-know-you gathering for aperitifs, a Frenchwoman sat sucking on a slender cigarette com-plaining about the disdain she thought many Senegalese people felt for the French.

"We built this country, after all," she fumed as she took another drag, unable to fathom the derision.

The West was busy offloading into this region its dirtiest fuel exports that no one else would take, its unhealthiest fast food that it had stopped serving elsewhere, its cast-off clothing nobody else wanted, its middle-of-the-night flight departures that in the global interconnected web of air travel allowed for reasonable daytime itineraries elsewhere, and even its substandard maxi-pads that gave women rashes.

So I knew that, to some, I was always going to be too much of a novice, too American, too Nebraskan, too uneducated, too focused on violence, too dismissive of violence, too privileged or too white. There wasn't much I could do about that, other than try to see things from other people's perspectives.

Meanwhile, my stories filed so far from West Africa, even the one I wrote about the oil pipeline militants, were landing in the middle of the paper, far from the visibility of the front page.

———

BACK IN DAKAR, we hosted our first houseguests several months after we arrived—a family we knew from Brooklyn. Just having them around reminded us of home. I tried my best to be a good tour guide.

I took them to the biggest fabric market—a scene that is as chaotic as Times Square on a weekend—where vendors peddle thousands of meters of bold, colorful designs that women wear every day as dresses and head-wraps. I'd never paid much attention to the fabric before. The prints almost blend into a rainbow blur—until you stare at them. From a distance, what looked like swirls and squiggles and blobs printed on some of the fabric actually were images of tubes of lipstick, designer handbags, laptops and electric fans—tributes to pop culture and innovation.

I looked closer. Some conveyed feminist messages. One popular pattern, called "The Family," shows a hen surrounded by eggs and chicks. A disembodied rooster head is positioned alongside them. The message: a woman may be married, but she's the center of the home; the father just floats around nearby. Another pattern illustrates birds soaring from the open doors of cages, wings spread wide. It's called "You Fly, I Fly," and is a warning to wayward lovers. If you betray me, I'll do the same.

During election time here, politicians hand out reams of the fabric with images of their faces plastered across it, the same way politicians in the United States hand out caps and T-shirts. Women who oppose the candidates still gladly accept the material but tailor dresses so the politician's face fits snugly across their rear ends.

The market was a hit with our friends. Todd and I were trying to ensure they had fun in unfamiliar terrain that we ourselves were still figuring out. We took them to the beach, sent them off to a desert lodge and arranged for sunset drinks overlooking the ocean. They loved it. Mission accomplished.

The kids and I crammed into the car to drop them at the airport for their flight home. In my rush, and swept up in patting myself

on the back for having successfully hosted our first guests, I'd forgotten about the strenuous scene of the Dakar airport, with throngs
of people and taxis vying for spots. I joined a long line of double
parkers outside the terminal, pulling alongside an already parked
car, where I told our friends to hop out. As they disentangled
themselves from the backseat, my girls trailed them. While unload-
ing luggage, I looked up to see the car alongside me backing up—
with Zola behind it. "Stop!" I shouted.

The driver, a well-dressed Senegalese man about my age, yelled
at me to move my car.

"You almost hit a little girl!" I yelled back.

He poked his head out the window and kept hollering at me to
move my car. I kept yelling at him that he'd almost hit my daughter.

"Va te faire foutre!" he said, swearing at me.

"Oh yeah? Well, *va te faire foutre, aussi!*" I returned the insult.

All of the sudden, he pushed open his car door and rushed
toward me. And, before I could move out of the way, he punched
me in the mouth.

My lips were throbbing and I could taste blood. I fought back
tears as I gathered up the girls and pulled them into the car, where
my son was waiting. The man kept screaming at me to get out of
the way. I was shaking.

An airport police officer heard the man yelling at me and came
toward us.

"Move your car," he said.

"This man just punched me," I told him.

The officer's eyes widened.

"Who saw this?" he asked me.

"I don't know—probably everyone," I said, gesturing at the
crowd around us. "If you need proof, look at my mouth!"

"What happened?" he asked me.

With a reporter's diligence I tried to recount the story, telling
how I had pulled my car alongside his, he nearly ran over my

daughter, I told him to stop, he yelled at me, he swore at me, I swore at him . . .

The officer stopped me. "You swore at him?"

Yes, after he did the same to me, I explained.

"You can go," he said to the other driver, who slinked back into his car and sped off. The officer looked at me. "And you need to get in your car and follow me."

I texted Todd. No response. I tried again and again.

"Where are you? I'm being arrested!" I typed.

The messages didn't seem to be going through.

My kids were bawling. I argued with the officer, trying to take a photo of him and of the man's car as he pulled away—and the policeman insisted I hand over my phone.

I gave in and drove behind him as he walked to guide me to a makeshift airport police headquarters just outside the parking lot. Everything began to happen in a blur. Me trying to contain my terrified children; me explaining to the officer in charge that I believed I was the victim; me beating back a man who I turned around to find was pawing Maude with a hand he had jabbed through a chain-link fence.

I tried pleading my case to the officer, to no avail. I showed the commanding officer my lip. By now I was spitting out little chunks of torn skin where the blow had crushed the inside of my top lip against my teeth. Meanwhile, a sobbing Luther was begging me to stop arguing. So I did.

In the end, the officer in charge wrote me a ticket for blocking traffic and made me pay the equivalent of a $10 fine. I handed over the money and he let me leave.

Here, as it turns out, the unspoken rules say women are supposed respect men. Even if they have insulted you in the first place. I had crossed a cultural line by swearing and getting upset. The ticket said I blocked a driver but the loud and clear message was don't insult a man.

On the ride home the kids and I had a long, frank and somewhat panicked talk about seeking justice as a woman.

"This is what it's like for women in other countries," I told the kids as we drove. I worried whether this man had a wife and, if so, how many times she had been hit during a heated argument.

"Women are abused and no one is punished," I said, half blind with rage over what had just happened.

Zola started wailing, shouting again and again, "I want to go back to America. The police don't do this to people in America."

"Oh yeah?" I said, sensing another potent teachable moment. "You know what the police are doing in America? They're killing black people!"

The three kids let out a collective scream and all began to sob.

The wails continued as we drove. Deciding we all needed to get our fury out, I told the kids that, for the rest of the ride, they could scream any curse word they wanted without penalty, just this once. We continued down the dark and empty seaside road, a stunned foursome in a foreign land, with *fucks* and *shits* hurtling out the windows to anyone who might be listening.

CHAPTER 4

Call Your Husband

I SHOULDN'T HAVE sworn at the guy. I should have been more compliant with the police. I shouldn't have let the kids swear. But was this what it was going to be like as a woman living here?

The usually logical Todd didn't quite know what to make of the punching incident. He tried to find sense in it, some explanation or deeper meaning that made us all feel better. But he couldn't. I think we both just wanted to forget about it.

The night that I spent getting punched, he was out at the embassy field playing Ultimate Frisbee, the first time he'd played since before we had three kids. When we were younger living in Seattle, I made fun of him for liking such a hippie sport with players who all liked to talk about "the spirit of the game," and professed it was all peace and love and just having fun. When I tried to play, I was so bad nobody wanted me on their team. It was not fun. But Todd liked the game, and I think it made him feel young again to be on the field and still be able to outrun 20-year-olds. He was starting to find a bit of enjoyment in Dakar, even if it was through an import from America.

But for me, getting punched in the face really tainted my view of this place. I started hating Senegal. *Teranga,* my ass.

Instead of sparkling tinsel, the trash that piled up on the roadsides revealed itself to me in new ways, along with the stagnant rainwater that pooled in the streets in the rainy season. My running route along the seaside bluffs I nicknamed "pet cemetery" for all the abandoned farm animal carcasses that rotted along empty stretches of the road. It reminded me of the back roads in Nebraska where people dumped old refrigerators and stoves into creek beds, leaving them to rust and decompose. Here, roadway shoulders were every shepherd's dumping ground. The smell of death lingering in the moist air, which I had been ignoring, now made me gag. I shuddered at the rats bigger than our cat prowling the streets at night, and the bats with raptor-like wingspans screaming as they commandeered the trees outside our bedroom window. I complained about the chemical aftertaste of the powdered Nescafé, the only caffeine option in most restaurants. Amid the symphony of birdcalls in our yard, I picked out the one menacing cackle that sounded more like the threatening caaaaaw that rang out when Scooby-Doo and Shaggy were about to encounter trouble.

I tried to tune out this new sense of revulsion with the world around me. Compartmentalizing can be a beautiful thing. And, like most reporters, I excelled at it.

Journalism required mental distance. It wasn't that I didn't care about the awful things I had reported on. I cared so much, in fact, that I had accepted and lobbied for sketchy assignments. I was evangelical in my belief that the power of journalism is to help make the world a better place. I knew that to do my job I had to keep building a mental wall between myself and my subjects and surroundings.

I learned how to do that over time, by covering a lot of bad news. It started back in the United States with crime scenes—seeing bullet casings and pools of blood on the sidewalk, the aftermath of gang violence. Then came the tough interviews: the stoic father of a boy who survived being shot in the head by a stray bullet comes to mind. I moved on to domestic killings, freak accidents and plane crashes. I watched American soldiers poke at four corpses of scrawny young men shot execution style in Mosul, Iraq, rotting on the street because everyone was too afraid they were booby-trapped to touch them. I sat with a man whose lungs were full of cancer at a San Antonio Krispy Kreme, as he cried about what we both knew were his last months of life. I arrived in Haiti after a massive earthquake, and within five minutes got stuck in traffic behind a garbage truck scooping up stacks of rotting bodies that had been set out on the side of the street like the week's trash. The smell of death leaked into my car, penetrating my hair and clothes, which stank of it for days. So many people were killed then that rotting corpses were piled up or squished between layers of pancaked buildings and strewn about along the streets. On one corner two corpses lay on a bed inside a brothel—a man and woman struck dead in missionary position. The brothel's outer walls had fallen during the quake, exposing this couple to passersby, who amid all the gruesomeness and sorrow had become hardened and couldn't help but point and laugh at such bad timing.

In my first job at the City News Bureau of Chicago, I covered crime in some of the most dangerous neighborhoods in the city. The old cigar-chomping, smoke-filled newsroom movie *His Girl Friday* was based on City News. This was the place that came up with the journalism mantra: "If your mother says she loves you, check it out." Trust no one, the thinking went, not even your own mother until you've done a thorough job of reporting.

It was journalism boot camp with long hours and a lot of yelling. An editor barked at me for mistaking Wentworth "Avenue" for Wentworth "Street." I was required to call to check in with the home office five or six times a day as I hopped between assignments and crime scenes, even when it meant competing with drug dealers for payphones.

"You have to have some goddamn natural curiosity," one editor yelled at me after I'd failed to sufficiently grill the cops about a high-profile art gallery heist.

Curiosity didn't come natural to me. In my church growing up we read aloud Bible verses that commanded us to be *in* the world, not *of* the world. The world was sinful and full of sinners. Best to walk around with blinders on, they taught us. Leave that apple on the tree. It'll only get you into trouble.

I trained myself to be curious by writing out all my questions in advance in my notebook for every single story.

At City News, we all dreaded being made to work the overnight shift. It involved stakeouts at some of the bloodiest crime scenes, and in-person trips to the coroners' office in the wee hours to pick up a list of the day's body count. Only a select few reporters had ever managed to escape the shift. I was one of them. A top editor shielded me. I was grateful. But I also wondered, was I a disappointment? Did he think I was one of those women who couldn't handle it?

I've had editors on the other extreme, who tried to finesse the image of their women reporters as extra tough. When I was pregnant and working at *The Wall Street Journal,* a male editor once suggested I time the filing of a major story so that I would be in the middle of final edits while in labor. It would improve my reputation inside the paper, he assured me. He wanted to make me look invincible. I just wanted to get my baby out of me. I politely declined.

A special sort of parsing is done of women reporters willing to go to war zones and disasters. Outsiders label you "hard" for working where others won't. And you live in fear of bosses labeling you "soft" if you complain about harsh conditions.

My career had been filled with tough assignments documenting tragedy and despair. But journalism helped me feel like I could do something about events in places where everything seems so mercilessly unfair.

So yeah, I got punched. How could I feel sorry for myself when other people had been through so much worse? I got over it and got on with my job.

———

THE BIGGEST STORY in my region was playing out with incredible violence and sheer terror for the few million people who lived in one of the poorest places on earth: northeastern Nigeria.

Nigeria is a huge, diverse country, with not just skinny creeks patrolled by militants in the Delta but big, sprawling cities like Lagos with its Manhattan-esque skyline and rollicking music and art scene, and a band of territory in the middle that turns emerald green in the rainy season, with miles of farmland and huge herds of migrating cattle.

But for seven years in the nation's northeast, a group of Islamist extremists called "Boko Haram" had been roaming the country-side, raiding villages, burning homes, murdering people and steal-ing livestock in rural communities where the families of farmers and fishermen lived hand to mouth.

The group was hell-bent on returning the region to a state where a harsh interpretation of Islam ruled. They wanted a caliph-ate. The government and military were targeted as the enemy. They were emblems of Western, sinful leanings. Any arm of the government—civil servants, police and, notably, public school teachers and students—became enemies, along with anyone who didn't believe in the cause of Boko Haram, a name that translates as "Western education is forbidden."

It was easy to dismiss the group as a bunch of religious extrem-ists.

I understood devotion to religion. I had spent much of my youth at the redbrick Church of Christ out by the highway in my small Nebraska town. My mom took me to Sunday morning services, Sunday evening preaching, Wednesday night Bible studies and the occasional revival. I memorized Bible verses, played on the Bible Bowl team, sang in the church choir and lined up for Jell-O and Cool Whip salads at fellowship dinners. I knew all the hymns by heart. I surveyed the wondrous cross. I was redeemed by the blood of the lamb. Amazing grace saved a wretch like me.

When I was about 10, a preacher wearing rubber hip waders guided me down the stairs of the small, rectangular pool. My white baptismal gown floated to the top of the chilly water. I quickly pushed it down so I wouldn't flash the congregation with my Strawberry Shortcake underwear. The preacher said a prayer, and I went under, baptized into the name of the Father, the Son and the Holy Spirit.

"Now I belong to Jesus, Jesus belongs to me," sang the congregation gathered to celebrate the event. "Not for the years of time alone, but for eternity."

Religious-based terrorism back then in America involved abortion. Our church never participated in the movement that advocated bombing abortion clinics—Operation Rescue was headquartered just 200 miles due south of us—but I had heard people in the congregation say they supported that kind of violence.

The group ravaging northeast Nigeria was far more deadly, of course, and was acting out of far more than just religious fervor.

Back when it was first getting started, Boko Haram's charismatic founder, Mohammed Yusuf, had a legitimate beef with the state. Corruption in Nigeria was out of control. The inequalities it produced riled the population. In Nigeria, northerners were almost entirely Muslim; the capital and other urban areas in the south were largely Christian, and many Muslims felt left behind because of their religion. The Northeast, where Yusuf was from, was the poorest region in the whole country, with vast areas of little or no real government, let alone government services like electricity or running water. As people there struggled to get enough to eat, politicians and government workers were stealing public money to build fancy houses, drive nice cars and send their children to London or somewhere else in the West for their education. Those kids then would come back and take their parents' place in government in order to continue stealing other people's money, sending off their own kids to British boarding schools and universities, only to start the cycle all over again. *What are they teaching those kids in the British schools?* the illiterate rural population must have been wondering. "Western education is forbidden" was almost a reasonable rallying cry.

As Yusuf drew more followers to hear his sermons at the local mosque, the government became more nervous and paranoid. In Maiduguri, the northeastern Nigerian city where this was all playing out, local officials passed a new motorcycle helmet law. It outraged riders who didn't want to wear helmets any more than many American riders did when those kinds of laws came on the books in the United States. In Maiduguri, many of them couldn't even afford a helmet. It threatened the livelihoods of people who relied on motorbikes for work and was yet another way government showed it was out of touch with regular people. Some clever protestors zipped around the city wearing hollowed-out squash shells and rubber tires on their heads to express their annoyance at the new law.

In June 2009, Boko Haram members were on motorbikes, helmet-less, riding in a funeral procession. Police stopped the convoy to ticket the men without helmets. The grieving riders were furious. Violence broke out. And it has been going on ever since. Police later detained Yusuf and killed him. No charges, no trial—it was extrajudicial murder. They didn't even try to cover it up. His successor was Abubakar Shekau, a ruthless and reckless man who made his presence known in a series of propaganda videos where he waved his AK-47 and ranted with bulging eyes. Security officials called him insane. His message of violence drew even more outraged followers.

I paged through books and articles about Shekau and was struck by one fact: he and I were the same age. By his early 40s, Shekau had taken over complete swaths of territory in northern Nigeria, holding open-air sermons that drew hundreds of people. I sat in my office internalizing this, staring out the windows that I had not yet found the time to cover with curtains, while he was probably out there plotting no less than a presidential coup. I was intrigued.

Poor village schoolgirls were the reason most people had heard about Boko Haram. More than 250 girls had been kidnapped from the small community of Chibok, Nigeria, in 2014 when fighters stormed their school as they slept. They shoved the terrified girls into trucks and sped away.

Not only did the Nigerian government fail to organize a search party immediately, but it spent days denying the kidnapping had even happened. Officials must have been embarrassed that such a hideous event had occurred on their watch. It was also proof they were losing the war against the militants.

Later, when officials admitted the kidnapping was real, the government turned down the help of other nations' armed forces. It was a matter of pride. Bringing back the girls was a national issue, they said, to be handled by Nigerians. Parents of the girls were so desperate, one father had hopped on his motorbike and set out to search for the girls himself. He found shoes and bits of their clothing but the trail petered out. He came home empty-handed.

Boko Haram taunted the government by broadcasting videos of the girls in captivity, with Shekau pledging to sell them in the market. The images were striking for their awfulness—dozens of teenagers gathered together in dark hijabs that exposed only faces stricken with terror.

Their parents started speaking out, criticizing the government for doing nothing. Activists in the capital took up the cause, holding signs and marching through the streets demanding action. On social media, a hashtag was created: #BringBackOurGirls. Soon after, the sad images of these girls in captivity hurtled across the Internet and the world.

The kidnapping turned the war into a celebrity cause. On the red carpet during the Academy Awards, Sylvester Stallone and Ellen Degeneres held posters that read, "BringBackOurGirls." Michelle Obama released a photo of herself doing the same. Schoolkids in America, France and South Korea marched in support of finding the girls.

The Nigerian government was compelled to act. But by the time the military began an earnest search for the militants, the girls were long gone, hidden in the forest. The Nigerians later relented and enlisted the help of foreign governments with their drones and intelligence gathering operations. The government even tried to negotiate with Boko Haram for the girls' release. But years of mistrust, infighting between militants and a change in the Nigerian presidency complicated the talks. The girls remained in Boko Haram's hands.

The Chibok girls had become the symbols of the havoc the group had caused throughout the region in a war that had spread across Nigeria's porous borders. Their captivity was the unfinished story of this long war.

After I had accepted this job, one of the former *Times* West Africa bureau chiefs had cautioned me to avoid the lure of conflict reporting.

"A war story will always get you on the front page," he had said. "I guarantee it."

Why, he argued, should we cover African countries differently than we cover anywhere else? Places here also have political issues, economic struggles and art scenes that are worthy of stories. Why make it seem like every nation on the continent has a war going on and little else?

He had a good point. But I couldn't ignore wars. In fact, I felt I had a responsibility not to. People in power paid attention to the *Times*. The best I could do, I decided, was aim to strike a balance with my coverage. For every war story, I would try to find another story on another part of life in the country where I was reporting. Onward to the war zone, then, I decided.

———

I WAS FEELING good about heading out for my first war assignment covering Boko Haram. Jaime was in place in case anything happened. I'd done my homework. I called my editor to let him know I was thinking about hitting the road, heading out to report in the danger zone.

"How often should I call you to check in?" I asked.

"Call your husband," he said.

That answer stopped me. It seemed so cold.

I thought back to the few weeks I had spent in Iraq to report on the war, a decade earlier, and had finally reached Todd via satellite phone. It was Christmas and he was at his parents' house, probably sitting by the fire, glass of wine in hand. I was on the other end of the line in the middle of the desert, standing alongside a stalled military convoy and picking bits of ash out of my hair after having fallen asleep in the sand near what turned out to be a burning trash pile.

"Merry Christmas," I mumbled when he picked up.

"I wish you were here," he said.

"Yeah."

We hung up without saying much more.

At this point in our relationship Todd could go for a week without noticing I hadn't checked in. It wasn't that he didn't care about me. It was the opposite. He had absolute confidence I could take care of myself in any situation. It was nice. And a little lonely.

And yes, I get it, I get it, my editor is busy. The paper also had a security expert who advised reporters about dicey areas. But that was the moment I realized how very much on my own I was out here. No editor was going to hold my hand, let alone tell me where to go or what to do.

To be fair, a lot was going on in America. Donald Trump was drawing thousands of people to his unruly rallies, where he bragged about his wealth, threatened the opposition, told lies and disparaged the media. My competition in the news cycle was a blustering guy with a wild comb-over who was starting to act like some of the worst politicians in Africa.

The more I learned about my new region, the more the whole Trump dynamic had a familiar ring to it. Just like Trump, presidents around here had no qualms about flaunting their wealth—their fleets of luxury cars and fancy real estate holdings—even as most of the population only dreamed of such a lifestyle. "Lock Her Up" became a rallying cry at Trump rallies, as presidents running for re-election across West Africa were plotting the arrests of their chief opponents. The president of Senegal did wind up putting his opponent in jail.

Trump's domination of the news cycle would all be done soon enough, after the U.S. election, I thought to myself. The world would be dazzled by the news of the first female American president and then the nation would be back to business as usual—and my stories from West Africa would have a shot at getting noticed.

I ignored America and carried on.

My predecessor in the bureau had been on this beat writing about Boko Haram during the heat of the battle, when militants were roaming the streets killing at random. He covered the war exhaustively, telling stories of children burned alive or kidnapped, women who were raped, entire villages set ablaze, abusive military practices as soldiers killed scores of civilians in their hunt for militants—the awfulness went on and on.

By the time I arrived in West Africa, the war had been going on for the better part of a decade. Boko Haram had since been driven from its strongholds, no longer controlling large towns and other territories. Fighters had fled into hideouts in the forest. The group was unable to muster the power to mount attacks on military convoys and installations. Instead, they carried out cheaper and easier-to-organize suicide bombings.

Covering Boko Haram likely was going to be the most dangerous assignment I would encounter and, in truth, I wanted to get it over with.

My best chance of breaking new ground, I calculated, would be to try to interview a Boko Haram fighter. That might help explain what was still fueling the rank and file in the group, long after they'd proven their point, to carry out even more violent and heinous attacks. And why so much violence? Who were these fighters? Where did they get their weapons and explosives? What motivated them? What was their background? I could think of dozens of questions to ask a fighter that would help illuminate what this war was even about at this point.

Boko Haram was one of the most secretive terrorist organizations in the world, communicating only through a handful of videos it released starring Shekau, often wearing a brown stocking cap and headband made of a ragged strip of camouflage fabric. An AK-47 resting on his shoulder, he flailed his arms while bragging about his prowess on the battlefield and leveling various threats. Shekau didn't call up reporters to chat, so beyond the propaganda videos and the string of corpses left behind, the group largely remained a mystery.

In Nigeria, the military had detained a few fighters, and from time to time, they trotted them out before news cameras, where the men disavowed Boko Haram and talked about the gallantry of the Nigerian military. It seemed contrived. It was impossible to know if the people making these claims were actors or if they had been tortured—or paid. Nigeria's military had a terrible track record when it came to transparency, not to mention human rights.

If I was going to find a fighter I needed to get to the war.

CHAPTER 5

The Terrible List

THE WAR WITH Boko Haram had begun to spill across the Nigerian border, ravaging a skinny sliver of land thousands of miles from urban anything in the country. The paper had never covered the war from the Cameroon side of things, so it seemed like a chance to break some new ground.

A lot of regions have nicknames for less populated, rural areas. In Nebraska the western panhandle was known as "outstate," a sort of derogatory name for the smattering of small towns that didn't hold much political clout. In New York, "upstate" is the name for entire populations that, because they exist outside the city, are lumped together into one term. This slice of Cameroon was called "the Far North." In French, its literal translation was "the Extreme North," a name that better reflects the severity of the area, a palomino-colored, treeless moonscape littered by piles of big boulders that the sand seemed to have belched into existence.

In the Far North, even during good times, food and work were scarce. But now the main sources of income, farming and herding, had screeched to a halt. Farmers were afraid to stray too far from home to go into their fields, for fear of being killed or kidnapped. Those who dared to farm were allowed to grow only crops that grew low to the ground, like onions, so soldiers could keep a clear sight line for approaching militants. Herders no longer freely moved their cattle from place to place to graze. Many fields were left fallow and animals were dying of hunger. People were struggling to get enough to eat.

Boko Haram fighters weren't in better shape. Since the military had chased them off the territory they controlled, they had relied on looting to support themselves. If the farmers had nothing to eat, the militants also had nothing.

I had no idea how I would find a Boko Haram fighter in the Far North. But I knew that I needed to understand the situation on the ground before I could even begin to make a plan to go there. I emailed a diplomat working in the area to see if he could update me on recent events in that part of the country. A few minutes later he had sent to me what he called the "Terrible List." I clicked on the attachment.

February 4 An adult male detonated explosives behind the house of a tailor. They both died. The attacker was looking for a larger group of civilians to target, but since the latest increase in suicide attacks people cannot be found gathering on the streets. Later, two suicide attackers detonated and killed themselves, seriously wounding a high-school student.

February 6 A village was attacked by presumed Boko Haram assailants. Five civilians were killed and numerous homes set on fire.

February 10 A twin suicide attack killed eight civilians and wounded forty-five, nine of whom are in critical condition. Two women suicide attackers coming from Nigeria sought to join a group of people gathered for a funeral. One attacker detonated soon after, at around 6:20 A.M., but the second attacker died in the blast, before she could detonate.

February 11 Cameroonian military members discovered a Boko Haram camp. They killed 12 Boko Haram members.

February 13 Boko Haram suspects launched an attack on troops, but it was successfully repressed. Source says there were about 50 assailants. Boko Haram assailants killed 13 civilians. After preaching to the detained crowd, assailants randomly beheaded and shot civilians chosen from the group for no apparent reason.

February 14 Cameroon launched an early attack on Boko Haram positions, killing 162 assailants. Four bomb-making facilities were dismantled.

February 15 In the evening, twenty-five individuals suspected of belonging to Boko Haram, including ten children, nine women and six men carrying guns, were apprehended.

February 19 In a market frequented by women, two females detonated explosives, possibly carried in water tanks, killing 35 and wounding 115.

February 22 Boko Haram killed one man about 50 years old. Reports say that the man was killed when, out of desperation for drinking water, he went to the border to get to a well near a school, where he was apprehended and then killed by the assailants.

That was only part of the list. In full, it was a stunning near-daily accounting of wartime horrors, any one of which would be front-page news had it occurred in America. The violence had been playing out in this particular border area for months. The nation's leaders no longer flinched at a report of a bombing or the slaughtering of a man killed filling his bucket at a well.

But among this list of tragedies, a couple of the entries held a detail that stood out to me right away: the use of female suicide bombers.

In recent wars, suicide bombings had become a common militant tactic. Women bombers were a rare phenomenon. Yet it made sense as a strategy. Women draw less suspicion than men, and in conservative societies, they are subject to less thorough searches by male security officers afraid of breaching cultural mores by patting down their bodies.

Perhaps the most famous women bombers were those deployed by the Tamil Tigers in the 1980s and 1990s, who worked in all-female bomb squads in Sri Lanka and were equipped with grenades and cyanide capsules in case of capture. Recently, too, women had gone on suicide missions for various militant organizations in places like Palestine and Bangladesh. In Chechnya, the so-called black widows had carried out bombings. And my colleagues had written about women who had lost brothers and husbands in Iraq during the war and sought vengeance by putting on suicide vests and blowing up checkpoints and police stations.

ISIS also had been accused of deploying women bombers. But two scholars writing in *The Atlantic* contended that this notion was largely mythology, hyperbolized by patriarchal societies captivated by the notion of chicks with bombs. "The idea of the female badass sells," they wrote.

> Burqaed and belted-up to the nines, she is the ultimate Other, transgressing not only civilizational prohibitions against murder and suicide, but also deeply ingrained assumptions about what it means to be a woman in patriarchal societies where women are accorded lesser status. She is a deviant among deviants, exploding the most elemental code of the jihadist worldview: namely, that men are men—which is to say, first and foremost, warriors—and women are women—which is to say, first and foremost, wives and mothers.

I knew that Boko Haram had used women suicide bombers in a few attacks but I had thought it was more of an anomaly than a trend, and something that had happened in Nigeria. The entries on the Terrible List—two bombings by women occurring within days of each other—made me wonder if this was becoming a regular thing in Cameroon now, too. Authorities had reported some of the bombers looked young and might even be teenagers.

Finding a woman bomber offered a new way to look at Boko Haram, and a new twist on finding one of the group's fighters. I wondered what would motivate a woman to carry a bomb for a group that didn't exactly seem to hold up feminist ideals as a key tenet.

It wasn't going to be easy to find anyone who would reveal their intentions to blow themselves up. And anyone who actually had pushed the detonator button already was dead. So I figured my best bet for a story was to see if I could piece together details about the women bombers from talking to people on the ground. I started making calls.

Several aid agencies were working in the area, one of which, a group under the United Nations, had been angling for me to visit their operations in the field. I would pay my own way, and they would guide me to hospitals where I could talk to Boko Haram bombing victims and be introduced to local officials. They also would take me to a desert refugee camp for people who had fled Boko Haram.

The aid group had been working in the region for months, knew the area well and was aware of security risks. International NGOs often angle to play tour guide for journalists. They want the free advertising, hoping for publicity that will bring donations to their programs. Because the groups have workers on the ground and often employ local staff, they offer safer passage into danger zones than if a reporter was to travel on her own.

The arrangement came with no strings attached and usually benefited everyone.

But first I had to get to the Far North. I went to work on logistics. I would need to fly into the capital of Cameroon and from there get to the Far North city of Maroua, where I would meet my contacts. Luckily one domestic airline flew into that city. I looked online for its flight schedule but instead came across an article in a Cameroonian newspaper complaining about the operator's safety record, with the hyperventilating headline "Flying Coffins!"

Maroua hadn't been attacked for weeks and was considered for the most part safe. But in some areas the United Nations vehicle I was to travel in would need to be escorted by the Special Forces of the Cameroonian military. Convoys of military vehicles sometimes attract terrorists. But I decided better a heavily armed escort than none at all.

"It's going to be a little dicey," I told Tyler Hicks, the photographer the *Times* had assigned to accompany me to Cameroon, "but you've probably been through much worse."

For the past two and a half decades, Tyler had hopped between just about every war zone and natural disaster on the globe. A blond with hunky good looks and an ash-strewn résumé that included a pile of photography prizes, he was a legend in the photojournalism world.

Some reporters preferred to go their own way and be spared the hassle of working with a photographer. I'm not one of them. My brother, nine years older than me, became a photojournalist when I was in elementary school. I was the kid sister tagging along on his assignments and in the darkroom, back when that existed. In my own career, I always found my stories benefited from joining a photographer who got out the door at dawn to chase the good light or stuck around on the scene of a story for a few hours after I'd already filled my notebook while they snapped away.

I also missed having a work husband. At the *Journal* my work husband and I used to slump over an orange couch at the base of a staircase in the newsroom and gossip or rant for hours, or sneak out for a second breakfast of Cuban sandwiches, sitting on barstools at a diner as our pores soaked up grease from the grill while we hashed out reporting problems.

Being assigned to work with anyone in these conditions was a bit like being cast in a season of *Survivor*. Strangers heading to an entirely new place, for days at a time, trying to come up with at least one front-page story for one of the biggest newspapers in the world. It would be easy to see how we could turn on each other.

Before we carried out any actual journalism, there were permissions to secure, visas to get, hotel reservations to make, drivers to find, cars to rent, translators to hire and schedules to coordinate of various aid workers who needed to clear their calendars to show us around. All those tasks usually fell on the reporter.

Tyler and I agreed on a few ground rules, for safety. 1) We wouldn't board a flight on that sketchy domestic airline. 2) We wouldn't stay in the war zone for more than two nights. 3) We'd keep a low profile, not wandering around town, alerting terrorists to our presence.

I booked us two nights at a hotel in Maroua and asked the aid workers if we could tag along on a charter humanitarian flight to avoid the Flying Coffins airline. They readily agreed. Everything was falling into place, and I felt more at ease knowing someone experienced like Tyler was coming along. My husband did, too.

Some husbands might be jealous of their wives jetting off for a few weeks alone in the middle of nowhere with a famous war photographer. Mine wasn't one of those. Todd was simply practical.

"Either you want to be with me or you don't" was the way he always framed our relationship.

I did, and that was that.

Besides, I told my husband, Tyler had a reputation for dating younger women. I assumed that to him, working with me would be like working with his great-aunt Mildred.

"YOU DON'T GET to control things while you're away," Todd kept reminding me before I left. The kids' teeth might not get brushed every night and their hair wouldn't be combed, probably ever, but they would be safe, fed and happy and would make it to school on time, I was certain.

The key to a happy, two-career household in America has puzzled some of the brightest minds of our time. We had been one of those rare dual-working couples that had never had to sacrifice career ambition. Most successful working moms I knew in America all had husbands with flexible schedules or even a trust fund to fall back on. Our careers magically had progressed together.

But now, for the first time, the balance of career power had tilted toward me. My predecessor had a stay-at-home wife who took care of their kids; the three West Africa bureau chiefs before him were childless.

The standard tour for international correspondents was three years. But we had a rip cord. The editors had assured me that if "special circumstances" merited it, I could leave after two years and still be in good graces with the paper. I guessed a shaky marriage would qualify. I hoped it wouldn't come to that.

Overseas reporting has been blamed for the start and demise of many romances. In Iraq's Green Zone, babies were conceived and marriages disintegrated. The sites of deadly earthquakes and tsunamis were also the settings in which reporters fell in love with their fixers or slept with philandering photographers. One friend's relationship had ended after an affair while covering the Ebola outbreak—hooking up with another journalist when most people were too cautious about spreading the virus to even shake hands.

But it wasn't infidelity I was worried about. There comes a point in time when the idea of putting up with another person's quirks seems like a whole new level of exasperation. And who has the energy for that? Or the time?

I just didn't know how we were both going to do our jobs and raise our kids in this totally new scenario.

"It would have been easier if we'd had a *wife*," explained one female reporter who had been in a similar dual-career situation while working on the *Times* international desk. She'd wanted the mythical third spouse—the one who would stay at home so mom and dad can work. Instead, she had juggled raising kids and two careers while abroad. And now she was divorced.

I tried to put that out of my mind.

I said goodbye to Todd and the kids, who still were too enamored with their new lives to notice a missing parent. Besides, my husband had done the same thing a dozen times in the past few years. My leaving wasn't a power imbalance, not at this point at least. It was my turn, is all. Todd was fine with it, and the kids were excited to have him to themselves for a while.

I landed in Yaoundé, the lush, hilly capital of Cameroon, and set up a few meetings with ministers and other officials, biding my time as I waited for Tyler to arrive so we could catch our flight to Maroua in the Far North. One diplomat picked me up at my hotel to take me back to his house for lunch.

"I'm going to drive around for a while now," he said, as I buckled my seatbelt, "so we can talk without being spied on."

I had no way to gauge if he was being paranoid. Did the Cameroonians really bug a diplomat's house? It seemed kind of James Bond to me.

The car rolled over hills thick with short, emerald banana and palm trees, a land so green it was the polar opposite of sandy Dakar. We passed open air restaurants lit up with neon blue mosquito zappers and block after block of people selling folding metal chairs with ribbons and lacey coverings, decorated the same way my junior class had gussied up the folding chairs for our high school prom inside the metal shed that served as the community center. Yaoundé's central market wound round and round, up several floors of a concrete building that looked like a car exhaust–stained version of The Getty but with hawkers crammed together selling vegetables under umbrellas. Another vegetable market outside the city center, where yams the size of newborn babies and softball-sized green peppers were on display, was covered in knee-deep mud. Vendors had placed thin wooden planks on the ground so shoppers could cross some of the worst patches.

As we drove, I learned off-the-record military secrets and unbridled criticisms of the government in very undiplomatic terms. Everyone knew where most of the Chibok girls were—in a swath of forest near the border between Cameroon and Nigeria, the diplomat told me. They weren't missing; they were impossible to access with any guarantee that Boko Haram wouldn't start executing them if they heard rescuers approaching.

Tyler arrived and we headed for the Yaoundé airport to catch our humanitarian flight to Maroua. Inside the bare-bones terminal, a worker holding a clipboard with passengers' names seemed to be taking an awfully long time staring at her list.

"I'm sorry," she said as she looked up. "Your names aren't on here."

"But we have to get Maroua today," I pleaded.

"Sorry, the flight is full," she said, walking away.

The aid group had forgotten to arrange for our tickets.

I made a few panicked calls but there was nothing to be done. Putting us on board would mean pulling two humanitarian workers from the plane. The next flight didn't leave for two days. Our whole trip, coordinated with the schedules of a half-dozen busy aid workers, was in jeopardy.

On the loudspeaker we heard a call for the Flying Coffins airline, announcing a flight to Maroua. Or at least we thought they said "Maroua." It was just a few miles away from the similarly named Mora. And Maroua also rhymed with nearby Garoua. These Far North names seemed like practical jokes to confuse outsiders.

The loudspeaker crackled again. The voice definitely said "Maroua."

Tyler and I looked at each other. We had no choice. It was the only way to keep our trip on schedule. I went through the familiar lecture in my head. *Hundreds of people fly this airline every day. Flying is safer than driving in a car.* And so on. An hour later we had tickets on Flying Coffins Airline. The new flight would get us there too late in the day to accomplish much real reporting—the government had put in place a curfew that started at nightfall. We'd need to stay an extra day in the Far North.

We hadn't even left the capital city and already were about to breach two of our three safety rules.

We wandered Yaoundé's airport, where outside one giant plate glass window on the main floor sat a blackened jet that looked like it had caught fire on the runway. Tyler photographed it and texted the picture to his girlfriend, telling her we were about to board that plane, just to freak her out. I started to do the same thing to Todd and then thought better of it. This kind of joke doesn't always translate well to the father of your three children. I asked around and learned the plane belonged to a carrier that had run out of money, leaving its fleet, a single jet, to the elements. The charred-looking fuselage was covered in mold.

We got in the security line, where a big white sign announced the prohibition of cocaine, morphine, opium, "uppers," ecstasy and—I wasn't quite sure why—palm oil and honey.

A security officer asked me to hand over my backpack. He unzipped all the pockets and started going through every single zipper and pocket by hand. He pulled out a mini tin of Altoids.

"What is this?" he barked.

"Mints," I said.

"What?"

"It's just candy."

"No candy allowed on the plane," he said, confiscating the tin. Next he pulled out my pack of gum.

"No gum allowed," he said, taking that, too.

He dug deeper into the little outside pocket of my pack and his hand emerged around a single tampon. He held it in front of his face to inspect it.

"What's this?" he demanded.

Embarrassed, I glanced over my shoulder to check whether Tyler was watching. His nose was buried in his phone screen.

"It's a tampon," I said quietly.

"A what?"

Oh right. Tampons aren't widely used in this part of the world. I wasn't quite sure how to duck out of this situation without embarrassing myself further. Men here didn't talk openly about Woman Things. But I didn't want him to confiscate my tampon stash because I was pretty sure I wasn't going to find a Walgreens in the Far North.

While I was trying to decide what to tell him, he called over another guard. Both of them were manhandling the tampon, and starting to open the packaging.

"No, wait," I said.

I decided just to be blunt. Being a woman wasn't a crime or anything to be embarrassed about, I reminded myself. In the heat of the moment, though, I couldn't remember how to say menstruation in French. The guards were looking at me, waiting for my response.

"It's for my monthly blood," I said in French, trying to piece together two words that would get the message across.

"Your what?" the guard said, looking baffled.

I remembered then that Jaime had made fun of me for sometimes confusing the French word for blood—*sang*—with monkey— *singe*. I had, I realized, told the guard that the small cylinder he was clutching was for my monthly monkey.

"It's for that thing that happens to women to make them have babies," I blathered on.

"Ooooh, it's a toy for babies. OK, great," he said, handing the tampon back to me.

I stuffed it in my pack before Tyler looked up, and raced up the stairs to the plane.

In time I would become accustomed to the choppy West African skies, full of dust and brutal heat waves that pilots always cautioned were going to rock our descent. I even grew fond of the one pilot who broadcast ABBA's "Mama Mia" on the loudspeaker, as he warned passengers of turbulence before guiding the plane onto the runway.

But back then, I was new to the unfriendly skies and still a little rattled as I made my way down the aisle after the bumpy landing of our Flying Coffins flight. I approached the front of the plane, and the flight attendant stopped me.

"Where are you headed?" she asked.

"To Maroua," I asked. "This is Maroua, right?"

"No, Maroua is our next stop."

Next stop? What was this, the crosstown bus? This was another part of air travel around here I needed to get used to. Planes wound up where they were supposed to go, but sometimes it took a while to get there. Flights often made unannounced stops in several other cities or even countries before they reached their destinations.

Already this one trip had been a steep learning experience about travel in this part of the world. On the other hand, unlike travel in America, West African airlines served meals on every flight and practically no one ever reclined their seats. Flight attendants were polite, and usually so were the passengers.

A COUPLE HOURS later, we made it to Maroua and were guided to a U.N. building for a briefing before the sun fell and curfew began. Ten aid workers sat around the table, and one by one they started to talk.

I was anxious to hear about conditions in the city and the camp we'd be visiting. I wanted to know about the biggest problems the refugees were facing and the security threats in the area. Were people living in fear because of the suicide bombings? And why were so many women willing to die for Boko Haram?

All that came out of their mouths was bureaucratic mumbo jumbo. The conversation was a blur of "livelihood strategies" and "persons of concern" and "community-based enterprise develop-ment tools." They droned on about their mission to "develop poli-cies that promote a range of comprehensive solutions."

I began to tune out, staring out the window at the cattle market across the street, where the last cows were being led away after a long day of haggling. The town had been hit by suicide bombers a few months back. I scanned the area for debris. Nothing. Just a kid using a stick to swat the butts of cows that were four times as big as him. I tuned back in to find one of the workers reciting passages of text from the United Nations 1960s protocol on the status of refugees. I couldn't take it anymore.

"I didn't come all the way here for information I could get on the Internet," I blurted. "I want to know what's going on—here in the city and out in the camp."

"We'll go to the camp another day," one of the workers said.

"Isn't there anything you can tell me about the situation here?"

The room fell silent. Maybe they were afraid of saying anything real to a reporter. Or maybe they just sat inside their office all day and wrote reports. I wasn't going to get anything useful out of this meeting.

"Why don't we go back to our hotel and talk more tomorrow?" I suggested. At least tomorrow we had a few meetings scheduled around town.

Maroua didn't feel that unsafe. Schoolkids walked the streets in yellow uniforms. Men rode motorbikes covered in bubble wrap to keep out the dust. A few yellow taxis rumbled down the dirt roads. Kids pedaled Mary Poppins–era bicycles—rusty old cruisers they were barely big enough to maneuver. We passed a couple of empty restaurants and women hawking balls of deep-fat-fried cassava frit-ters. A connoisseur of unhealthy food, I'm game to try anything deep fat fried. But we couldn't stop. It was in our interest to stay out of sight.

A guard lifted a rusty metal arm for our car to enter the hotel grounds. In the lobby, a few soldiers in camouflage milled about.

The receptionist handed me a menu and I ordered chicken, picking at a scrawny, greasy drumstick as I sat outside by a pool watching bats dive-bomb the mosquitoes hovering above water so green I wondered if it had ever been cleaned. Exhausted, I crashed in my room, on a hotel pillow that smelled like stale sweat and maximum-strength cologne. I had brought a little door-stopper with me to wedge under my hotel door so an intruder couldn't push it open, a poor-man's security lock. But I forgot about it. I spent the night swatting at mosquitoes that had stolen inside one of the holes in the hotel's flimsy net that hung over the bed.

The next morning I rose early and stumbled out to the poolside restaurant, stirring powdered Nescafé into a cup of boiling water in hopes a caffeine jolt would help get rid of the bags under my eyes. The frizz sprouted from my hair in the morning humidity.

Tyler emerged from his room, fresh-scrubbed and ready to go, with a dreamy-smelling cup of high-grade caffeine in his hand. He had brought his own Kenyan coffee beans, mini grinder and personal travel pour-over filter system, which made a strong, good cup of coffee wherever he was in the world. I was such a rookie.

"Did your room have a lot of mosquitoes?" I asked, making small talk. "They were swarming inside my net."

"I always bring my own net," Tyler said.

Of course.

I gulped down my Nescafé before the driver arrived. Tyler stayed back at the hotel but I had a few early appointments, one with the governor of the Far North. I wanted to be on time.

At the governor's compound, I was guided to a small waiting room where a photo of a spry-looking President Paul Biya hung on the wall. It was at least three decades old. Biya had been in office since I was in fifth grade. He was in his mid-80s now. Workers shuffled by, paying no attention to me as they went about their day. One hour passed. I was assured the governor would be available any minute. Two hours passed. Then three.

An aide emerged and said it was time. He led me into a dim office, where the governor sat behind a large wooden desk. I reached my hand across the desk to shake his.

"Just a minute," he said, and nodding to his aide, he got up and walked around his desk toward me.

A large velvet curtain flung open on one side of the room. Floodlights flashed on, momentarily blinding me. I could make out the silhouettes of what must have been a dozen cameramen from various news stations, tripods splayed. They were training their lenses on me.

"Are you ready?" the governor asked them.

They nodded, and he extended his hand for me to shake, smiling for the cameras.

"We can begin the interview now," the governor said.

So much for keeping a low profile; rule Number 3, shot to smithereens. Every TV network would be broadcasting on the evening news that a *New York Times* reporter was in town. I didn't know whether to be terrified that my cover was blown or furious that competitors were going to be sitting in on my interview. There wasn't a thing I could do to change any of it at this point. I rolled with it.

"You invited the local guys, huh?" I said to the governor.

"Yes, yes, of course. Let's begin," he said.

So we did.

The governor complained about how the war with Boko Haram had hurt the local economy.

"People are making half as much money as they used to make. Animal breeding is disrupted. Farming is disrupted. Social life is totally disrupted. Tax revenues have plummeted," he said. "Everything is upset.

"They're looting everything," he continued. "They even loot our hospitals for medicine. They steal everything. They're not just a religious sect, they're like some kind of monster group of bandits.

"And now they're bombing us. They change their tactics all the time. They're using women now, so you never know who is going to be a suicide bomber. Everyone is a suspect."

I thanked the governor and waved to the cameras and we headed for my next stop, a Catholic bishop.

We pulled into the diocese, a cluster of a half-dozen weathered concrete buildings, and stepped into an office lined with shelves stuffed with religious books, rosary beads dangling from a portrait of Jesus, and a copy of Hemingway's *A Farewell to Arms*. A rifle rested on a table underneath it.

The bishop talked of the war's disruptions to regular life the same way the governor had, emphasizing the fear that came with suicide bombings and not knowing who was the enemy anymore. Refugees from across the border, where the violence was even worse, were flooding the Far North, he said, living in inhumane conditions in camps where cholera raged and security was a problem.

"There are more than 100 babies born in these camps each month," he said.

Here is where I thought he would whip out a Bible verse or two, maybe from the New Testament—"whatever you do for the least of my brethren, you do unto me" or something similar. But that's not where he was headed.

"I just don't understand why anyone isn't trying to get these people out of here and send them back to Nigeria," he said.

"But there's a war going on in Nigeria," I said.

"Nigeria is a huge country. There should be a safe place for them somewhere there. It's not good to have all these people here."

"Where would they go?"

"I don't know, but it's a drain on our resources. I know generosity is good, but this is just too much. We have to think of our own future. If these people stay here for too long, they'll never go back."

If I were a missionary this is when I would have dug into my stash of WWJD—What Would Jesus Do—rubber bracelets to hand to him. But I'm a journalist, so I thanked him for his time and moved on.

We picked up Tyler and spent the afternoon at an eight-room local hospital—accustomed to treating stomach illnesses and motorbike accident victims—that had been turned into a triage center. The hospital had no X-ray machine, no blood bank, and often no electricity. Surgeons had to be flown in from the capital to tend to the severed limbs and shrapnel suffered in bombings in nearby towns. The single long, dark hallway gave way to rooms filled with bandaged people. Most of them were recovering from injuries suffered from an incident I recalled seeing on the Terrible List, when a woman detonated a bomb at a market in a nearby village.

The patients described that day to me, how they were just going about their routines, working in the market, when the bomber showed up. The deaths and injuries were awful enough but many of the survivors also lost their entire inventories in the blast.

In one room, a nurse sat fanning a woman who looked to be in her early 20s as she lay on a cot, her hair braided in narrow, perfect rows. The blast had knocked her unconscious and she had yet to wake from a coma.

"I just don't know exactly what Boko Haram wants," said one woman in a nearby bed. Crowded around her lap were three children whose skin was pockmarked by shrapnel.

Inside another room, sitting on a plastic mat on the floor, was Kaltoun, a 25-year-old woman. She was a vendor at the market, selling dishes that day, she explained. Bandages circled her head and covered a giant gash on her shoulder.

"What were you doing when the bomb went off?" I asked her.

Kaltoun seemed to ignore my question. Instead, she started telling me about a recent transaction.

A customer had approached her wanting to buy a stack of six plastic plates, she began. He had only a 10,000 franc note, the $20 bill of Central and West Africa. The six plates cost 2,000 francs.

"Uh-huh, OK," I said, unsure where this was going.

He handed the money to Kaltoun, and she searched her pockets to see if she had change for him.

"I couldn't find any small bills," she said.

She hollered to her grandmother, who operated a nearby stall, to see if she had any change. But she was low on small bills, too.

"He gave me 10,000, he gave me 10,000," she kept saying, over and over.

"Then what happened?" I asked, trying to keep the conversation on track.

"I got up to go look for change to give him," she said. "And I heard the loudest boom I've ever heard in my life."

The bomb had exploded. The blast knocked Kaltoun to the ground. She must have lost consciousness for a moment. When she came to, she stood up and looked around. Her customer was gone, disintegrated by the bomb. She was still holding his 10,000 franc note in her hand.

Kaltoun saw her grandmother lying on the ground. Her legs had been torn off. She died a few hours later on the operating table. Kaltoun watched her neighbor die, too, bleeding to death before help arrived.

But it was the guilt over her dead customer's money that she just couldn't shake.

"I never got him his change. I know it's a minor injustice . . ." she said, trailing off. "I just never thought something like this would happen here."

Her account was awful and dramatic. Yet I knew that stories like hers and the others at this hospital would never make it into the paper. The bombing that caused their injuries had taken place more than a week ago. It was no longer news. Especially when it was indistinguishable from all the other bombings, and all the other victims.

CHAPTER 6

Rahila

BACK AT THE hotel, Tyler turned in for the night, and I lingered by the green pool to decompress for a few minutes. Two soldiers were sitting at a table across the patio, empty bottles of beer in front of them and their AK–47s slung across the backs of their plastic chairs. I stood up to go to my room and one of them beckoned me over.

"Who are you?" one of them asked.

"I'm a reporter from America working on stories about Boko Haram."

"Sit with us," he said.

I sat down at the table and in an instant regretted it. The smell of alcohol on the soldiers' breath slammed into me. Hanging out at a hotel alone with drunk soldiers was a bad idea. I scanned the patio for Tyler, but he was nowhere in sight. No one was in sight. No waiters. No hotel workers. Nobody.

"You want to know more about Boko Haram?" the soldier said pulling out his smartphone. "I just came back from the border." The other soldier sat silently, eyes closed and arms folded. He was teetering in his chair, about to pass out. "I'll show you Boko Haram."

He opened up his photos and shoved the phone in my face. A video began playing. A group of men stood in a field behind a woman and barked an order to her. She knelt on the ground over a hole in the dirt. One of the men whipped out a knife and started sawing at her neck. I was watching a beheading video.

After *Wall Street Journal* reporter Danny Pearl was beheaded in Pakistan, I had made a personal vow to not watch his or any of the other beheading videos that circulated in dark corners of the Internet. I'm not particularly squeamish. I've seen dead bodies. But Internet beheading videos? I just couldn't see what I had to gain from viewing that kind of thing.

I tried to look away from the soldier's screen. But wait—was he the one doing the beheading? I focused on the grainy face on the screen of the man sawing back and forth and looked up at the soldier. I couldn't tell if it was him. Maybe he was the one behind the camera filming the video, which was just as troubling.

"Who filmed this?" I said, my heart beginning to pound.

"There's more," he said.

He scrolled through his camera roll. He had dozens of photos of dead people. Some were detached heads. Others were just piles of pieces of bloody flesh. Some were the limbless torsos of uniformed soldiers.

"That was my friend," he said, pointing to one.

"What is this?" I said, breathing quickly. "What am I looking at? Who took these?"

Was this his own personal file of snuff videos? Did he murder these people? Did he get these videos from Boko Haram fighters? Was he actually a Boko Haram member, just in a military uniform?

The soldier was too focused on the photos and too drunk to respond.

"Did you kill these people?"

He ignored me.

"I really need to go," I said, and jumped up, leaving him staring into his screen.

I speed-walked to my room and dug in my suitcase for the wedge to slip under the door.

During the Iraq War, I saw American soldiers watch videos of bloody killings and their aftermath carried out by Iraqi "infidels." It was how the Americans psyched themselves up for the battle-field. That must be what those images were—propaganda videos released by Boko Haram that the soldiers were using to muster all the hate they could to steel themselves for dangerous missions. But I didn't know for sure. I spent the night in my room googling "Boko Haram beheading videos." Was the video the soldier showed me unique, or could anyone get it on YouTube? I fell asleep watch-ing beheading videos before I figured it out.

The next morning, over my Nescafé and Tyler's gourmet AA Nyeri Ichamara medium roast Kenyan coffee, I told him what had happened.

"Yeeeeah," he said, scanning the empty patio, where flies circled the drunk soldiers' beer bottles still on their table from the night before, "I think two days maximum is the most we should stay here."

We had overstayed but there was nothing we could do about it. The plane didn't leave until the next day. We geared up to head to a refugee camp outside the city. I had a few good pieces of report-ing but still hadn't found a solid story, and I hadn't learned much about Boko Haram fighters other than the misery they left in their wake.

The aid workers showing us around wanted to stop in a small village along the way where refugees from Nigeria were staying in the homes of local people—a far better situation than living in a squalid camp. These were residents who themselves had too little to eat and now were hosting and feeding dozens of others in cramped quarters. Generosity abounded in the Far North, the aid workers assured me. I thought back to the bishop and snorted. But I didn't have a story yet, so I agreed.

The workers said they had one woman in mind who would be perfect for my story. We pulled into a small village and she was standing on the side of the street waiting for us. She led us inside her one-room concrete house. It was clean; the only thing inside it was a thin foam mattress. I sat on the ground beside her as Tyler got comfortable on the foam.

She started telling me how she had left her home after rumors spread that Boko Haram was in the area. She headed to the Far North because it's where she had distant relatives. When she arrived at their house, she was told she could stay but she'd have to pay rent. She sold jewelry to make ends meet.

It was clear to me that this was a nonstarter of an interview.

Finding people or a situation—an anecdote—to illustrate a story can be among the most frustrating parts of a reporter's job. You can interview all the experts, collect all the charts and statistics and government reports, but without any humans to illustrate your point the story falls flat. And if I was honest, her story wasn't that dramatic.

War reporting offered its own particular maddening aspect when it came to finding anecdotes. I knew that after a few years of any war, with so many stories already written, victims' situations need to be *special* if they were going to make it onto the pages of a newspaper. The hardships need to be different than past hardships or far more severe. In the world of war reporting, it seemed like every story published had to depict a new threshold of suffering.

In my head I had to make a cold calculation. I'm sure this woman was having a hard time paying her rent. Her hometown probably wouldn't be safe enough for her to return to for months, if not years. But she had a place to live. She had food to eat. She had an income. It wasn't enough but it was more than most.

I felt deeply unqualified for this new position as jury and judge over whether the world would ever know her story, which she clearly wanted told. It was an enormous power to wield over a powerless human being.

"Thank you for your time," I said to the woman, and turned to Tyler. He had almost dozed off while she and I were talking. I guess I made the right call about whether her story was captivating.

I got into the car and watched the aid worker escorting us walk over to the woman and slip her some cash, a huge breach of ethics in journalism. He should have known journalists don't pay our sources. Even if her story were perfect, I couldn't use it now.

I barked at the worker for paying her. He was all I had to rely on out here where I was a stranger to everything. Surely there were other people we could visit in the village who might have better stories to tell. He started dialing numbers on his phone.

"Let's go to a different village," he said.

At the new village, which was no more than a smattering of huts made of dried cornstalks, I found more undramatic stories: people who had fled after hearing vague rumors about militants.

"Did you run through the night?" I asked, trying to tease out some awful details.

"No, we live right over the border," one man told me. "Took about an hour to get here."

They were hungry but not starving; the soles of their feet weren't bloodied from a terror-filled trek; their family members weren't killed by militants; they hadn't stared into the eyes of a bloodthirsty bomber. Some even had managed to bring along all their clothes and furniture.

How could I write about them when so many other refugees have lived through worse? Most people here in this new village were getting by on their own, without any help from locals, who might have resented their presence anyway. Maybe that was a story I should pursue. Everyone I met seemed to complain about not enough food. Was that my story?

I was looking through my notes when some of the soldiers who had been escorting us ran into the road.

"Get in the car!" they shouted, herding us toward the convoy.

"What's going on?" I asked.

"We have a credible threat of an attack here. We need to get out. Now."

They pushed us toward the vehicles and we sped away—the

journalists, the aid workers and the soldiers leaving behind the refugees. In the moment I didn't realize the absurdity of the situation. Rushing from the scene were the only people who could possibly help thwart an attack or deal with its aftermath. I don't even know what ended up happening at that village. Our convoy kept going.

GUIDED BY THE military, we headed far outside the town, turning off on a skinny dirt road that headed toward an empty, scrubby horizon. About 20 minutes up the road we started seeing dots of figures that soon revealed themselves to be a long line of girls dressed in bright blue pinafore uniforms and holding hands. It was almost midday and they were standing in the already blazing sun, facing the road. The line must have stretched for a mile.

"What are they doing?" I asked the aid workers.

"A dignitary from the U.N. is visiting today and the camp workers have lined up the girls to greet him."

Dozens of girls in school uniforms were living proof that the organization was having success at schooling young girls during a war where just across the border more than 200 students trying to go to school in Chibok were still being held captive. But didn't the dignitary already know that?

As we continued, square structures covered in white tarp several feet apart from one another in the sand became visible. The structures grew closer and closer together as we drove. Soon, they formed a metropolis of temporary homes tattooed with the blue United Nations logo. There must have been thousands of them.

In between the shelters women carried batches of sticks for firewood on their heads. A group of men tucked their knees onto small prayer mats and bowed their heads. Little girls and boys trudged barefoot through the sand, using both hands to lug yellow jerry cans of water.

My thoughts turned to Jaime. I wondered if this was what life was like for him growing up. He and his family had fled Sierra Leone's civil war. He had spent most of his childhood across the border in Guinea moving between a half-dozen refugee camps, sometimes losing all of his family's meager belongings in the transitions. He even had been shot in the knee. He lost family and friends to the violence.

In the Cameroon camp, children surrounded the car when we pulled to a stop. They thought we might be bringing food.

We got out and one of the aid workers shooed the children away, while another started leading me inside tent after tent to talk to families. All of them complained they had very little to eat at the camp. Sanitation was a huge problem, with more than 20 people sharing the same toilet. Many of the residents had lost relatives who were killed by Boko Haram. Some of the people of this tent city had been captured by Boko Haram and lived for weeks or months with militants until they escaped.

An aid worker flung back the flap on the home of one woman, Rahila, and I sat beside her on the ground in the dark room. There were no openings in the tent and the sun bearing down on the tarp created suffocating heat. The aid worker crouched next to us.

"She was kidnapped by Boko Haram," he said.

When I approach people to interview them I try to find some kind of common ground as I launch into questions. Reporting is a series of human interactions, one of my old editors liked to say. And that phrase is always in the back of my mind.

Shared experiences help both my sources and me get comfortable with each other. I once convinced a high-powered criminal defense lawyer to return my calls on deadline by being honest and telling him that I was just doing my job and didn't want to talk to him on a summer Sunday afternoon any more than he wanted to talk to me. It made him laugh and open up. I settled a nervous group of Senegalese migrants by pointing out the scar each man had on his forehead. My little boy has one, too, I told them. Just like my son, they all had smacked their heads while roughhousing when they were little kids. A universal rite of boyhood passage, we all agreed.

I didn't know how to find common ground with someone who had been kidnapped by tyrannical militants. But it didn't matter. Rahila was eager to tell me what she had seen.

Rahila was about my age. She told me she had been stolen from her home one morning when Boko Haram arrived in three vehicles, scooping up as many women as possible and spiriting them away in trucks to a nearby town the group had taken over.

The first thing Rahila noticed when fighters pushed her out of the vehicle and into their camp was a sea of women, she told me. So many of them, huddled on the ground or standing over cooking fires.

"It was as if they were mobilizing all the women there," she said.

Rahila wound up spending 10 months as a captive of Boko Haram. They didn't have a lot to eat, she said, and all the women started to shed pounds. Rahila, whose cheeks were sunken now, must have lost 20 or maybe 30 pounds she guessed.

"She was a really big lady before all this," said her nephew, who was huddled in the tent with us. "Really big."

Rahila nodded.

One day the fighters loaded Rahila and a few others into trucks and drove them to an old cement factory. Inside, the fighters displayed another group of captives. All of the girls were plump. Their girth was the first thing Rahila noticed. Some of them were crying and told her they had been kidnapped from a school in Chibok.

Rahila realized right away who they were: Boko Haram's famous hostages, the Chibok girls.

"If you do what we say," the leader of the fighters said, "you can have all the food you want and be as fat as these girls."

They took Rahila and the others back to camp and told them that now they would begin their training.

"We went to Koranic school every day," she said. "And they would teach all of us, even the children, how to kill people."

"Really?" I stopped her.

"Yes," she said, "how to bomb people's houses and things like that."

She went on to explain the six-level training program that Boko Haram employed to teach its captives to become killers.

The first level—first grade, she called it—was day after day of Koranic school. Hostages were made to memorize verses of the Koran and learn about Prophet Mohammad's teachings. Then, in "second grade," students graduated to weapons training. Children lined up in the front with grown women behind them. Everyone was given a stick and told to pretend it was a gun. They were shown how to hold it and how to fire it.

Graduates of weapons training went on to decapitation school. Always cut from the back of the neck, they were told, to prevent the victim from squirming. They'll die quicker that way.

After that, she said, came suicide bombing school. Keep the bomb tight in your armpit, fighters told their students, to stop it from shifting around and exploding too soon. When you reach a crowd of 10 or 20 people, detonate.

"You press this," she said, mimicking pushing a button. "They taught us that as soon as you pressed it you'd go directly to heaven."

The training went on every day, mornings and evenings. One night, however, classes were canceled because an important preacher from another Boko Haram camp was due to arrive for a big night of preaching. It might have been Boko Haram leader Shekau himself who was speaking; she wasn't sure.

"It'll be good for you to hear this," fighters went around the camp telling the captives.

Rahila knew everyone would be there. As the crowd assembled and the sermon began, she gathered her grandchildren and slipped away into the surrounding bush. They walked for seven nights, trudging along a narrow passage through the mountains along the border between Nigeria and Cameroon until she reached the desert camp here.

Rahila, a suicide bombing school dropout, was now stuck in a refugee camp that stretched to the horizon, in the middle of the Extreme North, in a country that didn't want her there.

Rahila wasn't a Boko Haram fighter, but she was trained as one. *This* was my story. The group was systematically schooling its women captives. In all the coverage I had read about Boko Haram, I had never heard that before.

I interviewed other refugees and we piled into the U.N. vehicle, passing the same set of blue-uniformed schoolgirls who, two hours later, were still lined up in the sun, forced to wait for the dignitary from Geneva who was supposed to discuss with their families the difficult living conditions in the camp. They were somber and looked like they might faint in the heat.

LATER, I INTERVIEWED government officials and tried to square what I had learned in the Far North. I asked a defense spokesman about those awful videos I'd seen.

"They take our officers and cut off their arms and slice open their stomachs and then they send us the videos," he said.

I told him about the suicide bomber training school for women. He said all female bombers were either high on drugs or unrepentant. They were ruthless Boko Haram members who didn't need any prompting to kill, he said.

"You saw the videos," he said. "Don't you see what they've done?"

I thought about Rahila. She didn't seem like a drug addict and she didn't seem ruthless. Maybe she was an outlier and that's why she dared to escape. Her life in the camp, in a region that rejected refugees like her, wasn't going to be easy in coming months, or even coming years.

Boko Haram was so despised that anyone who had spent time with the group, even by force, was suspicious—especially women. Many lied if they had been raped and bore the child of a fighter.

Women were introducing their babies as little brothers and sisters so no one would beat them or their children.

The stigma all stemmed from fear. In a place where women were blowing up mosques, soccer games, markets and restaurants, the suspicion was growing.

I was caught up thinking about Rahila and forgot my pledge to find another story that had nothing to do with war in Cameroon, a nation so diverse with its multitude of languages and landscapes that it is called "Africa in Miniature."

OUR PLANE DESCENDED into the capital city. Tyler's phone, back in the land of a reliable network, began to light up with texts from his girlfriend.

When my husband was on work trips, I had stayed up late after the kids went to bed to write him missives about what he was missing at home while he was traveling. I kept him posted on sibling spats, classroom drama, skinned knees, soccer performances and lost sweatshirts. I had kept an almost daily journal of family life so he could roll back in, all caught up to speed.

"I love the long emails you send while I'm away," he always told me.

I scrolled through my inbox. Nothing from my husband. He probably just was busy with the kids. I tried not to care.

CHAPTER 7

"I Cannot Watch This"

A FEW YEARS back, before we had kids, Todd and I cashed in wedding present plane tickets from his uncle who worked for an airline and took a vacation to the islands near Micronesia. We were there to snorkel and swim, but in Palau, Todd spotted a sign advertising an overnight kayaking trip. We could kayak for several hours out to one of hundreds of tiny islands and spend the night in a tent.

"We'll have the whole place to ourselves," he pleaded. "And we'll get to sleep on the ground."

I love to travel but I am more interested in the kind of travel where you walk around a foreign city, hit a few cool museums, eat some street food and go back to your dingy hotel. Maybe tack on a day of hiking or few days at the beach. Camping is not my favorite thing.

But Todd was excited about the idea. And I was still feeling guilty for nixing his honeymoon suggestion that we go on a two-week camping trip in the Grand Canyon. So I decided to be a good sport and agree to this plan.

A few hours later we were in the open ocean, wind blowing like crazy, the waves lapping over my kayak as we weaved within the rocky archipelago. I began careening toward a narrow overhang that left about a foot of horizontal space between the top of the water and a jagged layer of rock. I struggled with my paddle to slow down. It was no use.

"I'm going to get torn to shreds," I screamed to Todd, who was just ahead.

"Just lie down," he shouted, and kept paddling without turning to look at me.

"There's not enough space!" I screamed. "We have to go back!"

He ignored me. I watched him lie back in his kayak and slip through without a scrape. I did the same thing. It was fine.

At times Todd's unflappable personality, his Spock-like logic and lack of emotion, is maddening. Other times, it comes in handy. In the emergency room in Brooklyn when I was freaking out after Luther's forehead was sliced open at the playground and he calmly spoke with the plastic surgeon who was about to stitch him up. And on September 11 after we stood on our rooftop and watched the towers fall. I vomited. He talked about the war on capitalism, globalism and imperialism. And, again, on a turbulent Pacific Ocean, when our kayaks bobbed and weaved and glided onto the sandy shore of a lush, deserted island. We watched sharks circle in front of the setting sun as we cooked fish over an open fire and listened to monkeys rustle through the leaves.

Todd and I always made the extra effort to go to unexpected places, to take risks, in order to experience life to the fullest. We didn't mind the mishaps and hazards as long as they came with the ecstatic triumphs. And we were a good team in travel—together, we pushed ourselves even further than we might have otherwise.

Now, though, we were both on our own. Me in a war zone and him on the home front.

WHILE I WAS in Cameroon, Todd, understandably, had grown antsy about his own job. Pinned down with three kids and working from what was designed to be the maid's quarters—a musty one-room cottage positioned in the backyard—he was going stir crazy. He missed office life and he missed his colleagues.

"I have to fly to London for a conference," he announced upon my return from Cameroon.

"Have to?" I asked.

I was skeptical. His job wasn't chasing news. He made slides and spreadsheets and ran conference calls. He didn't *have* to go anywhere. In my view he could always designate a colleague to go in his place. But, then again, I'd been on the road for two and a half weeks with no family responsibilities.

"Fine," I relented. "Just try to come back as soon as you can."

And he was off. I was on my own, left to manage the family and do my work, just like he had done. Tag-team parenting.

The kids were getting into a groove at school. Luther joined the boys' volleyball team. Maude had a new friend from Mauritius. Or maybe it was Massachusetts. She couldn't keep the two straight. Zola kept mixing up "missionaries" with "mercenaries"—both were part of her new patois. They all liked their teachers, and they seemed to like their new life.

A lot of expats patted themselves on the back about raising "third culture" kids. The idea was that children who lived abroad with expat parents adopted a culture that transcended those of their parents' homelands and that of the nation of their own passports. They were children of the world and citizens of nowhere, global nomads with broadened minds and multicultural tendencies.

It seemed a bit rich for me. Our kids went to an international school where English was the primary language. The student body overall was diverse, with kids from Senegal and all over the world, but most all of them were into Taylor Swift and Minecraft. And every child at that school had parents who could afford the hefty tuition, or whose companies were footing the bill just like mine was.

We hadn't sent our kids to a Senegalese school. We were scared off by stories of rote learning and corporal punishment. We had even been too timid to send them to a French school. It seemed cruel to move them thousands of miles from home and plop them in a classroom where they couldn't understand anything. We had been chickens and now we worried they were missing out.

Dakar was entering one of the biggest holiday seasons, which is also one of the bloodiest: Tabaski. Known as Eid elsewhere in the world, Tabaski is the celebration of Abraham's willingness to sacrifice his son Isaac, a story my children were familiar with from the comic book version of the Bible, which my mom had bought them after realizing that was the closest thing to church they were going to get. The Senegalese celebrated the holiday by sacrificing a sheep, often right in their front yard.

Around this time of year loud baaaas wailed from neighbors' homes, confusing our cat. Sheep markets popped up on sidewalks all across town like Christmas tree lots in New York. Radio stations and mobile phone companies offered sheep giveaway contests. On the highways, people strapped live sheep to the tops of cars and buses as they traveled to their holiday destinations.

The editors at the *Times* were starting to embrace new storytelling methods on social media and asked if I could do a short live video report from a sheep market. The idea was nerve-racking. I've always been terrible on live TV. I don't speak in sound bites, I lose track of what I'm talking about and I fill my speech with *ums* and *uhs*. The idea of operating a device as well as trying to sound coherent was terrifying. I considered outsourcing to Jaime then decided I should just do what was asked of me and get it over with.

I took a taxi to a giant sheep market, one of the biggest in the city. There were hundreds of animals baa-ing and struggling for freedom from the rope tied around their leg. It smelled like the county fair. I stepped around piles of sheep poop to find the owner. He told me how the market was an amalgamation of flocks from shepherds who had come from hundreds of miles away, marching their sheep to Dakar in hopes that someone would choose their animals for sacrifice. When Tabaski was over, they'd march the overstock back home. I fired up my phone to start the interview and was a few minutes in when a sheep clenched its jaws around my skirt and started tugging. It almost disrobed me before deciding instead to eat my notebook. Interview over.

The Tabaski celebration was a daylong event, starting with a trip to the mosque and then a sheep bloodbath that gave way to a meat feast. Heaps of grilled mouton, shredded carrots, fried potatoes and peas slathered in mayonnaise were arranged inside a shiny aluminum platter, covered with a silvery lid and wrapped in wax fabric or a flimsy sheer scarf dotted with rhinestones. It made for a fabulous presentation.

One of my daughter's second-grade teachers, Mr. Papis, had invited us to his house for the highlights of the day. Luther had scheduled a playdate with a friend, and even though I was sad he would miss out on the festivities, I let him go. Making new friends was important. My girls tagged along with me to chez Papis.

As we drove across town that day to get to his house, the sharpening of knives echoed off the walls of buildings. It was as if the whole city were slaughtering in unison. Mr. Papis and his brothers were holding a long silver blade when we arrived. They had chosen his apartment building courtyard as the sacrifice spot. A savory white sheep was tied to a fence nearby.

My girls and I got settled in the upstairs apartment, perched on the back of a sofa to peer out the window overlooking the courtyard. The Papis children cozied up beside us.

"Girls, you know what's going to happen, right?" I asked my daughters. "Are you sure you want to look?"

They assured me they did.

Mr. Papis entered the gate of the courtyard, knife in hand. His brother led the sheep toward him.

"I cannot watch this," Maude said, punctuating every word as she slumped down onto the couch.

"Honey, you don't have to."

Zola covered her eyes with her hands. In an instant it was done, and blood leaked from the neck of the animal that lay flopped across the dirt. My girls peeked at the aftermath.

Later that day as we were leaving the apartment, we got stuck in traffic and I scrolled through my phone. Someone had tagged me on Facebook. I opened the app and found a photo of my son holding the leg of a skinned sheep. Looks like he had had his own Tabaski experience.

Most parents I knew in Brooklyn called to ask if it was OK to serve ice cream to my kid on a playdate. I would have thought sheep-skinning might have merited a phone call. I stared at the photo on my screen. Luther wasn't smiling but he didn't look traumatized. *Oh well,* I thought, *I guess the kids aren't missing out altogether on getting to know this new culture.*

CHAPTER 8

Maiduguri-apolis

I HOLED UP in my office to write my story on Rahila's suicide bomber school, going over the wording with my editor as we tried to find the right opening lines for the story. We settled on this:

Hold the bomb under your armpit to keep it steady, the women and girls were taught. Sever your enemy's head from behind, to minimize struggling. "If you cut from the back of the neck, they die faster."

The story went on. *Of all the many horrors of Boko Haram's rampage across West Africa . . . one of the most baffling has been its ability to turn captured women and girls into killers.*

Tyler filed his beautiful, somber portrait of Rahila sitting in her dimly lit temporary home. The story wound up on the front page. I was thrilled. Everyone would have a new reason to turn their attention to the war with Boko Haram.

People tweeted it. Apple News sent an alert about it to iPhones across the country. Readers chimed in on the comments section of the *Times* website. People from Philadelphia, Connecticut, Kansas, and one reader from Santa Fe who wrote:

> I am thinking of the girls and women who man-
> aged to escape after being held prisoner. I am think-
> ing of the families who rejected them upon their

return because they had been "used." I am thinking of the young women certain that they have no value left to their family and the only escape from the hell they are in is to die. . . . I don't think their decision to die is the least baffling. Tragically many recognize they are considered already dead.

People were paying attention. It felt like success.

The story published just as my husband was arriving home from his London trip. He was happy for my small victory, but he wanted to talk about his own career.

Todd's organization was trying to stop the rampant deforestation happening around the world. He was trying to get governments and companies to agree not to cut down one of the only things holding the climate together. It was important work, and in some places he and his colleagues were succeeding. While Todd was at his London conference, he realized that to be effective he needed to attend even more conferences that brought together researchers and representatives from corporations and environmental ministries to iron out their differences.

"To get anything done, I need to be in the room," he argued.

For either of us to be successful we needed to be away from home. That was going to be a struggle. But it wasn't the only one. We were moving in different directions on a more meta level. It was getting harder to connect with each other on almost everything.

I was getting pulled into places that couldn't be more different from the chandeliered hotel meeting halls where he had been hobnobbing. The differences in our job settings were the starkest they'd ever been. Our home in Dakar of course offered common ground. But until now I had almost always been able to communicate the behind-the-scenes of stories I had reported. He could visualize boardrooms, courtrooms, political rallies and crime scenes. But how could I really help him understand what it was like to meet a suicide-bomber trainee? Or to walk through a refugee camp that stretched for miles? The other truth is that I didn't have the energy to try. Instead, the work was taking over and I was starting to systematically shut Todd out.

While all this was sinking in, Boko Haram, with all its suicide bombings, was named the most deadly terror organization in the world by the Institute of Economics and Peace, an outfit that tracks terror groups. I needed to get to Nigeria to write about what was happening at the center of the fight. I was getting sucked into more war coverage. But I felt like I had to go. Or maybe the chaos was addictive. One big adrenaline rush that was far more exciting than life at home. I booked a flight.

My plane landed in Maiduguri and I headed out to meet my fixer there, a man named Shehu. He was listed on our official roster as the number two guy. The paper's top fixer in the area was away for the year on a fellowship. Shehu was the agriculture and fisheries reporter for a local newspaper. How he was going to help me find Boko Haram stories, I wasn't sure, but I had to make do with him until the main fixer made it back. Knowing already that he was someone's second choice, I had low expectations.

The small restaurant in Maiduguri where we agreed to meet had dirt smudges on the walls and empty tables littered with crumpled napkins stuck to surfaces that looked like they hadn't been wiped down for days. A worker was pushing a mop around. It smelled like it had been used to wipe up vomit and never cleaned. Every time it swooshed across the floor it let off a whiff of bile.

At the only occupied table sat a bald gentleman with a graying goatee. He was dressed in a crisp, white caftan that reached midthigh and matching white pants underneath. The material had shiny white swirls throughout, and the light that bounced off them created a hazy glow. He was staring into a cup. He looked almost angelic against the dingy restaurant backdrop.

He must be my guy. I approached, introduced myself. Shehu looked up from his tea and burst out laughing.

"What is it?" I said, baffled.

He looked me up and down, laughing so hard he had trouble catching his breath to talk. His eyes even watered. The waitstaff was staring.

"What?" I demanded, getting annoyed.

"You told me you were the bureau chief," he said, between his gasps for air.

"Yeah, so?"

"In Nigeria," he said, wiping tears from his eyes, "women with big titles are very big women. But you—you're not big at all," he said, eyeballing my praying mantis frame.

I wasn't sure if that was a compliment.

Shehu regained his composure and started asking me about the stories I wanted to pursue now that I'd made it to the heart of the insurgency. Boko Haram's men—and women—were still creeping back from time to time to blow themselves up in mosques or markets or at the gate of the main university.

Not long before I arrived in Maiduguri, a group of several dozen women had been arrested in a Boko Haram hideout. The government had detained them in a special, ultra-secure compound in the middle of Maiduguri. The military said they were wives of high-level Boko Haram commanders and were deemed so vicious they needed to be segregated from the rest of the jail population. The governor of Borno State, where Maiduguri is situated, decided he would take charge of them himself to ensure that they were kept far away from society so they could do no harm.

"I'd like to try to meet with the women," I told Shehu. "Can you help me set up an interview with the governor so I can ask him whether this is possible?"

Shehu sighed.

"The whole thing comes down to arrogance of our elected officials," he said. His Nigerian English was so proper it seemed stilted. He even rolled his r's, adding another level of elegance.

"What are you talking about?"

"The governor is right here in Maiduguri and won't talk to us. He will not even answer my call. We local journalists want to talk to him so, so badly. He will talk to only foreigners. We are Nigerians and he is right here in our community and could answer so many questions, and he will ignore us."

"So you're saying I should call the governor myself to set up the interview?"

"That is what I am telling you."

I dialed the governor's assistant. He guaranteed me an interview in the afternoon. Shehu let out a muffled I-told-you-so harrumph.

We had a few hours to kill before the meeting. Shehu told me he had lined up some people he wanted me to meet; he thought they might be good for my story.

We got into Shehu's car, an old navy blue Honda station wagon with worn shocks that was covered in dust both inside and out. His colleague was driving and we pulled out of the hotel, the car creaking every time we hit a bump on the sandy side roads.

Maiduguri was the capital city of a farming state. It was a small city but huge for that part of the country, otherwise dotted by tiny villages. It was a cultural hub in the region, home of universities, a history museum and a zoo inside a sprawling park where lovers picnicked next to the raptor cage. It had a decent soccer team and outdoor restaurants. In better times it was an island of music and bars and young people cutting loose surrounded by a conservative farm belt. The city's attributes reminded me of Minneapolis.

But now the backdrop was a raging war that had its genesis right within the city limits where the founder of Boko Haram first preached his fiery sermons. Security forces had razed his home near the railroad tracks and still kept watch over the area, should anyone want to pay homage.

Maiduguri was a city transformed by the war. Instead of motorcycle taxis that had been popular for decades, canary-colored motorized tricycles called "kekes" clumsily weaved through traffic. Motorbikes had been banned after Boko Haram used them to carry out missions—they allowed for sneak attacks and a quick getaway. They were outlawed across the entire state now, even in rural areas. Anyone caught with a bike was presumed to be Boko Haram and killed on sight.

Every square inch of space in Maiduguri seemed to be occupied by people who had run from the war raging in the countryside. The city's population was thought to have doubled to about two million people since the war first broke out seven years ago. Nobody knew for sure; there were now too many people to count. A former electoral commission building, a school, a bus garage, a teachers' college all were overrun with squatting farmers and their families who had fled their fields in fear. The town's polo grounds—where the hometown soccer team, the El Kanemi Warriors, went up against the Sunshine Stars, the Tornadoes and the Super Eagles—sat abandoned after being targeted by suicide bombers. The Warriors played their matches in a different state now.

The levels of desperation varied. Some people running away from Boko Haram lived in official government camps on the edge of the city, biding their time in white United Nations tents and living on handouts of macaroni and corn, trying to sell embroidered caps they stitched by hand and junky plastic jewelry they picked up from I don't know where. Others lived in camps that had been more hastily put together. There were no tents, only shelters made of sticks and scraps of rice bags or fabric or whatever they scrounged to keep out the wind and dust and rain. Most of the time it didn't work. The structures were so shoddy that when the rain started everyone ran out of their porous homes and clustered together, squatting on the dirt in groups of 20 or 30 while holding a large sheet of plastic or tarp over their heads, sometimes for hours. At least they had shelter, and usually the trucks came with food handouts. But not always. Sometimes food convoys got blown up by Boko Haram. Sometimes workers and managers stole bags of rice and sold them at the market. Large plastic sacks of rice stamped with World Food Program logos were on sale all across Maiduguri. One group of people running from war settled along the trash-strewn banks of the Ngadda River where leather-makers dried and dyed their cattle hides. They were so desperate for food they fried and ate the scraps of hide the leather-makers tossed aside.

Camouflage-painted trucks rumbled down the Maiduguri streets, passing little beds and sofas and other dollhouse furniture lined up for sale across one sidewalk. An armed man in blue jeans with a Spider-Man mask that covered his entire head stood in the middle of one traffic roundabout. The city's massive Monday Market was open other days of the week, too, always hopping with a sea of people walking between the stalls, everyone looking over their shoulder for signs of a suicide bomber.

At one intersection, I did a double take, craning my neck in the backseat of Shehu's station wagon for a better look. Out in the middle of the mayhem was a traffic cop wearing a single white glove, moonwalking as he directed cars and military trucks through the intersection. People called him MJ Traffic.

Pictures of the honorable Governor Kashim Shettima were posted all around town, on billboards and painted on old, crumbling walls. He was never smiling and always dressed in a flowing robe and often in a giant overstuffed chair that looked like a La-Z-Boy.

We pulled outside one building where a man was squatting along the curb, expecting us.

I got out of the car and Shehu helped me make my introductions. The man reached into the pocket of the threadbare caftan he was wearing and pulled a card from his wallet. "Lake Chad Hunters' Association," it read, along with his headshot and name, Abba.

Abba told me he had spent many weekends since he was a boy going into the desert scrub and hunting black-and-white-speckled guinea fowl, rabbits and other small animals. The hunters in his club worked in packs, organizing outings where they fanned out in droves of 100 or more with their homemade weapons—hand-crafted shotguns, some with duct tape and lines of tweed securing the barrels.

On a recent trip as they combed the bush looking for prey, Abba said, they accidentally surprised some fighters from Boko Haram. The militants armed with AK-47s opened fire, mowing down some of the men in the hunting club. Other hunters returned fire and soon Abba was in the middle of a hail of bullets on either side. It went on for what seemed like hours. He watched his friends drop alongside him.

"But I survived," he said, as Shehu translated, "because these protected me."

Abba extended his hand and uncurled his fingers to show me a fistful of small, round, red and black knobs of leather. I realized right away where this was going. Those must be amulets, or gris-gris or good luck charms or whatever you wanted to call them. And I wasn't going to write about them.

"The bullets passed right through me as though I was invisible," Abba said, explaining the powers of these little charms.

"OK, thank you," I said, wrapping up the interview and turning to Shehu. "Let's go."

We got into the car and I had to bite my tongue. I didn't want to insult anyone's beliefs, but this was the kind of interview Shehu was going to lead me to? A black magic folktale? My editors were careful about playing into Western stereotypes of Africa as the land of voodoo and the occult. They would never go for it. And frankly, I wasn't interested either. It all made about as much sense as God sparing Daniel from the lions' den.

"Do you believe in this stuff?" I said to Shehu.

"Yes," he said, with all the earnestness in the world. "Sometimes it can help."

I snorted. He stared straight ahead. We drove in silence for a few awkward minutes.

"I have another person for you to meet."

We still had a couple hours before I was supposed to interview the governor so I didn't protest. Who would he take me to next, I wondered. A voodoo priestess?

We crossed a bridge over the Ngadda River, which this time of year was nothing more than a trickle that wound its way through a solid stream of trash in the dry riverbed. I'd never seen anything so filthy.

"Yuck," I said out loud.

"What did you say?" Shehu said.

"Oh, sorry," I said. "I was just looking at the trash in the riverbed."

"What trash?" he said.

Some locals never seemed to notice the trash even when it was heaped all over public spaces. But I suppose it was a matter of perspective. I remembered how my mom on a visit to Brooklyn complained about all the trash bags stacked on the sidewalk on garbage pick-up day. I'd never even thought about the bags, passing them for years.

"We don't have alleys here, Mom," I told her. "Where else are we supposed to put the trash until the garbage truck comes?"

Maiduguri, caught up in the war, didn't even have a functioning Streets & Sanitation Department.

We entered a neighborhood surrounding a primary school. Displaced people had been coming there for a few years, abandoning their farms and squatting inside the school until there was no more space. People had started building ramshackle structures that looked like they were made of nothing more than straw. Shehu led me to one of them where chickens were pecking at the dirt and a 30-year-old woman named Hauwa was waiting for us.

"So what's her situation?" I asked Shehu as the woman got settled, hoping to get a quick understanding before I launched into questions.

"Let's ask her," Shehu said.

Interviewing her without knowing why we were there was like

shooting darts with the lights off. She was looking at me, waiting, and I had no choice but to start in. What's your name? Where are you from? What kind of work does your family do? How long have you lived here?

That last one was the bull's-eye and was all it took for her to begin telling me about her experiences with Boko Haram.

About two years ago word spread in her town that militants were on the way. Everyone knew the fighters stole any livestock around and killed any man of "fighting age" who refused to join them. Hauwa and her husband agreed he should flee with the family's small herd of cattle before Boko Haram arrived. She planned to gather the children and join him in a few days, once he found a safe place for all of them.

He took off with the cows, arriving at a military checkpoint just outside town. Soldiers demanded a bribe to pass. They knew he was desperate and fleeing and seized the chance to make money off of him. He was outraged and argued with them. They shot him to death.

Not long after, Boko Haram did invade. In the melee, they killed Hauwa's teenage daughter. They captured Hauwa and her two preteen sons and took them into their hideout in the bush. While they were there, the militants must have convinced her sons to join them in the fight. Hauwa couldn't be certain about that but she never saw them again. She spent months as a captive.

One night while everyone was asleep Hauwa managed to sneak away. She walked through the darkness and arrived at a nearby town, where she spotted soldiers manning a checkpoint. Hauwa begged them for help. Suspicious, they locked her up. For a week, they kept her in jail, taunting her with insulting questions.

"How many bombs did you bring with you?" they asked.

She didn't have any bombs, she told them.

"If you're so innocent, why didn't you go straight to a camp for help?" they asked her.

Hauwa was on foot, alone, and the camp was far away.

"Why are you alone?" they asked.

One child was murdered and she had no idea where her sons were, she explained.

After each round of questions, the soldiers threw her back in her cell, she said.

I looked over at Shehu, and he was sitting with his head in his hands.

Soldiers had been locking up hundreds of Boko Haram victims who had run away from the militants. The military even detained people they themselves liberated from terrorists. In particular they were suspicious of women, locking them up even if they had infants.

Some of the newly freed hostages were placed in large rooms, crammed with other women and children, where they sat on the floor and awaited questioning that they hoped would vindicate them. Most had no idea why they were even there. No one had explained. One woman wound up with her seven children in a holding pen with 130 other women and kids. The soldiers would call for them and ask them only one or two questions before sending them back. Other times they went for days without seeing a soldier. Some spent months in detention. All of these people thought they had been freed, only to be locked up again without any indication of when they would be released. Some were never heard from again. One woman peered out a small window in her cell to spot her husband being led for questioning. She saw him pass three separate times while she was detained. Eventually, she was released. She never saw her husband again.

Soldiers did later set Hauwa free, convinced the 30-year-old widow who had lost her husband to angry soldiers, her teenage daughter to militants, and her two sons to who-knows-what wasn't a terrorist. She found her way to Maiduguri, where she was squatting with other people who also had fled the violence. Hauwa was trying to earn money by braiding hair but mostly was surviving off of handouts from aid groups, if the food trucks managed to show up.

"Life is not easy," she said.

As we walked to the car, I noticed Shehu's eyes were glassy.

"That was quite a story," I said.

"Listen," Shehu said, "would you mind if in a few days I come back and bring her a bag of rice? Would that violate your ethical rules?"

Journalists abide by a strict code of ethics. We can't accept big gifts from sources, and we aren't supposed to pay anyone for a story. It was a punch in the gut knowing that giving a single paycheck to some of the people we were meeting probably could have changed their entire year for the better. Journalists are observers not activists. We are not supposed to get involved. It keeps our stories honest. I played by the rules. But what were the rules about a Nigerian fixer arranging for an $8 bag of rice to go to a nearly starving widow in a war zone long after we interviewed her? I decided I would take the heat for any perceived violation.

"I don't think so," I told him. "Go ahead."

WE STILL HAD time to kill before the governor's interview and Shehu suggested we stop for tea. We pulled alongside the Liberty Tea Shop, a small outdoor café. Workers and students were lined up for a morning cup of Lipton mixed with condensed milk, and dining on oil-fried yam or an egg on white bread, loaves of which were stacked inside plastic sacks that reminded me of Wonder Bread. Next door to the shop, kids crammed into a little arcade around two ancient PlayStations. I sipped my tea from the same plastic cup as the guy in line before me and watched a woman dipping fried dough into a pot of boiling oil. Behind me I heard a squeal and turned to see two little boys in blue school uniforms clinging to Shehu, squeezing him with all their might as he patted them on the head. Without a word, they let go and continued on their way.

"I'll tell you about them later," Shehu whispered.

I settled into a rickety bench to let the time pass. I noticed a silhouette inside a building beside the café. I got up to peer inside. It was a man with his back to the street, sitting cross-legged on the ground, his face just inches from the wall.

"Shehu, is it prayer time?"

"No, why?"

"Well, what is that man doing back there?"

"Ah," he said, gearing up for what I could tell was going to be a lengthy explanation, which I would soon come to recognize as his signature way of answering questions.

"The whole thing comes down to irresponsibility, poverty and selfishness," he said.

"You see," he began, drawing a deep breath, "a man will have enough money to marry a wife. Some will have enough to have two wives. They will have children. But when it comes to feeding his family, it is the man who selects what is used in feeding them. When it comes to breakfast, for example, rather than prepare tea and a meal at home, instead what he will do is make the wife stay home to warm the remnants of what they ate in the night as dinner."

The word remnants had three syllables. "Rem-a-nants," he practically purred, rolling his r and adding a sharp point on the t.

"You mean leftovers?" I asked.

"Yes. Leftover food, which is usually local soup—without even meat. Then the man will go out by himself to a tea joint and will ask them to fry eggs with bread, milk and everything. Then when eating he will face the wall blocking the door so that not everybody will see him and recognize him. That is, he is eating well at a restaurant while feeding his family at home leftovers. He is ashamed.

His back is to us because maybe he lives in this area. Maybe his children live in this area. His in-laws also live around here, and he doesn't want anybody to see him eating. That is what he does."

"So these men stick their families with leftovers and go out for a fancy breakfast?" I said, shaking my head at the selfishness. "What jerks."

"Honestly," he said, nodding his head in agreement.

We walked back to Shehu's car and I spotted a pregnant goat. Pregnant animals always made me uncomfortable because their outsized bulge reminded me of carrying twins. But pregnant goats were the worst because they looked like the baby was wedged inside them perpendicularly.

"Check out that pregnant goat, Shehu."

"Dionne, that is not a goat," he reprimanded me, "that is a sheep."

Argh, I mixed them up again. I was beginning to like Shehu and needed to explain myself so he didn't think I was a stupid American.

"Sheep look different in America," I began my defense. "They have furry wool."

Shehu stared at me.

"They're fluffy," I said.

He kept staring.

"Look," I said, googling a photo of a woolly sheep and handing my phone to him.

"What *is* that?" Shehu said.

"That," I said proudly, "is an American-style sheep."

"It's ridiculous," he said.

Shehu's phone started blaring an annoying set of chimes at maximum volume. He answered the call before he told me where we were headed next.

Our car turned down a narrow street, passing burning trash piles where kids in plastic flip-flops or no shoes at all picked through the ashes in search of anything valuable. Women sat on the side of the street knitting microscopic geometric patterns into caps popular with men in the north of the country. People climbed across chunks of concrete in dilapidated buildings that had become their new homes. One street had long rows of mud walls, and we stopped outside a doorway carved into one of them.

Shehu, phone still to his ear, guided me through a maze of narrow hallways until we came into a small dirt clearing where a woman who was in her late 60s greeted us. Like many older people in this part of Nigeria, she had thick scars starting at the corners of her mouth; they looked like cat whiskers and had been carved into her cheeks when she was a child. The tradition was largely banned now. Shehu ended his call and grabbed a plastic bucket in the corner and turned it over for her to sit on. He stretched out a plastic mat for us to sit below her on the dirt.

I had no idea what this woman had to offer but, just like last time, I launched in. It didn't take more than a couple questions for her to tell me her story.

She had moved into the mud-walled compound just a few months ago, after Boko Haram attacked her village, guns blazing in the middle of the night. It was a brutal invasion. Her arms waved as she pantomimed the beheadings and shootings she'd witnessed, mostly of men who refused to join the group and were gruesomely killed on the spot. Fighters kidnapped all the young women and girls, herding them into one part of the town. They had decided she was too old to be of use so they left her. Terrified, she holed up in her home alone for days as militants carried on with their rampage and takeover of her village.

"Then what happened?" I asked.

One afternoon she heard the roaring engines of approaching motorbikes. Then she heard yelling. She peeked out her door to see in the distance a screaming man being chased on foot by fighters on the bikes. He was running straight toward her house. She stepped from her doorway and began sobbing as she witnessed the awful scene unfold. The man seemed to be heading right for her.

More and more motorbikes arrived, encircling and finally trapping the man, who was still in the distance. She knew he didn't stand a chance. The tears flowed, she said, blurring her vision so she couldn't clearly see him as the inevitable happened. It was only after the insurgents shot the man repeatedly, his body collapsed to the ground as the fighters fled, that she realized she was watching the murder of her own son. Seized by pure terror, he had been running for his mom.

I was stunned. We expressed our sympathies, wished her well and thanked her for her time. What was there to say? I had never heard such a tragic story. It was nauseating.

Pretty much everyone in this city had an incredible story to tell. All you had to do was ask. They wanted to share the terrible things they had witnessed. They wanted the world to know. Maybe someone somewhere would find a way to stop this senseless violence.

I thought about walking around Manhattan on September 11 and reporting in the hours after the World Trade Center collapsed. I had pedaled my bike through snow-like piles of soft ash on the Brooklyn Bridge as hundreds of other people were streaming in the opposite direction. I stuck around a makeshift triage center near City Hall, where volunteers waited to receive the injured who never showed up, because all the victims had been vaporized. That afternoon, I managed to get a call through to a wise ex-colleague who was watching the scene on his television on the West Coast.

"Remember," he counseled, "everyone you meet today, no matter who, will have an amazing story to tell."

He was right. And Maiduguri, at the epicenter of such an awful war for years now, was no different. I realized even that voodoo hunter with the amulets had been worthy of hearing out. To be fair, any American who had emerged unscathed from a gun battle after watching his friends drop dead around him probably would proclaim their thanks to an all-knowing mysterious spirit who lived in the heavens after having created the earth in six days. Was crediting such a miracle to tiny pieces of leather that different?

I also was getting the hang of Shehu. He wasn't big on prepping me for interviews, but it didn't take much work for me to extract information. "What happened?" That was really all I needed to ask anyone. And yes, Shehu's explanations went on tangents, but getting to the end was usually worth the wait.

Shehu drove me around the city to introduce me to important figures—the head of the local vigilante group, people in charge of displaced-persons camps, local aid group leaders. If someone happened to speak one of the area's languages he couldn't, he called in two translators—one to translate for me and one to make sure the translator was doing it right. Accuracy was important to him. We developed an interview rhythm between us where he sat back and let me ask questions of sources even when he already knew the answers. If the source wasn't straight with me, he interjected. If one of our sources became combative, I was the good cop and he was the bad cop.

Finally, it was time for my interview with the governor and we headed for his office.

"So, who were those two little boys hanging on you earlier?" I asked.

"Ah, those boys," he said, shaking his head. "I wrote a story about them for my newspaper."

The two boys were Hudu and Abbani. Hudu was seven when Boko Haram invaded his home and locked him in a room, where he listened as they slaughtered his parents. The militants took Hudu with them and put him on top of an armored vehicle, where he was in charge of feeding an ammunition chain into a mounted weapon. They told him they would kill him if he refused.

Abbani was 10 when he watched Boko Haram behead first his father, then his mother. Fighters took him to their camp, where he was forced to run errands. One day, they heard the military heading toward their hideout. The group's leaders shoved a gun into Abbani's hands and told him to fight. When soldiers arrived in the Boko Haram camp, Abbani ran away. As he raced through a field he spotted a teenage girl crouching in the weeds. She was also an escaped Boko Haram captive, pregnant with the baby of a fighter who raped her.

She and Abbadi ran together and came across Hudu. He was holding an AK-47, shooting wildly into the air before he dropped the gun and fell on his face.

The girl rushed to Hudu and gathered him to his feet. The threesome together kept running until they were safe. Abbani and Hudu were now living with her and her newborn in Maiduguri. They call her "mother." They were the world's most amazing blended family.

This place. These stories. They were unfathomable. I was unintentionally assembling a collection of terrifying stories. And again, I knew not all of them would make it into the newspaper. I documented them anyway. And I vowed to find a place for Hudu and Abbani in my reporting, no matter what.

CHAPTER 9

Aisha

THE KINDS OF stories Shehu's newspaper had published didn't endear it to its hometown audience, Boko Haram. This was nowhere more obvious than at the newspaper's local headquarters, where Shehu brought me to find a copy of his article on Abbani and Hudu.

A newspaper delivery truck was the only vehicle in the parking lot. A few years back fighters had strapped six bombs to the underside of it. A reporter noticed something strange jutting from the undercarriage and called the police. Back then, some officers were so afraid of Boko Haram they had barricaded themselves in their station house. It was the start of the war, and Maiduguri's police department didn't have a bomb squad. Officers didn't know how to remove the explosives. Reporters weren't qualified to do it. Three weeks later someone finally came to detach the bombs. The paper put the truck back in service, a moving monument to journalism refusing to back down in the face of threats.

Shehu's own reporting had put him in personal jeopardy. Or maybe it was more accurate to say that he put himself in jeopardy to tell important stories about Boko Haram.

One in particular stood out. Shehu had heard about a market where Boko Haram members openly traded fish, vegetables and other supplies with wealthy Maiduguri businessmen who were profiting from the war. Such a big marketplace couldn't have gone unnoticed by soldiers fanning out across the countryside. They must have been getting a cut of the proceeds in exchange for looking the other way.

The trade that went on at the market technically landed within Shehu's Agriculture and Fisheries beat. He convinced his editors to let him do the story. He wasn't officially a war reporter, but really, everyone in the region had become one.

Shehu was desperate to expose the market—he was sickened by the idea that elites were helping sustain the war. But he knew he would be killed if he showed up there with a reporter's notebook and started asking questions. So he developed a plan to go undercover. For two weeks, he went barefoot to rough up his feet so they looked like "village feet," the blistered and calloused feet of poor rural people who can't afford shoes. He pretended to be deaf and mute and headed out to the market. Soldiers and even militants stopped his vehicle at various checkpoints. He just smiled and nodded. They were convinced by his shtick and let him pass. He arrived at the market and walked around openly to observe what went on and went back home and published a story about what he saw.

The article achieved the best result an investigative reporter could ever hope for—it upset everyone involved. The militants, the military and Maiduguri's elites all were outraged. Like many journalists who reported the truth about the war, Shehu for a while was a wanted man.

Earlier in the war when Boko Haram was roaming more freely around town and targeting journalists, Shehu had kept three apartments, moving often to avoid detection. He sometimes took refuge hundreds of miles away in the capital, where he kept his family for safety. Now that the military had chased Boko Haram from Maiduguri, working as a reporter was safer. But Shehu hadn't been afraid to expose the truth at whatever cost.

I was a foreigner with vast resources who could drop in and out of a conflict zone. If I made someone mad with a story, they'd have to fly to Dakar to threaten me. My company could pull me back to America if things got scary.

Since I'd been on the West Africa beat, a few people commenting on my stories had called me a "badass," in a complimentary way. I was a badass for reporting from the scene of a terrorist attack or a badass for writing about war victims. It seemed like a gendered word used to praise women for doing jobs men did without gushing compliments about their bravery. Regardless, I always believed that half of a reporter's "skill" comes from just showing up. Here, I was on the sidelines of the battle. Shehu waltzed right into the middle of danger. He was the real badass. I was riding his coattails and I was in awe.

The car arrived at the governor's compound, passing through checkpoints where guards searched for explosives. I opened my door and realized I was the only one getting out of the car.

"Shehu, aren't you coming?" I asked through his rolled-down window. "It's your chance to talk to the governor."

"I refuse to go near that man," he said. "The governor has failed us."

He must have sensed my hesitation. I was getting used to having him guide me through interviews.

"He speaks English, you don't need me to translate—you'll be fine."

I guess I should have been upset with Shehu for leaving me on my own. But I saw his point. I show up with my *New York Times* credentials and am escorted right in. His anger was deep. The war had no end in sight. Maiduguri had been inundated by hundreds of thousands of newly homeless people, straining already strained resources. The awful stories of war victims were endless. The governor had made a lot of empty promises about caring for them and about ending the war. It wasn't getting better.

I admired Shehu's skepticism of authority, especially after what he'd witnessed. He didn't need to be granted an audience to kiss any government ass.

I wandered into the main building and was directed to a small office, where I was told the governor would receive me any minute. Four hours later, I was escorted into a living room–sized office, where Shettima greeted me. His huge hand swallowed my smaller one.

"Governor," I started in, "I'm curious about these women you are keeping who were married to Boko Haram commanders."

"Yes, I have secured them here in Maiduguri," he said.

"Are they as vicious as you say?"

"I see them as largely radicalized," he said. "Some of these women, they might become suicide bombers if we release them to the world."

The governor's plan for the women, he explained, was to "de-radicalize" them, indoctrinating them against Boko Haram much in the same way they apparently had been convinced that Boko Haram was a force for good. Once that was complete, the governor would set them free, giving each woman a packet of seeds, an irrigation kit and some livestock to set up her own farm. But that was a long way off, he cautioned.

One of the women, in particular, was loyal to Boko Haram, he told me. She was married to a top commander.

"From the way she was defending her husband, obviously she has some affection for the idiot," he said.

"Can I meet with her and the others?"

"Why not?" the governor said. "I will personally drive you to their safe house."

As a foreign reporter, I was getting special treatment. The governor grabbed a set of keys and walked me out to a shiny black pickup truck. He got behind the wheel and we were off, his parade of siren-blaring security cars trailing us.

As we lurched through the slow-moving traffic, it began to dawn on me that we were heading to meet with women who might view me as the very symbol of Western civilization that Boko Haram abhors. What would they do to me? Spit on me? Swear at me? Surely the governor's bodyguards would hold them back. I steeled myself.

The safe house was a compound of several buildings surrounded by tall, concrete walls lined by coils of razor wire. As soon as we stepped through the heavily guarded door, a dozen kids rushed the governor. They gathered around him, tugging at his arms and clinging to his gown. Their fathers were said to be some of the fiercest commanders of Boko Haram. They just wanted a hug. The governor told me he even had decided to adopt one little girl. She was just 11 and had been raped by a fighter.

The kids' mothers were all sitting under the shade of the only tree on the grounds. It was Ramadan and we had a short time until they were allowed to eat a meal, breaking their daylong fast, so I gathered a few of them as quickly as I could.

The women—56 of them in total—were all from poor farming communities where low rainfall and years of war had left their families struggling even to find enough to eat.

I pulled one of the women aside. Her name was Aisha and she had been married to the high-ranking emir, or religious leader, of the militants. She hadn't run off and joined Boko Haram. In fact, she was captured along with other people when fighters invaded her village, killing some of her friends and neighbors.

For months she lived as a captive, scrounging for food in the forest and living a limited existence, reined in by fighters who refused to let her move around much in their sprawling camp. She gave up hope that she ever would return to any other way of life.

"I thought, forgive and forget. I was just staying with Boko Haram," she told me.

Eventually, the emir started bringing up the idea of marriage. Some Boko Haram members violently raped their captives. Others believed the Koran had taught them they needed a woman's permission for "marriage"—if that's an appropriate word for the union between kidnapper and hostage. Aisha refused.

The emir persisted. He offered her rice and told her if she became his wife she would have that for a meal every day. It was tempting. She had been getting by on watery porridge and roots she dug up. Still, she didn't budge. He told her she could roam wherever she wanted in the camp if she married him. This also held appeal. Even in her own village she was expected to stay close to home. Still, she refused.

Finally, the emir offered her the equivalent of a $500 dowry. She knew she could spend that at Boko Haram–controlled markets, for food and clothing. It was far more money than she would have fetched for a dowry in her home village. She was finally swayed.

Aisha moved into the emir's quarters. She cooked for him and did his laundry. In her own village she would have been saddled with those tasks as well as been expected to spend most of the day in the fields doing grueling farmwork. The wife of a Boko Haram commander wasn't something she'd imagined for herself in life, but in reality she probably wouldn't have married someone of her own choosing anyway; her father or other relatives would have selected her groom.

Being married to Boko Haram guaranteed Aisha an easier and, in some substantial ways, better life than she had at home.

"But what about the violence?" I asked.

At one point her husband showed her his weapons cache but she didn't ask any questions. She knew Boko Haram killed people— she'd seen some of the murders firsthand in her own village. But she tried not to think about it. Besides, she felt powerless to stop it.

"What can I do about it?" she offered.

Elsewhere in the region, when the terrorist group had captured women, Boko Haram had portrayed itself almost as feminist.

"You are now in an Islamic kingdom," one fighter had told another kidnapping victim, according to Hilary Matfess in her book, *Women and the War on Boko Haram: Wives, Weapons, Witnesses*.

"Here," the fighter continued, "women's rights are respected, not like (other places) in Nigeria where women are made to farm, fetch water and firewood, and where you have all types of discrimination."

While the men were out marauding, Aisha and the other commanders' wives had the camp to themselves, she told me. They were basically mafia wives. Like Carmela Soprano, they turned a blind eye to their husbands' violent lifestyles and reaped the rewards.

"When you marry Boko Haram you are free," one woman told Matfess in her book. "All you have to do is clean a little."

The governor thought of these women as vicious. But I wondered if maybe they were clever, making the most out of a situation that would have left them miserable even in times of peace. I found out later that after the women were released from their detention, Aisha went back to her Boko Haram husband.

CHAPTER 10

Bad Mom

I SAT IN my kitchen with a splitting headache, being bombarded by complaints from my kids about all the terrible things their father had done while I was away. I had just returned home from Nigeria and they already had started in.

Zola griped about the too-small Band-Aids that Todd had used on her scraped knee. Maude was outraged that he wouldn't let her have Nutella crepes in her school lunch. Luther was angry that Todd let the kids watch only one movie for the whole two weeks I was gone.

I should have scolded them for complaining when their dad was outnumbered. But all I could concentrate on was how their whining was so jarring and their complaints so inconsequential given the stories I had just heard. I decided I was going to tell them, within reason, about the people I met and the stories they told me. It wasn't a scared-straight approach but it was close. Todd and I had never hidden negative news stories from our children; rather, we have explained them, in terms they could understand.

Boko Haram, I told the kids, was started by really, really poor people who were tired of the government and rich people stealing from them. First they protested, I said, but nothing changed. They got angry. Then, just like the militants in the Delta who had cried out for so long with no one listening that they resorted to blowing up oil pipelines, in Maiduguri things also got out of control. The police killed Boko Haram's leader without even a trial. War broke out. A lot of people died. Even kids their own age had been kidnapped or killed.

My girls were still young, only nine years old now, with short attention spans—they were already tuning out. But when I started talking about Shehu and the bombs on his newspaper truck, Luther's eyes widened.

"Is it dangerous for you to be there?"

Uh-oh. That wasn't the outcome I had been aiming for. I wanted him and his sisters to realize how lucky they were to have the life that they do. But of course that is the conclusion a child would leap to—worrying their mother is in danger. Bad mom move.

I thought about how a journalist friend had sought my advice about applying for an international posting at the paper.

"You'd be perfect for my job when I'm ready to leave here," I told her.

"Oh, I could never do that," she said. "I have kids."

It was a slap in the face. I wasn't walking into battlefields, I explained. I was interviewing victims on the periphery, once they had escaped to safety. I weighed the risks, talked to sources on the ground and never knowingly put myself in danger. In America, with all the mass shootings, classrooms, churches and sidewalks were becoming dangerous places to be. Is that any safer?

I had sought counsel from other moms who worked dangerous beats. At my paper, there were quite a few of them. One told me she reassures her children that "mama knows how to help herself if she gets hurt." She had emphasized the elaborate safety and first-aid training the *Times* makes us all go through.

I tried that line of reasoning with my son.

"I don't go near the dangerous areas," I said. "I just talk to the people who have been there."

He seemed satisfied.

But was I taking too many risks? *Hundreds of reporters had done this kind of work in the past*, I reminded myself. Most of them were men but some must have had kids, so why was it any different for me? The ones who were good dads probably trained their brains just like I did, to temporarily tuck away the part of them that is a parent the moment they walk out the door. No one stops loving their kids while they're on a work assignment. The focus just shifts, sometimes fully and completely, to the job ahead.

And unlike a 9-to-5 job, mine was in the office inside my house when I wasn't traveling. I had 90 full extra minutes of time each day, instead of my old Brooklyn commute, to spend with my family. Sometimes I went to Luther's afternoon volleyball games, the girls' swim meets or lunch at the Lebanese café on the school campus, where I could spy on the kids during their P.E. classes.

Some days, I had more freedom than most working moms.

THE NEXT DAY, the kids were meant to go to school, and I had planned a big day of writing to finish my story about the Boko Haram wives. As it turned out, though, Luther had some kind of stomach bug and needed to stay home.

Todd was stuck on a conference call for the better part of the morning, so I situated my boy in bed with a comic book and holed up in my office, hoping he would read quietly or nap so I could wrap up my story.

My phone rang. A European number popped up on the screen.

"Hello, Dionne, this is Bono," the voice said on the other end of the line.

"Bono?"

It took me a minute to remember that I had seen a press release announcing that the star of U2 had been touring Nigeria and was even passing through Maiduguri on a humanitarian trip for his nonprofit organization. I had emailed his spokesperson asking why I hadn't been alerted to this ahead of the trip. He was there right around the same time as me, and it would have been nothing short of bizarre to see a rock star celebrity in a war zone. It at least would have made for an interesting paragraph or two in a story. His staff had regretted not telling me about his travel plans and had him call me instead.

"I've been reading your stuff. You're just incredible. Keep it coming," Bono said. He was flattering but I wasn't quite sure he was telling the truth.

He launched in with what he'd learned while in Maiduguri. It turns out the governor took him to the safe house of commanders' wives, too. Bono didn't tell me anything I didn't know already, but I was heartened someone famous was aware of the issues there. And I was hopeful that through his celebrity he would help spread the word and bring attention to the situation.

"There are two million displaced people, one million of them are kids, and even as the military is pushing back on Boko Haram, these people have no homes to go back to. They've destroyed them. As you know, their homes are gone; their villages are gone. It's pretty shocking. I'm used to a scandal. I'm used to natural disasters, but this is a disaster that's being caused by neglect, by 20 years of misgovernment of the region and of this conflict. This conflict is development in reverse. It's pathetic. If Nigeria fails, Africa fails. If Africa fails, Europe fails. If Europe fails, America is no longer America."

Bono was on a roll. In one breath he went on to broaden the topic to just about everything. He rambled about ISIS, Brexit, Syria, migration, immigration, right-wing fervor, the North Atlantic Treaty Organization, Hillary Clinton, Angela Merkel, Bill Gates, polio. . . .

"Mom!" my son burst through my office door shouting as Bono carried on in my ear. "I just had diarrhea!"

I was petrified Bono had heard him. I covered the phone's mouthpiece with my hand and whispered, "Honey, I'm on the phone with Bono."

"Who's Bono?" he said in an even louder voice.

"I'll tell you later," I whispered. Thank goodness Bono was talking so much he apparently didn't hear anything. By this point he was on to the Cold War and the World Bank and . . .

"But my diarrhea . . ."

"Out!" I swatted away Luther as Bono continued.

In truth, I was a bit annoyed at Bono. He was explaining issues that as the West Africa bureau chief for the *Times* I already understood. But at the same time he was interested in this part of the world—so interested that he had gone to Maiduguri. And he was as curious about the commanders' wives as I was.

"I woke up this morning thinking those girls were so beautiful. They had such a kind of . . . a look in their eye, and I was trying to figure out what it was," he said. "They were being really welcoming and everything to visitors, but there was defiance—a little bit of 'fuck you' just behind their eyes. I just, I don't know, I'm still not sure."

I FILED MY story, my son recovered, and I had a bit of freedom to reconnect with my kids. I started by explaining who Bono was.

My job was starting to really click. Some parts of it were dangerous, but it was exhilarating all the same. And it seemed worth it. I had a chance to make a difference. That was why I got into this business in the first place.

My brother, an early pioneer out of my hometown, had urged me to work at my campus newspaper. I showed up at the *The Daily Nebraskan* and editors assigned me a story about a space artifact—a capsule that was part of the Apollo program, donated to the university. Officials had displayed it outside the museum, exposing it to the elements. The capsule had been designed to withstand the extremes of outer space, but that was no match for Nebraska's four-seasons-in-one-day weather. It had begun to rot. Space enthusiasts were outraged.

I bumbled my way through interviews about the capsule with university board members, calling them back after forgetting to ask basic questions. I walked around campus interviewing regular students to hear their thoughts, finding it impossible to take notes as fast as they talked. I tapped out my story on the newspaper's clunky IBM keyboards and submitted it. My editor looked at the article and let out one of those long, exasperated sighs. She clicked on the cursor to push the top of my story far down on the page so she could clear a path for a dramatic rewrite.

My story cycled through three editors, who kept handing it off out of frustration. Make more calls, they told me. Write another version—and another. I skipped classes to work on the rewrite. I planted myself in front of a screen at the messy newspaper office in the basement of the student union, eating takeout from the Burger King upstairs for every meal. At last, I scored an interview with an astronaut—Eugene Cernan, famous for being the last person to ever have walked on the moon. He criticized university officials for failing to take care of what was a piece of our nation's space exploration history. His quotes redeemed me, and my story was published on the front page.

I had found justice for what most people considered space junk. But I didn't care. Friends read my article. Professors complimented me. The campus newspaper editor-in-chief hung my story on the kiosk in the middle of the newsroom, where he circled my byline and marked up the page with a black grease pencil to congratulate me. The praise was nice, but most important, the university was shamed into acting. I was thrilled. And I got paid. It was my first real job.

At *The Daily Nebraskan*, I went on to cover legislative hearings, Gulf War vigils and a gruesome murder trial of a student. I also made dumb mistakes. I once reported that some 30,000 students at my university had been diagnosed with sexually transmitted diseases—more than the entire student body. The real number was something like 3,000. I confessed my sin, moped for days, worked hard at other stories to redeem myself and fell in love with journalism all over again.

I haven't stopped reporting since.

At urban newspapers across the country, I specialized in being a generalist. I showed up at crime scenes and house fires in Chicago. I wrote about new shopping malls in Naperville, a state budget crisis in Olympia, a plane crash off the coast of Southern California, nefarious lobbyists in Albany, a parking ticket scandal on Long Island. I got tear-gassed outside the World Trade Organization meetings in Seattle. I was an embedded reporter during the war in Iraq, assigned to an all-male combat unit after the military thought *Dionne* was a male name. I covered one of Michael Jackson's molestation trials, staring at his face day after day, unable to place what seemed so familiar. Finally, I realized what it was: his pink-tinted lipstick was the same shade as my mom's.

I was getting all the more excited about journalism, but my industry was dying. I worked at news organizations that slashed editions, laid off prize winners, paid old-timers to quit and stopped handing out free copies of the paper to their own employees, or shut down altogether. Finally, I landed a job at *The Wall Street Journal*, one of the most prestigious newspapers in the world.

The editors assigned me to the telecom beat. I spent hours in conference rooms listening to executives drone on about market capitalization and ARPU—Average Revenue Per User, I eventually figured out. I went on to write about scheming corporations and watched their CEOs get sentenced to prison.

Landing on page 1 at the *Journal* was an epic achievement, so difficult that most reporters were celebrated if they averaged just two front-page stories a year.

I gamed the system by writing a lot of A-heds, a *Journal* specialty of funny, front-page features on weird and quirky people, places and phenomena. Whenever I worried I was running a page 1 deficit, I'd stare at my keyboard and try to recall things we did in Nebraska that wealthy coastal elites—the *Journal's* readership base—would consider unusual. Collecting hailstones after a storm and storing them in the freezer. Hiring a traveling pancake man to cater a party. Dressing up as Joseph and Mary cradling a baby doll Jesus and sitting outside in the freezing cold and snow with barn animals to create a "living nativity." My ideas were exotic enough to sail onto the front page.

Those stories were nice distractions from the daily grind. But the real work there, covering corporations and business interests, was less fun for me. The *Times* was a better fit, but my beat writing about the economy still involved plenty of sitting in auditoriums listening to academics talk about struggling human beings as data points in Excel spreadsheets.

For more than a decade in journalism, I had miscast myself. I was a general news reporter at a business newspaper, then a business reporter at a general newspaper. Joining the international desk at the *Times* felt like maybe finally I was getting it right.

But I felt guilty for having been so distant from my kids in past weeks, so I overcompensated. I took them to the only frozen yogurt store in town, letting them heap chocolate sauce, sprinkles and marshmallows on piles of dessert. We went to one of Dakar's fancy beachside hotels, where we paid a day fee to use the swimming pool and bouncy castle, snacking poolside on French fries and Fanta. At home, we took advantage of a city where everything can be delivered, even an ice-cream cone, and ordered the Senegalese version of Domino's pizza while we watched movies on school nights.

A colleague who traveled a lot for her job confided she had engaged in the same kind of fun-uncle parenting when she returned from her trips. Her husband, stuck with the day-to-day parenting, was outraged.

"You don't get to come home and be Disney Dad," he had scolded her.

I was falling into the same routine. My husband peeked in from his office to find us on our fourth round of the board game Sorry.

We left him behind while we went out in search of American pancakes and bacon and the one store in town that sold American Cheerios. The expiration date on the box was long past and I smelled a whiff of bug spray from what most likely was some kind of insecticide showered on containers at the port. Each box cost $10. I knew it was ridiculous, but I splurged. The kids wanted a taste of home.

I was certain my story on the Boko Haram commanders' wives would soar to the front page. But the paper was mired in presidential campaign hysteria. The editors didn't touch it for days. America's election was less than a month away and Hillary's emails and Trump's rallies were all anyone was talking about. My story got buried inside, running on page A6 of the paper.

I felt dissed even by the international editor, who had a quirky Instagram account where he posted photos of the lunches he made for his son to take to school, along with thoughts on the day's big news from abroad. My story didn't even make sandwich Instagram.

We had new technology at the *Times* that allowed us to check how many readers were clicking on our stories. A few thousand people had read my article. *Not bad,* I thought. Until I clicked around and realized a story on victims of the economic crisis in Venezuela had more than one million readers. It was crushing.

NEWS FLASH: HILLARY Clinton didn't win the election. The whole world became fixated on America's new bombastic president. Whether for or against him, Americans were reeling.

In Brooklyn, my friends' little girls were sobbing. In their confidence that their own daughters would witness a Hillary victory and the shattering of the ultimate glass ceiling, they had told their girls *Handmaid's Tale*–like horror stories about Trump. The morning after the election, one friend's daughter was convinced she would no longer be allowed to go to school because she was female. Another's daughter thought she would be thrown in jail.

Being abroad for the aftermath of the election offered a reassuring distance from the tailspin that liberal America was going into. The same women who were putting on their pussy hats and marching on the Capitol probably had never given a passing thought to the women I'd met who were making the most out of being victims of rape and kidnapping.

I was ashamed of myself for feeling like that; it was an unfair comparison. I wasn't being reasonable. Maybe I was just bitter I couldn't crack the front page with my own stories. It was hard to argue the increasingly valid fear that the Trump administration's seeming assault on issues important to many women wasn't front-page news. It was strange to straddle both worlds and at first hard to realize that women in each place were protecting themselves the best they could.

CHAPTER 11

Walk of Shame

IT SEEMED LIKE a century ago when Todd and I first met on a small bus with a smoking engine and a strong gasoline smell that filled the cabin as it hauled us toward a 5 A.M. tour of the old demilitarized zone between North and South Vietnam.

It was 1997. I was backpacking. He was the guy in front of me loudly chatting away about his courses in graduate school as I tried to doze until we arrived at our destination.

Annoying, I thought, and tried to tune him out. But the conversation kept jolting me awake. He had ditched a career in investment banking, I heard him say. He wanted to be a history professor. I opened my eyes enough to notice tiny brown curls on the back of his neck that had slipped from the mess of his Eddie Vedder hairdo he'd stuffed into a ponytail.

Annoying, yes; but also kind of cute.

I had been dating guys who worked in record stores or played in bands, whose life ambitions seemed to be getting to the bar before happy hour ended. One boyfriend had been so broke and aimless, I left lunch money on the bedside table for him while he slept in and I went to work. He spent it on beer.

This new guy was different. Todd spoke Mandarin. He was

working on his doctorate degree in history. He read Richard Rorty books, for fun. "There are no norms!" he shouted when he was drunk, quoting Portuguese poet Fernando Pessoa. I was captivated listening to his ideas about how the world works and how he would fit in and try to make it better.

After our DMZ tour, Todd convinced me to tag along with him on a side trip to Sapa, a village in the hills of northern Vietnam. I'd spent weeks sweating through a Southeast Asian summer. The cool temperatures of Sapa and the terraced rice paddies that coiled around the emerald hills somehow made a dorky, loud-talking, sort of snobby grad student incredibly attractive.

We spent the summer trading long emails, him from his dorm room in Beijing, and me from the back room of the post office in Ho Chi Minh City, where a kind worker let me use his computer. Once, I even flew to meet Todd in the industrial city of Wuhan in China, a spot he picked because of its lack of appeal to tourists. We were so happy to see each other we made out on the bus from the airport, oblivious to the fact that it had stopped and all the passengers had stepped off.

And the guy was a pro at adventure traveling. He had all the gear—Gortex raincoat, microfiber socks, quick-drying mini towel, even a titanium spork, just in case. I was wearing rock-climbing shoes that I had mistaken for hiking boots. I carried a bandanna for a towel. Worst of all, my backpack was too small. It was stuffed to the brim and dug into my shoulders.

When it was time to say goodbye, he insisted I take his REI specialty backpack with lumbar support and cushiony arm straps. It was the nicest thing anyone had ever done for me.

In our life in West Africa, I was the one with all the gear— a satellite phone, a satellite modem, Australian work boots, a Kevlar helmet. And I was the one getting to go out in the world. He wanted to be the kind of supportive spouse who didn't whine about his wife being away.

But he was the one left behind to ferry the kids to activities while dodging the horse carts and pedestrians who wandered into the lanes of the new toll road, the station wagons so stuffed with people the undercarriage almost scraped the road below and trucks so loaded with bags of flour, even on the roof, that they looked like they would tip. He watched over our three kids on his own when they swam in an ocean known for its snaking rip currents that had carried people who couldn't swim out to sea. He wrangled the kids every morning to slather them in sunscreen and took them to friends' birthday parties at a skate park with rental Rollerblades whose wheels had rusted in place. Working from the servant's quarters wasn't helping his self-image.

My own work was so difficult I sometimes forgot to be grateful. One of my male friends used to joke that he wished just once when he came home from work his stay-at-home wife would hand him a cocktail the way Samantha used to do for Darren on *Bewitched*. He worked hard, my friend complained, and when he got in the door he found more work to be done: unfinished school assignments, dishes in the sink and chaos.

Of course Samantha handed her husband a drink. All she had to do was twitch her nose to get all that other stuff done.

I didn't expect a martini, and I didn't expect home life to be perfect, but I expected Todd to hold up his end of the agreement. And he was. He hadn't voiced complaints, not yet anyway.

But once at a dinner party, I caught a comment under his breath as I nodded along during a conversation of parents discussing classes at our kids' school.

"How would you know?" he mumbled. "You're never even around."

I didn't respond.

I SHOULD HAVE realized that trouble at home was brewing, but the call of the road was too strong.

An invitation landed in my inbox from a branch of the United Nations, which was offering access for a few select journalists to areas in rural Nigeria that are difficult to get to, partly because they were crawling with Boko Haram but mostly because the military controlled who went in and out. The trip was part of a tour the U.N. was organizing for a delegation of high-ranking diplomats. The hope was that they would view the destruction firsthand and their countries would pledge money to U.N. organizations that help children, distribute food or set up camps for people on the run from the war.

U.N. officials had calculated that having us along to write about the humanitarian issues at a time that coincided with the diplomats' visit would generate bigger donations. Press trips that involve a gaggle of reporters, however, can be a drag as organizers try to satisfy the different needs and interests of every reporter. But the U.N. would secure permissions for us to be out in the countryside, something that was tough to do on our own. And I would be allowed to interview not just military officers commanding the war but people living in camps in parts of the region journalists hadn't been to in years.

It seemed too good to pass up, and I could tack on a few non-war stories while I was there.

The *Times* assigned a photographer to accompany me, Ashley Gilbertson. I had never met Ashley but I had a fixed image in my head of the person behind all those photo credits that appeared at the bottom of dozens of photos in the *Times:* an intrepid, pudgy young American woman with a brown bobbed hairdo who always wore one of those khaki, multipocketed photographers' vests.

I googled the name. Turns out Ashley was a man. And I rolled my eyes at his profile photo—he had a cigarette hanging out of the side of his mouth. His hair was a patch of dirty blond tumbleweed. He wore black skinny jeans with Chelsea boots and a black collared shirt, untucked with one open button too many, exposing his chest. He looked like he was on his way to a party in a Soho loft.

"He's going to be a total egomaniacal asshole," I said to my husband.

"You can handle jerks," he said. "In fact, I think you like them."

Back at the *Journal* I had once been handpicked as the reporter to collaborate on a complicated story with a belligerent colleague.

"You're the only person in the newsroom he won't make cry," the editor told me.

He was right. We wound up friends.

Breaking through the tough guy shell was a necessity for any woman who wanted to be successful in male-dominated fields. When I reported in Chicago, I had to win over mean, cynical, media-hating cops and detectives—almost all of them were men— if I wanted any information on unfolding cases or even just a place to camp out between assignments and use the precinct phone in that pre-cellphone era. I knew I passed their test when I got hold of the password to access a secret, unmarked cop bar.

Ash, as it turned out, may have looked like he was going to get drunk and punch someone, but after a bit more digging I found out he was an Australian journalism veteran known for his honest coverage of the Iraq War and the deep emotional toll it took on him. He had a reputation for going anywhere, doing anything and working like crazy.

The first thing he did when we met was shove a bag of high-end coffee beans from a hipster New York roaster into my hand. A reprieve from Nescafé!

Our plane landed in Maiduguri amid a storm; Shehu met Ash and me at the airport. The wind was howling in almost tornado-like fashion, whipping dust that swirled around our feet.

"Shehu," I said, taking in his crisp white clothing that was still crisp and white even in the blowing sand, "how do you keep that outfit so clean?"

"Ah," he said, taking a breath. "The whole thing comes down to the expenses of everyday life.

"To exist, a man needs food, shelter and clothing. These things can be expensive. Rent here can cost thousands of naira. A man may live in a small apartment or a big apartment. The big ones have one bedroom or two bedrooms, a proper kitchen and a toilet. They are very expensive. So expensive. Food is expensive. We have chicken. We have suya, which is roasted meat."

I wasn't sure where this story was going but I was savoring it, and I could tell Ash enjoyed it, too.

"The meat can be very spicy for your people. It is from the cow or the sheep. Our clothing we buy in the market. The clothing that is dyed—that is the clothing with color—is expensive. The clothing with no color at all—I'm talking about the clothing that is white—is less expensive."

"OK," I said, "so your white outfit is cheaper than if it was blue."

"Yes, yes," he said. "And I buy many white outfits and change my clothing often," he said, laughing at his own ingenuity. "That is what I do."

We piled into his car, the worn shocks heaving under our weight when we sat down.

"You're here at the invitation of the U.N.?" Shehu asked.

"Yes," I said. "They invited us to come take a look at their operations."

"They're doing nothing for us here," he said. "They are only making things worse."

"Come on, Shehu." I loved how he questioned authority but these were the people feeding the hungry and giving them shelter. "Clearly they're doing something. They hand out food, right?"

He pursed his lips in disgust. I didn't press him.

SHEHU HAD HEARD the military recently had been going through villages in the countryside and evacuating everyone, torching homes, Boko Haram–style, and rounding up people into camps near major towns. Clearing the countryside of regular people, the thinking went, would make it easier to spot and kill the bad guys even if it meant uprooting the slim part of the population that had felt safe enough to stay in their homes. I knew the military had a poor track record when it came to human rights, but how could they think that this strategy was going to win the war?

We were staying at a brand-new U.N. base camp, nicknamed "the Red Roof," a smattering of empty buildings with red metal roofs, large white tents and giant containers that looked like the bases the U.S. military contractors had set up in Iraq.

The small tent city was fancier than any U.N. refugee camp I had seen. The floors were concrete and the units were outfitted with IKEA furniture. They were even better than the hotels in the city with their old shag carpet that trapped visible chunks of dirt. At those hotels, the electric outlets sizzled when I plugged in my laptop, and the rooms were coated in toxic mosquito repellent that left a fake citrus smell I could almost taste, as if the humid air was so saturated it couldn't absorb the droplets.

I was happy to tag along with the U.N. and see what they wanted to show me, but I also was bent on finding members of Boko Haram. Shehu thought one of our sources might have a lead.

While he worked on that, we went with other reporters to the U.N. headquarters in town where an Irishman named Darren, the head of media relations for the agency that invited us, pointed us to a room set aside for the working press.

"You can file your stories from here," Darren chirped, proud of having cleared a space for busy journalists with deadlines.

All the reporters looked at one another. No one had the heart to tell him that beyond some kind of catastrophic attack that killed dozens, no news organization in the world would take breaking news updates from the front lines of the nearly eighth year of the war with Boko Haram.

We were herded into a room for a security briefing. U.N. offi-cials told us about their efforts to build relationships with the Nigerian military. They had hired a retired general as a liaison between the U.N. and the military and had arranged briefings for us with high-ranking commanders. They told us soldiers were carrying out humanitarian missions even when that wasn't their job. One commander had managed to find a copy of a *Tom & Jerry* cartoon in the local language and arranged a screening for kids in a camp for people who had been uprooted because of the war.

In the initial years of the war, the Nigerians had refused the help of the United Nations. By the time the country agreed to let the U.N. come in, the place was a wreck, with hundreds of thousands of homeless struggling to find enough to eat. If the U.N. didn't keep up good relations with the military, workers worried they would be kicked out. But buddying up to a military that had killed and detained innocent civilians seemed like an awkward undertaking for humanitarians.

Friends of mine who worked inside the organization were whispering worries that the U.N. in Nigeria was heading for another Sri Lanka–type outcome. In 2012, an internal investigation found U.N. workers had stayed silent in the face of human rights violations in the final months of a bloody civil war there when tens of thousands of people were killed.

During our Maiduguri briefing, officials talked about how the Nigerian military had said that parts of the countryside were safe for anyone to live now, but that we should keep our eyes open as we traveled. Were they trying to signal us that the military was lying? Why not just tell us what was going on?

"When you meet the military officers," one of the U.N. officials counseled, "be sure to congratulate them on their success."

I couldn't believe what I was hearing. The last thing I would ever do is congratulate this military, on anything.

Ash and I boarded a U.N. helicopter flight to a small community about 60 miles from Maiduguri. From the air we spotted long lines crisscrossing the scrub that looked like motorcycle tracks. Or maybe cattle tracks? It was hard to tell from up high. We saw remains of charred fields and burned villages. Soon, scattered piles of hay emerged. In fact, they were shelters assembled by the thousands of people who had fled their homes with nothing but the clothes they were wearing. It wasn't Boko Haram who had chased them away; it was the military that had evacuated them. A deep trench that looked like a waterless moat ringed the camp, to trip up terrorists should they invade. Or maybe it was to keep the displaced people from going home. It was hard to tell who was defending against whom anymore.

This is what success looked like, apparently. Congratulations, military, great work here.

Soldiers greeted the helicopter and escorted me, Ash and other reporters into a conference room where a commander stood behind a podium and other military brass sat across from us at a long table.

"Who is your team leader?" the highest-ranking officer in the room asked.

All the reporters were silent. We weren't a team. We were competitors.

"She is," Ash piped up, pointing to me.

"Madame Team Leader, please make a brief statement," the officer told me.

Ash smirked. I wanted to kill him. I didn't know what to say.

"Congratulations on your successes," I began, horrified at the words coming out of my own mouth. Why the fuck did I say that? What is wrong with me? I fumbled through introductions and tried to recover. I explained we were there to learn more about why the military had been evacuating the countryside and rounding up people into camps.

"We have not evacuated anyone," the officer said, and told us question time was over.

Was he flat-out lying? The other reporters had heard the same rumors. We went back and forth with the commander without progress. The military was controlling our access and they had guns.

It didn't seem wise to keep grilling them when they were done talking to us. The soldiers escorted us all outside for a group photo together. The sun was so bright all I could do was squint and grimace.

I spent hours interviewing people in the camp there. Everyone I talked to confirmed soldiers had been combing the rural areas for anyone who remained, telling them to leave and then burning down the entire village.

People complained they didn't have enough to eat in the camp. The military was afraid that Boko Haram would rob any large stores of grain or other food so they controlled how much was on hand at any time. Soldiers had shut down mobile networks and closed fuel stations. No one could leave. All of it seemed to violate international law. I met one old man who confided he had been sneaking out to go fishing in Lake Chad, smuggling his catch back home by stuffing it in his pants. There were strict prohibitions against fishing now, and anyone caught with fish was presumed to be a terrorist and killed. He was braver than most people, who played it safe, stuck in the misery of the camp.

We boarded the helicopter again and landed in Maiduguri. When I got back to camp I checked my email. My inbox included a news release sent to the public from the Nigerian military announcing our visit.

"Foreign Media Commend Nigerian Army in War Against Terrorism," read the blaring headline.

> The Nigerian Army has been commended for its professionalism in the war against Boko Haram terrorism in the North East of the country. This was disclosed by a team of international journalists from *The New York Times.* . . .

Good grief. The other reporters, Ash and even Shehu teased me for being an instrument of the Nigerian military. Shehu started saying, whenever he mentioned soldiers, "your friends from the Nigerian military." I deserved it.

BACK IN MAIDUGURI, Ash and I decided to check out the park surrounding the local zoo. Amid the monkey cages, the enclosure featuring a single cow and the elephant exhibit, where workers had decided to burn garbage as the beasts trudged aimlessly, young people sprawled across the patchy grass sipping Coke and pouring over textbooks or sitting on benches smoking joints with friends.

The city drew young people from all over the country to attend the University of Maiduguri, Ramat Polytechnic, Kashi Ibrahim College of Education and its several other colleges. Musicians touring the nation made a stop there on the way to bigger cities, knowing they could attract a crowd of college kids. Young people drank beer—it was outlawed now but everyone knew it was sold at a military bar called the Officers' Mess. One popular drinking spot was situated outside a hotel that had long ago been abandoned, its empty hull looming in the background as young people danced and smoked a shisha pipe under a single lightbulb. Drugs were popular, too. People popped opioids in hopes of improving sexual performance. Casual sex, in certain circles, took place as it would in any university town. The local supermarket had an entire section dedicated to erotica with erection-enhancing chewing gum and butt-tightening creams.

We came across a couple in the park, Kefas and Ruth, stretched out in the shade. We sat down with them and launched into a discussion about the local social scene and dating in particular.

Kefas, a typical 20-something with white headphone wires dangling around his neck, and Ruth, who wore a black scarf around her hair, were taking it slow.

Kefas explained the excruciating courtship he endured trying to win over Ruth, a Christian and a serious student who at first found him frivolous. He had seen her walking across campus at the

University of Maiduguri and slowly got up the nerve to introduce himself. They spent a lot of time studying together, but she
told him straightaway she didn't want to be his girlfriend. He pursued her for more than a year, begging for official boyfriend-
girlfriend status. He declared his love. He made big promises. He
recited Gambian poetry. The poems worked. She agreed to date
him.

Kefas wanted to have sex. Ruth wanted to wait. She wanted no
distractions from focusing on her environmental biology coursework. For now they settled on holding hands. But the couple already had planned out their future. They would be married and
have children.

At first they reminded me of couples I had met at church growing up in Nebraska. Girls there wore "purity rings" as a pledge to
God to stay virgins until marriage. They planned on being wives
who served their husbands as the Bible commands.

But that wasn't what Kefas had in mind. He wanted to support
Ruth's career, he told me. He planned to be the kind of husband
who helped with childcare and would do the dishes.

"Where did you learn these ideas?" I asked.

"My Gender Equity professor," Kefas said.

Of course the universities here were hubs of liberal thinking and
broad ideas, I had to remind myself. It was easy to forget a parallel
way of looking at the world existed in the same city that gave rise
to militants known for enslaving women.

LATER THAT NIGHT, some of the journalists—all of them men—and
I decided to head to the nicest hotel in town, the Pinnacle, and its
poolside restaurant for dinner and drinks. It was Valentine's Day
and we needed a break. We passed under the gate and walked
toward flashing lights to find rose petals floating in the pool water.
A DJ spun Afrobeats. A few people already were dancing.

The Pinnacle was hosting a special all-night Valentine's party.

Valentine's Day wasn't celebrated traditionally in Nigeria, but like many other Western holidays and traditions, it had gone global.

The Valentine's Day bash and the general party scene in Maiduguri was the opposite of what Boko Haram wanted. Because of a wartime curfew, which started as early as 6 P.M. in some parts of town, any evening party was an automatic all-night blowout. At curfew, the gates swung shut and everyone partied until dawn. The setting of these lock-in parties shifted, for security reasons. Boko Haram would like nothing better than to light up a drunken dance party. They had done it before, back at the peak of the war, when they stormed a disco and sprayed everyone with gunfire as they danced to "Billie Jean."

The Pinnacle that night could have been in a college bar anywhere.

Ash and I decided to stick around for the all-night bash. In our roaming around town we were accidentally collecting the pieces of a good story about showing the alter ego of the birthplace of Boko Haram. The other reporters just wanted to take a break and drink so they stayed too, buying large brown bottles of Star beer.

As curfew fell, the canned music started getting louder. People piled onto the dance floor on the patio. A woman in a hijab started twerking. One woman danced with a baby strapped to her back. Green and orange lights flashed across another dance floor that opened up inside the hotel. A couple stood making out in the corner of the room while others bumped and grinded.

I joined a group of women dressed in sparkly T-shirts, tight pants and sky-high heels as they sat by the pool. They had ditched their boyfriends for a ladies' night out, they said, because some of them were dating more than one guy and they didn't want to hurt anyone's feelings on Valentine's Day.

We talked about dating and love and one of the women complained to me how Maiduguri men all insist on having sex, to test a woman to see if she's good at it. She was confident she passed.

"I do it well," she said. "I do it very well."

All her friends howled with laughter.

The party dragged on. It felt like I had talked to everyone there. These college kids all had so much energy. I was beginning to worry how I'd stay awake until dawn.

"I kind of want to get out of here," I said, sitting down at the table of reporters.

They were tired of the scene, too, and decided they could continue the party back at the U.N. camp. One of the guys raced to the bar to buy a half-dozen loose bottles of beer for the road. We'd been at the party for hours. Hadn't they had enough? He stuffed them in a wispy black plastic bag, and we all walked out to the parking lot. The taxis were gone, of course, because it was past curfew. The U.N. camp was about a half mile away.

"I guess we're walking," someone said.

We ducked under the arm of the hotel gate and set off into the night. A far-off orange streetlamp cast subtle shadows that were even creepier than if it were pitch dark. We walked in total silence, minus the clanging beer bottles. The sound was like clashing cymbals in the otherwise still night.

"Can't you keep that quiet?" I hissed.

The guy tried to press the bag to his chest but couldn't muffle the noise.

We were only about a block away from camp when a truck approached, its lights drawing closer to us. That vehicle out at that hour, I knew, was one of two things: military or Boko Haram. Either one wasn't going to be pleasant to encounter. Not only were we violating curfew but we also had beer, which was illegal, or a sin, depending on who was driving that truck. We all looked straight ahead in silence and kept walking as it approached. The truck slowed when it got to us. A man who must have been a soldier peered out the window and looked us up and down. The truck sped away. We sprinted for the camp entrance and rushed inside.

We had been reckless and idiotic. Staying out that late was a mistake. In my quest to report on Maiduguri's wild side, and egged on by a bunch of reporter bros, I was getting sloppy. The consequences of some of those kinds of mistakes were on display at the headquarters of the *Times,* in a hallway of conference rooms named after dead reporters.

CHAPTER 12

Aurina

THE NEXT MORNING Shehu phoned with good news.

He had called our sources and found some former Boko Haram members. We'd need to interview them in private, he said, so he had invited them to his apartment. Ash and I went there to wait.

Shehu's apartment was in a little painted concrete complex of four or five other units. He had a front patio and had planted a few pansies in a flower box outside. The petals were falling off one of the plants and another was dead.

"I need to take better care of those," he said, when he saw me looking at them.

We stepped out of the bright sun and through his apartment door. The curtains were drawn, so it was dark inside, and it took my eyes a minute to adjust. He had no furniture other than a mini fridge, a small TV and a thin carpet stretched across the floor, where a few old copies of his newspaper were strewn. It looked like a CIA safe house.

"I prefer to sit on the floor," he explained away his décor and shrugged.

Soon enough a car pulled into the driveway alongside the apartment. Inside was our first subject, a former fighter with Boko Haram who was living in one of the camps in town. I finalized my list of questions. Why did you join? What did you hope to achieve? Have you ever met the leader, Shekau? Why did you believe in his teachings?

The car door opened and I heard the shuffling of plastic flip-flops against the concrete. I looked out the window and saw a teenage girl being led into the room. Shehu must have misunderstood me. I wanted a fighter.

She sat down on the floor in front of me and I had no choice but to begin an interview. I knew it had been a hassle for her to get out of the camp—the military and local security forces controlled the comings and goings, another violation of international law.

She was round-faced, with cheeks that looked like they still stored baby fat. Her name was Amina, she said, and she came from a small farming community outside Maiduguri.

"What is your relationship to Boko Haram?" I asked.

From time to time her community had brushes with Boko Haram. Fighters were regulars at the local market, where they bought food and supplies before returning to their hideouts. It's not like people in the village wanted to sell to them, but they knew if they shooed them away, they might be killed.

One day, she said, a lot of fighters arrived, on motorbikes and in trucks. They announced that anyone going to school would be killed. Some of the militants stormed Amina's house—she was 16 then—and tried to drag her away. Her older brother protested. They shot him to death in front of her. Amina watched them drag his corpse outside and leave it behind the house.

Fighters shoved her into their vehicle along with other women captives and drove to their camp. When they arrived, Amina marveled at how huge it was.

"There were so many people, and a lot of women—a good number of them pregnant or nursing babies," she said. "There were just so many women."

"Soon you will all be married off," militants announced to their set of captives.

"But I don't want to be married," Amina heard one woman protest.

One of the fighters shot her to death right there. He looked at Amina and told her she would be next unless she agreed to be married. She stayed quiet.

Soon, fighters started dragging Amina and a few other girls along with them on their operations to raid villages. The raids played out much like they did in Amina's own hometown, with fighters storming into a town, making proclamations, then targeting women and girls for kidnappings.

They enlisted Amina and the other women in the raids.

"They told us anyone who did not abduct a woman would be killed," she said. "So on my first outing with them I abducted three."

"You what?" I said, not comprehending what I was hearing.

"I took three girls."

So, then, I guess technically she *was* a Boko Haram fighter. This was not what I expected.

After a few raids, Amina began to notice a pattern. While fighters picked off with gunfire all the men they saw, women and girls would run inside their houses to hide. She soon learned that her victims were ridiculously easy to find, always hiding behind a door or crouching in a back room.

Sometimes fighters trailed Amina to make sure she was doing her job. They told her they didn't want elderly women or nursing women. They wanted younger women and girls, to "marry."

Amina targeted girls her size or smaller, because they were easier to manage. She grabbed them by the wrist or used her fingernails to dig into their shoulders to drag them into waiting vehicles. The process gave her flashbacks of her own capture. At first, she cried as she carried out her kidnappings. But after a few times, the tears stopped.

One kidnapping haunted Amina. Her captive screamed and sobbed as Amina dragged her away. On the drive to the camp, the girl talked about how she had watched fighters kill her parents. They had been terrified their daughter would be raped by militants. The girl trembled as the truck made its way, sobbing to Amina that she didn't want to be raped. She was only 14. As they neared the camp, she became hysterical and even fainted at one point.

Once they were inside the camp, militants left the girl alone for a few weeks.

"And then what happened?" I asked.

Amina closed her eyes and paused. She swallowed hard before she continued.

There was an empty room at the camp where fighters took girls of their choosing to have sex with. One night during dinner, Amina looked up to see the girl she had captured being led into the room. She kept her eye on the room for hours, watching fighter after fighter enter. There must have been a dozen men who went in and out of that room. The girl's terrified screams turned into whimpers. The last fighter left and Amina ran inside. The girl was moaning and badly bleeding.

For three days Amina stayed with her, trying to nurse her to health. But the brutality was too much. She died.

"There was a time when I dreamed about her often," Amina said. "I saw it in my dreams several times, when all those men came to have sex with her. I saw her as she was dying, how she was talking about how much pain she was in."

Amina decided that, whatever the cost, she had to get out of that Boko Haram camp. She couldn't kidnap anyone else. One evening she waited until prayers to tell a fighter she had to go to the bathroom. Unwilling to skip out on prayer time, he told her to go on by herself, without an escort. She headed toward the surrounding bush and when she was far enough from the camp, she sprinted. Night fell and she kept running, even when she couldn't see a thing. She kept falling and scraping her knees. She kept going.

At dawn, she came across a group of herders letting their cattle graze on the scrub. They gave her food and water but cautioned her against staying with them. Boko Haram wasn't far away. Fighters usually let the herders pass without much trouble, but they would spot her right away. The cowboys were Fulani, and their skin was lighter than Amina's. It would be obvious she didn't belong. They pointed her in the direction of a road and told her to keep going. Don't stop, they told her, or Boko Haram will find you.

Amina's feet and legs were cut up and swollen by the time she got to the road. She tried to flag down cars. So many passed her without stopping.

At last one pulled over. A man rolled down his car window and Amina approached. Calmly, so as not to frighten him, she explained her situation. The man grimaced.

"The same thing happened to my daughter," he told her. "Get in."

He drove her to safety.

That afternoon at Shehu's safe house, other so-called Boko Haram fighters filed into the apartment one by one. One kidnapped boy told me he went on raids with Boko Haram, firing his weapon when he arrived at villages. He insisted it was always so dark that he didn't know if any of his bullets hit anyone. I suspected he was lying—probably it was his way of coping with the guilt. A teenage girl told me how Boko Haram had taught her to shoot an AK-47. They took her on raids with them and she hopped off the motorbike yelling as she fired into the air. The men were impressed and complimented her ferocity. She knew it was messed up, but part of her liked the attention.

The last interviewee shuffled out of the house as Shehu's phone began to ring.

"There's been another suicide bombing," he said.

The attack had occurred outside a camp for people uprooted by the war that was known for being overcrowded, sometimes with hundreds of people waiting outside to get in.

Ash jumped up. It was the only chance for him to photograph something that was actually happening. He had sat through my interviews without complaint, listening with eager curiosity. But all that talking wasn't yielding any photos. Bombings seemed to be happening more and more often. The aftermath of an attack like this illustrated the devastation that so many people face in Maiduguri on a regular basis.

"Let's go," he said to Shehu, and started walking fast toward the car.

"Aaaaaash," Shehu said, drawing out his name to get his attention. "The area where this attack occurred is dangerous."

"I. Don't. Care," Ash said. "Let's go."

"If you insist on going, I will get someone to take you. But I am not going," Shehu said. "And I don't think you should either."

Ash looked at me. "You coming?"

I wanted to say yes. But I wasn't sure. Suicide bombings were becoming the signature element of this stage of the war with Boko Haram. There had been more than a dozen that occurred in Maiduguri in the past two months, many of them by women. But did I need to see the aftermath to tell the story? Part of me believed I did. I could interview people who saw the awful attack and wanted to talk about it.

One of my first assignments as a reporter in Seattle was covering the story of a high school girl in suburban Seattle who had drank herself to death during a night of partying. I was told to knock on her family's door for a quote. I knew her family deserved the opportunity to comment on a story we were writing. And I knew it was important to write about the incident to serve as a warning to other families. But I hesitated to intrude at such a sensitive time. It seemed crass and unfeeling. Of course her family and friends were heartbroken. What more would they say? My editor sensed my reluctance.

"We do these kinds of things for a reason," he said. "In times of pain people sometimes offer the most clarity of anyone. And some-times they want to convey that to us."

He was right. I had covered enough tragedies by now to know how the raw emotions of eyewitnesses could offer the kind of in-sight that is muted days afterward.

The world needed to know the impact of suicide bombings that were no longer anomalies in Maiduguri. But the area around the camp had a reputation for being dangerous, long before a suicide bomber pressed the detonator. Some people suspected Boko Haram even had a secret bomb-making factory there.

Was this the bridge too far that Arthur Sulzberger had warned me about back at the office in New York?

Shehu presumed that with my three kids expecting me home, I wouldn't be reckless enough to go. He pulled me aside.

"Dionne, Ash has a wife and child waiting for him in New York. Talk to him. Tell him not to go."

I called Ash over so we could talk it through with Shehu. No-body wanted to get killed, but we also didn't want to be paranoid for no reason. We were losing time if we were going to go, but I wanted to understand Shehu's concerns to make sure he wasn't being overly protective.

Shehu explained that militants sometimes struck twice at this particular camp, so we risked falling victim to another attack. But another threat came from security forces that would be swarming now, terrified that Boko Haram was nearby, with twitchy trigger fingers and a thirst for revenge. Bullets could fly and we could get caught in the middle.

Ash took a long drag of his 100th cigarette of the day.

"OK," he said. "I think we should stay."

The rest of the afternoon we pouted on Shehu's front porch like grounded schoolchildren, half mad at ourselves. Were we chicken-shit journalists or responsible parents?

Shehu came out on the porch.

"I have someone who wants to talk to us."

Another of Shehu's mystery sources. So far they hadn't disappointed so I was happy to move on to a new mission with him.

We drove to a local museum that was next to an outdoor amphitheater. A contemporary dance troupe was practicing, with a choreographer leading young men and women who twisted their bodies across the stage. Two men banged on giant drums. Another swayed as he played an algaita, a long wooden instrument that sounded like an Indian charmer's flute but more rollicking. Ash stepped in to photograph him, swaying like he was under its spell.

I entered the tiny museum, walking down outdoor halls lined with dusty framed photos of local politicians and religious leaders from decades past. Blocks of text discussed the history of the region that surrounded Maiduguri—and the jihad of the 19th century that had once gripped the area.

The jihad back then was so successful that an Islamic caliphate, the Sokoto Caliphate, was created and thrived for years. Its peak population was nearly 10 million. Its leaders had taken over villages and towns and enslaved more than two million non-Muslim people, schooling them in the Koran and trying to convert them.

Shehu led me to a dark back office, far away from the museum's collection, from the dancers, from anyone at all. A tall, stick-like man walked in holding a large envelope. Shehu offered him a chair.

This man, Babagana, sat down and began telling me his story.

One day a few months back, a missile had landed in the middle of his farming village. It was the calling card, he soon learned, of the Nigerian military. A convoy of trucks arrived. Soldiers in uniform poured out and started torching all the homes.

"Bring out your Boko Haram!" they yelled as people rushed from their homes.

For months, militants had been recruiting members from villages in the area. Fighters also shopped at a nearby market from time to time. Everyone in town knew Boko Haram was close at hand. But they were terrified of the militants, too scared to chase them from the market or to even rat them out to authorities. Babagana and the other families pleaded with the soldiers—they had no Boko Haram members there. The soldiers weren't listening. They gathered women and children in one area and told them to turn their backs and stay silent. Then, soldiers rounded up all the men in the village, even men out in their millet fields.

"Who among you is Boko Haram?" they asked again.

"No one," the men kept repeating.

Soldiers made Babagana and the rest of the men take off their shirts. Some who had been dressed in traditional gowns were left in only their underwear. Then they lined up the men.

"We said: Who among you is Boko Haram?" soldiers again asked.

"We ourselves have been attacked by Boko Haram," one of the men said. "We're here only because we can't afford to leave our crops and our cows."

The soldiers made the men lie down on their stomachs in the dirt. Babagana got down on his knees and joined them, his face planted in the sandy soil. Then, one by one, soldiers executed the men. They killed more than 80 in all.

When all the shooting began, Babagana's wife, Maryam, and her friends turned their heads toward the gunfire. They wanted to know whose husband was being killed. It turns out everyone's husband was dead. Almost.

Babagana felt the fire of bullets passing through him. His shoulder. His hip. He had holes everywhere. The shooting stopped. His body twitched. He heard the footsteps of a soldier standing over him. The soldier fired his weapon into Babagana again.

The military convoy left and women raced to collect their husbands' corpses. They began stacking the bodies in a pile. Maryam ran to Babagana's lifeless body. He was still breathing. She dragged him to the side of a building and propped him upright. He opened his eyes.

Babagana drifted in and out of consciousness as he sat there. People from neighboring villages who had heard the gunshots began to pour in. One of them, a distant relative, saw Babagana. He told Maryam they needed to get him to a hospital.

He and Maryam heaved Babagana's limp body into a wheelbarrow. They set off for the closest hospital, miles away, taking turns pushing him through the bush. Bleeding and in pain, Babagana felt every bump in the terrain. He was still alive when they got to the hospital. Doctors there saved him.

Babagana removed the giant envelope from under his arm. He pulled out the contents: X-rays of his bullet wounds.

With the military blocking access to the area where his village was located, I couldn't travel there to try to verify his account or to check on any mass burial of corpses. The X-rays were the only proof he had of what had happened.

"Do you have any scars?" I asked.

He tugged at his clothes to show me a patchwork of entry and exit wounds. His otherwise taut skin seemed knitted together by the scars left from stitches.

Babagana's story was incredible, but even with the X-rays and scars, it was still just one man's account. I needed other witnesses.

"Shehu, I need more."

Babagana arranged for his wife to talk to us but that wasn't enough. A security official we trusted thought he could track down other women from Babagana's village. They were living in a crowded camp outside town. Shehu planned to send a car for them in the morning, before the day shift of military guards arrived to question them about where they were going.

It was close to curfew and we decided to go back to the U.N. camp. We'd done enough reporting for the day.

I CHANGED INTO a T-shirt and shorts, grabbed my toothbrush and headed to bathrooms on the far side of the camp. I passed by a little outdoor common area that was usually empty except for the reporters in my group who went out for a night smoke. But this night, it was packed with all the suit-clad diplomats who had flown in to tour the war zone.

"Nice pajamas," one said, pointing at me and laughing.

I ignored him and carried on my trek to the bathroom, passing by a staff building for the camp custodians, where I noticed the flash of a TV. I went closer to see what was playing. An image of President Trump filled the screen. He was behind a podium, holding a news conference. Local workers from the camp were gathered around. One nodded to me and made space on the couch. I scrunched in.

"Many of our nation's reporters and folks will not tell you the truth, and will not treat the wonderful people of our country with the respect that they deserve," Trump was saying.

"The press has become so dishonest that if we don't talk about it, we are doing a tremendous disservice to the American people. Tremendous disservice. We have to talk to find out what's going on, because the press honestly is out of control. The level of dishonesty is out of control."

The guys I was sitting beside snickered.

"He's crazy," someone said, and everyone around me laughed.

Trump continued. "I've ordered a plan to begin building for the massive rebuilding of the United States military.

". . . I think one of the reasons I'm standing here instead of other people is that frankly, I talked about we have to have a strong military. We have to have strong law enforcement also. So we do not go abroad in the search of war, we really are searching for peace—but it's peace through strength."

"He's talking like he's one of our presidents," someone said, eliciting more snickers.

"It's Idi Amin!" the guy next to me shouted.

Everyone wailed with laughter.

On the TV, a reporter asked the president about Russian involvement in the election. The question made Trump angry, and he went back to attacking the media.

"The failing *New York Times* wrote a big, long front-page story yesterday. And it was very much discredited, as you know. It was—it's a joke."

This seemed like a friendly enough crowd where I was sitting. But what if some of them took Trump's *Times* bashing seriously? It was only a matter of time before someone there got curious and asked what I was doing in Maiduguri.

I slinked away from the couch and headed to the bathroom again to brush my teeth, thinking about a president trying to turn the masses against journalists. I was thousands of miles from America, risking my life to do my job.

And that night, I was doing it in my pajamas.

On my way back to my tent I passed the diplomat, still swilling booze with the others in the common area. He raised his beer to me and laughed. I just smiled.

All the back-to-back awful stories were starting to weigh on me. That night, explosions shook my United Nations cot, more than once. Suicide bombers. Maiduguri felt like it was under siege. *What if they come for us here? We're a sitting duck in these white tents in the middle of town. The security guys the other night let us in without question. They're a joke. And now the camp is filled with not only journalists but high-level diplomats, the perfect targets for a group like Boko Haram.*

MY ALARM BLARED. Shehu called to say the bombings took place alongside the very camp where our witnesses were living. He had called to check on them. Yes, they assured him, they were fine and on their way.

Ash and I started to leave for Shehu's house, when my phone rang. It was Darren, the Irishman who was spokesman for the United Nations agency that had invited us to Maiduguri.

"We're having a press conference this morning," he told me.

"OK, I have some interviews arranged for the morning but I'll try to come," I said.

"You won't try. You'll be there," Darren said, his voice turning hostile.

"Excuse me?"

"We invited you here. You're coming to our press conference."

"I didn't know that coming to your press conference was a requirement of this trip."

"Don't be dense," Darren said, and hung up.

He didn't explain what he meant. But I could guess. The press conference was his big show, and without the press, well, it wouldn't be much of a performance.

The massacre witnesses were already on their way to Shehu's apartment. I wasn't going to miss out on interviewing them in order to sit in a stuffy room and listen to canned speeches from diplomats.

I assumed Darren's idea was to show the diplomats that the international press cared about the crisis, so they should care, too. It wasn't a bad strategy. Goodness knows, the war needed the world's attention—and financial help. The press conference featured all the officials who were prepared to make donations in their countries' names. They would get a chance to show off their generosity in front of the press corps. If a gaggle of reporters didn't show up, Darren would be embarrassed—particularly because the person leading the delegation was his fellow countryman, the Irish ambassador to Nigeria.

I didn't want to seem ungrateful to the United Nations. But this media relations guy needed to work on the relations part of his job. My phone rang. Darren again. This time he made veiled threats that if I didn't come I wouldn't get a ride out of Maiduguri. I tried to explain that I would love to come under normal circumstances but that I had interviews scheduled with witnesses to a massacre. He didn't care.

I hung up the phone and turned to Shehu. "I think I have to go to this United Nations press conference."

"Don't worry," he assured me. "We will wait for you."

Ash and I arrived at the conference room, where other reporters told us they too had been harangued into attending. The event started an agonizing 45 minutes late. We took our seats and officials took turns reading from prepared statements that I knew they later would email to reporters. It was a huge waste of time, and I was getting worried the witnesses to the massacre might get sick of waiting and leave before we could talk to them.

If there's anyone who hates a boring press conference more than an international correspondent, it's a war photographer. But Ash was going crazy over the assignment, snapping his camera like some kind of paparazzi fawning over movie stars. Darren straightened his posture, preparing for his close-up. I scribbled one or two notes in my notebook.

The diplomats stopped talking and opened it up for questions. But what could the Irish ambassador to Nigeria and the other talking heads tell me that I didn't already know? My most important sources of information were sitting on a living room floor waiting on me.

It ended and we raced back to Shehu's apartment.

"That was a total waste of time," I said to Ash.

"It was unbearable," he said.

"Well, you certainly seemed to be getting something out of it. You took enough photos."

He leaned over to show me his images on his camera. He hadn't been shooting close-ups of Darren and the diplomats. Instead, he had photographed a bottle of water in the middle of the table from three-dozen vantage points. It was his silent screw you to Darren.

By the time we got to Shehu's apartment the women looked exhausted. They'd been waiting for us for hours. But, thankfully, they still wanted to talk. Some were from Babagana's village and some were from a neighboring town. His wife, Maryam, showed up, too. One by one, they confirmed what Babagana had told me.

"We were all covered in his blood," Maryam said of the day she wheeled her husband's bullet-riddled body across the countryside.

After soldiers were done firing on Bagagana and the other men, they went to the neighboring town and carried out a similar massacre. I took notes on everything that they said happened there.

As the women were gathering to leave, I asked if they knew anything about the suicide bombings that morning.

"Oh yes, we heard them," one of the women said. "We worried all the extra security around would keep us from coming to meet you."

That's why, she went on to explain, that as soon as they heard the blasts they ran out of their shelters and took off through the bush— the same bush where militants hide—because they knew soldiers would be on high alert after the bombing and never let them leave through the front gate.

"The bomber was a woman," Babagana's wife said.

"How do you know that?" I asked.

As they walked through the bush, Maryam had tripped over the detached head of the bomber, blown off by the explosion. She had stared at the head. It had long braided hair. It was certainly a woman.

I was speechless. These women had risked their lives to get to me, had stumbled on the most gruesome of scenes—all this after being witness to a massacre of innocents. I had re-traumatized these women who already had been through one of the worst experiences imaginable. And what if soldiers had spotted them roaming through the outskirts of the camp? Women wandering out there would surely have been mistaken for would-be bombers. They could have been killed. I was nauseous.

Reporters always know their actions have consequences and can sometimes put someone in harm's way. For the past decade, before I became a foreign correspondent, those consequences rarely went beyond causing market fluctuations as stock shares rose or fell depending on the nature of a story. But this? This was horrifying.

My phone rang. It was Darren again. I had to hold myself back from screaming at him for keeping these women waiting, considering all they had been through.

"I've booked you and Ash on a flight out of here tomorrow," he said.

"But I'm not ready to leave," I said.

"If you're not on that plane, I won't have any choice but to notify the military," he said, reminding me that the U.N. had secured our military permission to be in the city. "And you'll never fly on a U.N. plane again."

Other than in the custody of Boko Haram, the last place I wanted to be was in the custody of the military, given what we'd just learned. The U.N. had told the military all the reporters would be leaving after their big event, the press conference. I also was worried about being blacklisted from U.N. flights. It wasn't a huge problem in Nigeria—commercial flights flew to Maiduguri. But in some parts of the region, U.N. planes were the only option for safe transport. What if Darren spread the word to other areas that the *Times* was uncooperative?

We were stuck. I had filled several notebooks already and had used up all the ink in a half-dozen pens. I worried my recording app was running out of space. I could write at least three stories from what I'd learned so far. We gave in and went back to the camp and packed our bags.

At the airport, Ash and I ran into other reporters whom Darren had shooed out as well.

"At least we pissed on their camp," one of the guys said. The men all started laughing.

"What are you talking about?" I asked.

At night, instead of walking to the bathroom at the edge of the camp before bed, the men had walked behind the tents to take a leak together outside on the concrete. They thought it was hilarious. It's silly but it crushed me. I had been trudging all the way across camp, parading before diplomats in my pajamas, while they held a penis bonding experience out back behind the tents.

One of the guys looked up from his phone.

"Whoa, check out this email," he said, handing me his phone.

As we were heading out of Maiduguri, the U.N. was preparing to hold a donor conference in Oslo, the mother of all press conferences for the organization. In the email, one official was complaining that I hadn't rushed to Oslo, to the swanky hotel where the conference was taking place tens of thousands of miles away from the war zone, to quote all the talking heads gathered there.

That was my breaking point. I had a story to write that explained how young women are conscripted to do horrible things for Boko Haram, another story that exposed military atrocities—how security forces were pushing helpless people into unsafe areas—and this muckety-muck from the U.N. wanted me to go sit at a conference in Norway to listen to dignitaries mansplain the war?

I fired off angry emails to U.N. officials even as my story on the civilian massacre ran on the front page of the paper. The editors decided it was important enough that it merited placement alongside a story about Trump's budget plan.

I knew the story would get more traction being on the front page of the paper than tucked deep inside. But I didn't have the courage to check our online metrics to see how many people had clicked on my story.

It didn't seem to faze the Nigerian government. They didn't respond. But something unexpected was happening. People from my hometown, another off-the-radar spot in the world, were reading my story and sharing it on Facebook. They were outraged by the violence.

I didn't get a response from the U.N. to my angry emails, but one of the other reporters did after he sent his own set of pissy missives. He shared the email with me, from an official at the U.N.'s humanitarian affairs division, complaining about *my* coverage.

". . . I also saw the article of the *NYT* today on Maiduguri," the official wrote. "There is nothing humanitarian in the article or helping raise awareness on humanitarian needs."

It continued, "I believe we, the humanitarian community, need to find the right balance when it comes to media coverage. While we agree (on principle) with the journalists that they are invited to help us raise awareness on the humanitarian situation, some have different agendas."

My "different agenda" was trying to expose a military atrocity and find justice for innocent civilians mowed down by the Nigerian military. There was "nothing humanitarian" about my story exposing human rights abuses, according to the official who works for the branch of the United Nations that "promotes solutions to reduce humanitarian need, risk and vulnerability."

As I read through the email, I realized I was pursing my lips in disgust the same way Shehu had done whenever I'd brought up the subject of the U.N. with him.

A few months later, someone at the U.N. must have recognized the value of the story. Nigeria had sought to join the United Nations Human Rights Council. The organization cited my story as among the reasons to block it.

CHAPTER 13

Work Husband

IT HITS YOU in the face the moment you step off the airplane in Lagos. The heat. The humidity. But mostly, the hustle: The airport security officers who ask you for a little "small small" before they let you pass; the men dressed in official-looking yellow vests so they can help you with your airline issues but who just want a tip; the taxi drivers wresting your suitcase away from you to lure you into their cars; the money changers who brag about their rate, thinking you don't know any better; even the little girls selling small bags of peanuts.

"Can we dash you, aunty? Can we dash you?" they say, employing Lagosian reverse psychology. A "dash" is a gift. They shove a bag of nuts into your hand—that's their "dash"—but do they expect payment in return? How could they not? Everyone else did.

And all of that is before you even leave the airport parking lot.

It was story whiplash—out of the war zone and into the beautiful chaos that is Lagos, in one day's time. Into the choked roadways, the slums, the open sewers, the people seemingly everywhere. But also the elaborate weddings with impossibly long guest lists; the hotels with miles-long buffets; people lining the escalator at the shopping mall theater to see the latest hit from Nollywood, Nigeria's version of Hollywood; millennials at a karate class in a park on a Sunday morning; a solitary man in a black suit and skinny tie dancing almost on his tiptoes on a small balcony over a stage as a band plays in the same spot where famous Afrobeat musician Fela Kuti once performed.

Only the madness of Maiduguri could make Lagos seem like a haven of tranquility.

In my attempt to balance out my war coverage, I had set up a few interviews in Lagos with people in the music industry for a story about copyright issues—a record label owner, a copyright advocate, an executive who distributes digital music—and figured I could get some meaningful comments at least in phone interviews with famous musicians.

But that didn't help Ash much. He wanted to trail a pop star to capture him or her in different environments. That kind of access was more than I needed to write my story. But Ash had sat through how many hours of living-room interviews in the Maiduguri safe house for me? And I couldn't argue that hanging out with my subjects longer wouldn't benefit my story.

We did some hustling of our own, convincing a music industry source to find us a celebrity musician willing to let us tag along for a few days, but it would take some time to secure.

I was getting anxious to go home. I'd already been gone almost three weeks. I was out of toothpaste. I was on round two of underwear, turning it inside out rather than washing it; it would never dry overnight in all this humidity. My husband had called a few times to blow off steam about the kids. The kitchen drain was plugged. Maude couldn't find her overdue library book. I knew I needed to feign sympathy, but fielding those calls from here was like an out-of-body experience.

"Ash, I don't know how long I can wait," I said.

I could pack up and go home and carry out interviews over the phone. But that would leave Ash vulnerable to complaints from his own wife, who might question why he was running around Lagos for days after the reporter he was working with had already taken off to see her own family.

"How about this," Ash said, "Let's agree neither of us can leave for another week."

We shook on it. Sometimes work husbands are like real husbands. They require some give and take. Still, I had been on the road for days on end. I was doing a better job of managing a balance with Ash than with my real husband.

WHILE WE WAITED on a celebrity, we hung out with young musicians who lived in poor neighborhoods and dreamed of making it big. One afternoon we went to a recording studio in a place called Snake Island. Most people considered it a slum, a narrow stretch of tin huts not far from a pollution-spewing sugar refinery. The studio was a one-room home with a Winnie-the-Pooh comforter stretched across a bed, the only place to sit for the 20-somethings laying down tracks as chickens clucked outside an open window.

Back in the city, Ash and I went out for coffee and cruised the mall, where couples in their Sunday best posed in the aisles of a Shop-Rite supermarket taking selfies the same way millennials in Nebraska pose at Walmart on their Sunday after-church shopping trips. We ate Tex-Mex, took in a concert, met the emir of Kano— a former Central Bank leader-turned-traditional ruler who is trailed everywhere by a jaguar-skin-clad priest who shakes maraca-like gourds behind him—and went to a gym that had 16 treadmills, each broken in a unique way. Ash, after a few years of self-medicating, had turned to jogging as a healthier way to deal with the emotional toll of his war coverage. He ran so hard on one of the treadmills it blew up, smoke slipping out from the folds of the tread. We were running out of things to do until our celebrity musician came through.

Finally, an Afrobeats star named Seyi Shay allowed us to shadow her as she flitted about her celebrity days. But after waiting hours for her to arrive at an MTV studio where she was filming a video, and waiting even longer for a concert that started a full five hours late, it was clear this assignment wasn't going to be done quickly.

Ash and I arrived at a photo studio where Seyi Shay was filming a commercial at 10 A.M. We planted ourselves on a black leather couch to watch an assembly of technicians, photo assistants, makeup artists and members of her entourage arrive, with no sign of her.

By 1 P.M. she still hadn't shown up and we were hungry. Ash ran out to grab some food and came back to present me with a black plastic bag. I reached inside to find Doritos. I wanted to hug him. It had been months since I had American junk food. He was just as excited.

Before we could dig in, Seyi Shay arrived, tired-looking and frantic. She plopped down beside me on the couch.

"I'm starving," she moaned.

I looked at my bag of Doritos and then at Ash. He shook his head.

"But she's hungry," I whispered.

"Now, *that* would be a bridge too far," he said.

Downtime is a big part of reporting anywhere but seems particularly acute in West Africa. Politicians show up hours late for interviews. Cars break down in the extreme heat. Rain makes roads impassable. Dust storms can strand you sometimes for days.

But there was nothing more fun than killing time with Ash. I was captivated hearing about his experiences all over the world. We worked well together, brainstorming story ideas and dissecting each other's work and how to make it better. We gossiped. We shared a love for unhealthy food. We traded curly hair products. We mocked each other about our clothing, our work habits and pretty much everything. We both nodded off in weird places, like coffee houses, conference rooms or in the backs of pickups traveling down bumpy roads with soldiers' AK-47s bouncing on the truck bed alongside us.

I was six years older than him. That's 42 years older in dog years, which is pretty much how the world calculates each year of a woman's life after age 40. So we didn't flirt; instead, we showed each other cute photos of our kids. We talked about parenting. When we went our separate ways on assignments he sometimes left me little presents: a miraculously still-frozen ice-cream bar balanced on my hotel doorknob or a goofy greeting card. And he remembered all my stories, for days or even weeks later. I never had to repeat myself. He listened—a guy friend who pays attention. It was like winning the work husband lottery.

We even had accidentally developed a way to try to keep a reality check on our own privileged whining: the baby bottle emoji.

"I just want to say I've been out here for a few days and I'm unable to look at myself in the mirror," he wrote me from an assignment in the Hamptons, disgusted by wealthy people who were complaining about the thread count of the hotel sheets or whatever it was.

"You're complaining about being in the Hamptons?" I wrote, followed by a 🍼.

It became a regular thing.

"In my fourth country today," I texted Ash from Abidjan after a set of exhausting plane flights.

His response: 🍼

"I had to outrun a guy trying to steal my phone," he wrote me from Accra.

🍼

"A man with a lead pipe chased me while I was running," I wrote from Dakar.

🍼

"I got my wallet stolen," I texted from Berlin.

🍼

On assignment together in Douala, while he waited for me in the hotel lobby, I texted him: "I'm having trouble writing a top to my story. I'm going to be late."

"Here," he replied. "Try this as a draft."

Of course we gave up the bottle when things were really bad. Like when Ash was distraught after a troubling assignment at a children's hospital in one of the most poverty-stricken parts of the Central African Republic. Or when I found out one of my fixers was frighteningly sick. Then we mostly offered meaningless interjections. But it helped.

Sometimes I questioned the wisdom of grounding myself by reaching out to a man who had once stripped down and changed into his running clothes in the middle of the night as we drove through rural Senegal, 16 miles from the town where we were staying, saying nothing more than "see you at the hotel" as he slammed shut the car door and bolted into the darkness. But Ash's endorsement of my emotions was oddly reassuring.

Once, Ash and I were stuck in a Nigerian airport. We had made it to the ticket counter after muscling our way through a crowd of people yelling and shoving, to find what all the fighting was about. Our flight was delayed for hours. We hauled our bags upstairs to the waiting area, brushing off a demand for cash "for a little something to eat" from the security guard.

We settled into tailbone-bruising metal chairs, some of them broken with no backrests at all. Mosquitoes hovered. I had been sitting in the same spot a few weeks earlier when the ceiling caved, unleashing a waterfall of black sludge that coated passengers underneath.

We decided to spring for the VIP lounge, paying an extra fee for a separate area that promised unlimited snacks, Wi-Fi and air-conditioning.

None of it was working that day but the big, plush chairs looked like a cozy place to get some work done. We settled in behind our respective screens as the waitress brought us complimentary crackers and Nescafé.

At one point Ash held up his phone for me to look at.

"What do you think of this ring?" he asked, showing me a photo of a thin ring that snaked around the model's finger.

I was puzzled.

"You think she'll like it in gold?"

"Huh?"

"It's almost my wife's birthday."

"You're buying her jewelry?"

"Of course," he said.

"Well, I think it's ugly."

I stormed off toward the bathroom. In the stretch of my—how many years was it now?—relationship with Todd he had bought me jewelry exactly once, on our 10th wedding anniversary. It was a necklace I had asked for. I was the fiancée who picked out and bought my own wedding ring. Todd had argued that our finances were merged by that point anyway. *Get something you like,* he had said.

"It's a waste of money and a symbol of consumerism," he liked to say about jewelry. He felt the same about flowers ("They're going to die in a day anyway."), chocolate ("All that sugar is poisoning your body.") and clothing ("You'd never like anything I would pick out for you.").

The truth is, I didn't really like jewelry—I didn't even have my ears pierced, and I hated how rings made my fingers sweat. He was right about chocolate and clothing. Todd was always right. That was the maddening thing about being married to Mr. Logical.

But somehow finding myself with a work husband who was interrupting his work train of thought to think of illogical and unnecessary presents for his real wife made me jealous. I was being ridiculous. Todd was at home taking care of my three kids and I wanted a ring? I was in a place where people lived hand to mouth. *What is wrong with you?* I thought to myself.

Later that night, my phone rang. It was Todd. He was calling with another gripe about home life. This time it was the cat. He had never liked the idea of having pets.

"Animals belong in the wild," he was fond of saying. "I don't need a non-sentient being to take care of."

To him, the cat was my hobby. He resented the fact that while I was out traveling and getting to do my job without any family responsibilities, he had to remember to feed the cat and keep him from scratching the kids and the furniture.

"I don't have any hobbies that you have to *maintain* while I'm away," he liked to say.

I had asked him to take care of neutering the cat while I was gone. It didn't require much work. Just dial up the vet, who even made house calls. That afternoon, Todd had been racing around shuttling the kids to various activities when the vet showed up. Todd let him in and told him to do his thing and ran off to pick up Luther from soccer practice. I guess he thought the vet would take away the cat for surgery.

A couple hours later Todd came home exhausted, looking forward to a beer between the next round of errands. He cracked a bottle and sat down at the patio table and took a drink. Satisfied with his little break, he started to set his bottle on the table when he spotted a few drops of blood. Nearby was a crumpled paper towel. He tugged on one end to look inside. It was the cat's castrated balls. The spot where Todd was having a beer had served as the operating table. And organ disposal wasn't included in the vet's house call.

While I was out working, Todd was confronted with literal emasculation.

CHAPTER 14

The Mouth of Resentment

"I HAVE SOME news," Todd said to me not long after I walked in the door to our house in Dakar. I'd been gone a month. A lot had happened.

While I was away, he said, he was being recruited to become CEO of a small environmental consultancy firm. He was pretty sure he was about to get a job offer.

"I've always wanted to run my own company," he said. "I really want to do this."

The job was in a British university town situated along a river that was the home of top-notch public schools, museums and clean air. Todd already had cycled through several dramatic career shifts— banking, academia, management consulting and now conservation. But all the shifts had put him at a disadvantage in this new career. If he had started working in conservation in his 20s he probably would have been running an organization by now. This was a big opportunity. It was hard to argue it wouldn't be good for our family. The kids would go to high-achieving public schools, and we'd be a shorter plane flight away from relatives in America than we were in West Africa.

But for me, the timing was terrible. The *Times* didn't have a bureau in the exurbs of London. I was 14 months into my job as West

Africa bureau chief. I hadn't even passed the two-year emergency bailout mark yet. I had no standing to request any kind of transfer. I was sure the editors would be unhappy if I raised the idea. Half of me was furious at Todd for even considering it.

"You just can't take that job right now," I said. "It will doom my career."

"But what about my career?" he said.

He had a point. But he had also agreed to give our life in Dakar a try. It felt like he was trying to wiggle out of our deal.

We tangled over this for days, cramming in heated conversations after the kids went to bed. Todd stalled the company on giving them an answer. I fumed that he wasn't rejecting it outright.

"You're not even giving me a chance to do this job," I argued.

After a few rounds of fighting, Todd decided I was right. We didn't move all this way just to bail on everything here. But he wasn't happy about it. And I wondered if he was beginning to regret this whole arrangement. He had left academia because he hated working on his own and feared a lifetime all by himself buried in the library stacks. But here he was on his own, too, out in his little musty office, half the time with only a neutered cat as co-worker.

He turned down the job and launched into what I like to call The Month of Resentment.

Phase one: the silent treatment.

Phase two: snide jabs about how I was a part-time parent.

Phase three: starting dinner without me, leaving to walk the kids to school before I was ready, refusing to watch a movie with the rest of the four of us, and so on.

Phase four: booking a two-week work trip without checking with me about my schedule.

Phase five: giving up. That was the most terrifying.

"Since I can't have this CEO job," he announced one afternoon, "then I think you should lead."

"What do you mean?" I was confused.

His new idea was that he would shift into full-on "trailing spouse" mode.

"We go wherever you want, and I'll be a 100 percent stay-at-home, dedicated dad," he said.

I knew by this point that Todd wouldn't be happy without work. And more frightening, I knew the less than soaring salary scale I could expect as a journalist. I could never have as much earning potential as my husband, who had a graduate degree, marketable financial and management consulting skills and now experience in the conservation world. He'd become a licensed contractor when we renovated our house, leaving me at home to sleep away the first trimester of pregnancy while he put together our IKEA kitchen cabinets. He'd read all the literature to qualify him as a doula before I gave birth. He knew more about having babies than I did. If he didn't know how to do something, he figured it out and did it. I only knew how to report. Minus a couple weeks of bagging groceries, I'd never held another job. And I was terrible at the grocery thing, always stuffing brown paper bags too full, so they split open. Given the sorry state of my industry, I didn't even know whether I'd be employed in the next few years. No way could my salary alone carry us through three college educations. I didn't want the breadwinner responsibility forever.

It was starting to sink in that by forcing our move I may have jeopardized my husband's career. He had scaled back from his job to accompany me to Dakar, with no guarantee he could ramp up again. Being away from the home office made him feel like his employment was vulnerable, regardless of whether that was the case. This might be his last shot at a job opportunity outside his organization.

And what if he was fired? How many institutions are angling to hire a middle-aged, mid-career man with not-so-great French skills who lives in West Africa? One of the reasons I had left my job at *The Wall Street Journal* was to get to a better newspaper before I was too old for anyone to consider me for a new job.

"Who's going to hire us when we're 50?" I had argued to a friend.

Even if our overseas experience was just a blip, I had made Todd very vulnerable. Maybe it was all the resentment brewing at home, but this move was starting to feel like a mistake.

A friend once confided in me that when she took an overseas position in her late 40s, her husband quit his job to tag along and be the chief caretaker of the kids until he found work. But he didn't find work and shifted instead into full-time dad mode. He loved it. They were happy. But neither of them thought through the ramifications of the situation. By the time they were ready to move home to America, he was in his 50s and had been unemployed for the past five years. He couldn't find a good job. She took a job she wasn't that excited about to earn a bigger salary as she tried to move up the corporate ladder.

I hoped to avoid that outcome. For the first time, I understood the traditional male lament about the pressure of being the head of a household. And it made my brain hurt.

WE DECIDED TO take advantage of one gracious job perk the *Times* gives its correspondents who work in dangerous conditions. They call it a "breather": free plane tickets out of the country for the whole family to anywhere on the same side of the globe. And, after a month straight of work in Nigeria, I needed to get away.

Because we were on the far west coast of the African continent, we had a lot of choices. Paris was closer to us than Nairobi. We decided we would get to Kenya and other parts of the continent, but the kids had been complaining about missing snowy winters at my in-laws' house in Colorado. We settled on Austria, cheaper and less crowded than the French or Swiss part of the Alps, but it would give the kids the snowy mountain experience they had been lacking on the edge of the Sahara. We booked a little apartment in a small hostel in a mountain village not far from the ski slopes.

Todd grew up in what I called Swiss Family Robinson. His parents left their jobs to live in a tent in the woods for several months when he was five. They took family vacations hiking to the tops of peaks and biking for hundreds of miles together. When I was little, my mom took me to the Omaha Marriott for one night each summer to swim in the indoor pool. My big adventure was being allowed to run down the hotel hall barefoot all by myself to fill up the square plastic bucket at the ice machine. The ice was free!

With Todd, I grudgingly agreed to go along on camping trips that went poorly from the beginning. Setting up camp was intuitive to him, but I always stuck the wrong pole in the wrong place and could never get a cooking stove to work. Having three kids running around, stepping on flimsy metal tent poles and tripping over ties and stakes was enough to make him explode. He wanted a partner in outdoor exploring, but with me along, he pretty much had four kids. Especially when I had a tantrum after bonking my head on a low-hanging rock or tripping on a steep decline or some other minor calamity that made me vow never to go camping again.

Todd was sporty and good at most anything physical. His nickname in grad school was "Extreme." I'm the person who has been strung to the back of a motorboat more than a dozen times and yet never managed to stand up on water skis. In Little League I forgot to step away from home plate while practicing my swing and clubbed the catcher in the head with the bat. I got a bloody nose once playing tetherball, by myself, when I whacked my face on the pole. After racking up so many embarrassments in childhood, I was done trying just about anything athletic by the time I was an adult. It's a wonder I haven't broken my leg while out for a jog. Yet.

At my house in Nebraska, Todd once had come across stacks of yellowed newspaper clippings that my mom had saved from the 1950s. "Searcey Pitches No Hitter"; "Searcey High Scorer, Again." My dad was a bit of a local hero in high school. People came from miles around to watch him pitch or play basketball.

Convinced I must have inherited some of my dad's abilities, Todd thought that if I tried harder I would unlock my true inner athlete. When we first started dating and were living in Seattle, he tried to get me into climbing, mountain biking, hiking and, his favorite, Ultimate Frisbee. I wasn't good at any of it. He thought I should try harder. I gave up. It remained a source of tension.

"What are we going to do together during retirement?" he always complained.

"Take up gardening," was my standard comeback.

The topic didn't come up as much once we were locked into all-consuming jobs in the concrete jungle of New York. But when his parents retired to the epicenter of skiing areas in the Rocky Mountains, he pleaded with me to try skiing. It would be a great activity for our whole family, he argued. I set aside my stubbornness and booked some lessons. I came back from my first one having almost flown off the side of a mountain. The next lesson, the ski lifts had to be halted to untangle me from the chair. Back on the slopes, my own four-year-old daughter whizzed by me as I struggled, taunting me from her tot-sized skis.

"Need a diaper, little baby?" Zola cackled back then as she zoomed past.

By the time we reached the ski rental shop in Austria, I had psyched myself out of even trying again.

"Come on," my husband pleaded.

"I promise not to make fun of you," Zola said.

I lied and said I had work to do. I ferried them to and from the slopes every day.

As the kids piled into the car after skiing one day, I spotted a sign for sled rentals. Sledding would be fun for the whole family. My husband was a little sad to give up a day on the slopes but he saw the value in us all doing something together. He agreed.

The next day we put on our snow boots and puffy coats and headed to the sales booth where we could rent sleds. The agent was confused.

"You want to go sledding?"

"Yes," I said, pointing to the sign above her head. "It says we can rent sleds here."

She went into a back room and came out with a manager to talk to us.

"You get on the ski lift here, and once you get up the mountain, ask the workers for the sleds and the sled run," she explained. "You're going to have to walk a while. You understand?"

"No problem," I told her.

We boarded the lift with the other skiers. Todd was embarrassed to be ski-less on a ski lift. I was thrilled. It was going to be one of the only times I'd ever get off a lift without falling on my face.

It was snowing hard at the top of the mountain and the wind made it difficult to see where we were supposed to go. I approached one of the lift operators to ask where we picked up the sleds.

"The what?"

"The *sleds,*" I enunciated.

He asked around to other workers, who pointed him to a nearby storage shed. After a few minutes of fumbling around for the key, he went inside and emerged with five old-fashioned wooden sleds—the "Rosebud" kind from the last scene of *Citizen Kane.* They were dusty and looked like they hadn't been used since Orson Welles had made that movie.

"Where's the sled run?" I asked.

The worker shrugged and went to find someone else. We were pointed to a narrow, snow-covered trail that sharply zigzagged up the mountain.

"Up there," one worker pointed. "You're going to have to walk."

My kids were in third and fifth grades now. They were hardy and I was just happy to not be on skis, so up we trudged, dragging our sleds behind us. The trail was tight at points and lined by a steep drop-off, but it was easy enough to navigate on foot. I kept thinking we'd have to step aside for other sledders but we didn't encounter a soul. After about an hour of hiking we reached a clearing.

There were no signs, no guideposts, nothing to point us to the sledding hill. We wandered the edges searching for it.

"Hey, guys, I think I found it," I said, pointing to an opening that revealed a large empty field of snow that sloped down toward the top of a ski lift far in the distance.

The kids, anxious for the payoff of their long hike up, rushed over.

"Now, kids," Todd started in, "this is steep and these are old sleds, so we need to be very careful."

But before he finished his sentence the kids were off, tearing down the hill. We hopped on to follow.

The descent was steeper than we realized, and we were going fast—really fast. I tried to drag my feet but it didn't help. Zola got scared and rolled off her sled. She reached out to grab the sled's rope but missed. The clunky wooden sled kept going on its own, faster and faster, barreling down the hill. There was no way to catch it.

I hopped off my sled to help her stand up and the same thing happened to me. Now two sleds were hurtling down the hill at top speed, rider-less wooden torpedoes.

We yelled for everyone to stop. This hill was dangerous. The others managed to hop off their sleds but Maude also let go of her rope. In a flash, her sled was gone, too, barreling downward. I watched it go, helplessly. In the distance I saw a flashing light. It got closer and I realized it was the ski patrol snowmobile. The man riding it looked furious. He pulled alongside me, screaming.

"*Verboten! Verboten!*" he yelled over and over. "This is *verboten!*"

"What part is *verboten*?" I said, confused. Of course sending ghost sleds jetting down the mountain was forbidden, but he seemed to be talking about something else.

"You can't sled in this area!" he yelled.

"I didn't know," I said. "We're trying to leave as fast as we can."

"You have to leave!" he yelled.

"Fine, I'm going. But if this isn't the sledding area, where are we supposed to be?"

He didn't answer. And he didn't offer to help. Instead, he sped away.

By the time I got back up the mountain, the rest of my family already was huddled in a circle waiting for me. Luther was sobbing, certain we had killed someone with the empty sleds unleashed on a slope that we realized now must have led to a busy lift.

"I certainly hope that's not true," I said. "But we'll have to go down the mountain and face the consequences either way."

I hadn't considered the possibility we had hurt someone, and I turned my head to see if I could spot any skiers at the base of the hill. It looked clear.

"Daddy says this never would have happened if you could ski," said Luther, still sobbing.

"What? What did he say?"

Todd was glaring at me.

"It's true," he said. "If you could ski, we'd never be here in the first place."

I was furious, and my mind was racing with all kinds of mean retorts that were too awful to say in front of the kids. *I didn't grow up in a family that could afford ski vacations.* We started down the hill. Luther was sniffling, worried that we'd encounter a pile of bowled-over cadavers when we reached the bottom. *I didn't have a charmed life where every sport was a breeze.*

It was taking a long time to get down and every moment was accentuated because we were walking in stony silence. *I haven't had time to myself since we moved to West Africa—I've been too busy racing between nearly getting killed and making up for time lost with the kids.* I was so angry I couldn't speak. *What's he been doing? He couldn't even make friends with the other moms at the kids' school.* At one point Luther sat down on his sled to take a break, and when he stood up, his sled slipped away and cascaded down the tree-covered side of the mountain.

We reached the bottom and found a pile of splintered wood

stacked near the ski lift. I rushed over to a frowning worker standing beside it.

"I'm so sorry," I said. "Was anyone hurt?"

He waved his hands around and spat out some German. I took him by the arm and walked into the bar of the little ski lodge nearby.

"Can anyone speak English?" I hollered.

The bartender offered to translate for us. No one was hurt, I learned, but the sleds were destroyed. Obviously.

"I'll pay anything. I'm so, so sorry," I said.

We settled up as the bartender explained that the area we had tried to sled on was off-limits because it led to a ski hill. The "sled run" was the very cliff-lined trail we had climbed up. No wonder no one had been sledding at this ski resort in years. We'd all be dead now if we had tried to sled down that.

I was so relieved the whole episode was over without any broken bones and none of us arrested, I forgot how angry I was with Todd when I walked out of the bar.

"It's OK," I said. "I paid for the sleds and no one was hurt."

Everyone cheered.

"I think we all could use a hot chocolate," Todd said.

"I just spent all my cash back there paying for the sleds."

"If only you could ski," he said, "then we'd have more cash."

I opened my mouth to yell at him and then realized he was joking. He recognized the ridiculousness of what he'd said. It was his non-apology apology.

"Yeah, Mom," Maude chimed in. "If only you could ski we'd have snow in Dakar."

"If only you could ski," Luther said, "Boko Haram wouldn't exist."

CHAPTER 15

There Is No Peace at This Place

WE ARRIVED BACK in Dakar—and back to reality and resentment.

Todd seemed freshly exasperated by his position in Dakar, feeling his career had been put on the back burner and unable to gain steady footing as a part-time, stay-at-home parent. The mothers at school were warming, but just a little. He was never quite able to finish a work project before being called away to do something for one of the kids.

In my case, I didn't push for a big talk. Instead, I decided to ride out the resentment. It was also easier to let disagreements go—or, rather, fester—when one of you was always walking out the door. Next up was Todd's turn: he was leaving the country for a work trip in Uganda for two weeks.

I got the kids off to school and settled back into my office, finding the time to reflect on the clever ways the women had found their way through horrible circumstances in Boko Haram areas. I wondered how women were navigating everyday barriers they faced in peaceful parts of West Africa.

I called up an article a friend had emailed me from a Dakar newspaper. It said that more women in Senegal were filing for divorce than ever before. It offered no analysis, and didn't cite any source for its data. I wanted to know more.

Why were more women getting out of their marriages? It seemed like a bold move for a patriarchal society. In America, where women were more liberated than women in much of West Africa, divorce rates were going down. More elites in the United States were getting married, and staying married. People at the bottom end of the economy weren't bothering to marry at all.

In Nigeria, I'd already encountered women in a war zone who were navigating sexist social and cultural norms to their benefit. So what was prompting women in peaceful, cosmopolitan areas and in more isolated rural communities to break those norms altogether and seek a divorce? Most every young woman I had met told me they wanted to get married and have a family.

Even our office security guard was having his own marriage troubles. His wife had been fuming since he sent her to take care of his ailing mother in a rural village a 12-hour drive away from Dakar. She was a city girl and didn't want to be stuck with someone else's mom and no husband way out in the boonies. She rebelled. Either he move there, she told him, or she was leaving him.

Maybe she was part of some kind of societal shift that was happening to compel women to demand more from their husbands? And then if they didn't budge, to pull the plug altogether on marriage? Maybe this was occurring in other countries too? Had women's rights and independence advanced more than we in the West realized? My editor was anxious for me to explore this.

But how could this be happening in a place where atrocities against women are inflicted, like the ones I'd heard from women kidnapped by Boko Haram. It wasn't just in war zones where women were suffering. I'd also toured a fistula clinic in rural Niger, hearing terrible stories about the ramifications of child marriage.

Fistula occurs when the lining between the vagina and anus is punctured, which happens with alarming regularity when a teenage or preteen girl with an underdeveloped reproductive system gives birth to a baby. The girls suffering from fistula can't control urination or defecation. Smelly and dirty, they were sometimes banished by their husbands, and even their own parents.

The fistula clinic in Niger was situated alongside a leprosy clinic—that was how stigmatized women with fistula were. Many of the girls who had been healed at the fistula clinic refused to leave. Still ashamed and worried they'd forever be considered outcasts, they were terrified to go home. The hospital had built a set of small bungalows for them to live in. They called it "Fistula Village."

A few of the clinic's patients had been severely wounded during genital cutting. This practice involves removing the clitoris or labia, which some thought would ensure fidelity after marriage. But one of the clinic workers explained to me that if a young bride resists sex, traditional medicine workers might diagnose them with an affliction they call "concrete hymen." A cutter is called in to make deeper and deeper cuts to "cure" the affliction. Doctors who'd treated the girls in the aftermath of this procedure had repaired sliced urethras and other awful mutilations.

But there was a bit of bright news amid these horrific circumstances. These patients were in the minority; genital cutting was becoming more and more rare. Nearly every government in the region had outlawed the practice, though the laws weren't always enforced. Still, over the last 30 years, rates of female genital cutting worldwide had fallen 14 percent. This was, overall, a huge gain in the fight for women's rights.

Although it seemed counterintuitive in a place where something like "concrete hymen" is known as an affliction, women as a collective were slowly making gains. Fistula rates were declining. More girls were being educated than ever before. In new areas, women were being granted land rights after laws for centuries banned them from owning property. Child marriage was even starting to decline in some areas as views shifted and laws against it were being enforced.

Back home in the United States, officials for years also had led a charge abroad to ban child marriages around the world. But Americans were just waking up to the fact that child marriage was perfectly legal in 18 states and allowable in certain circumstances in all 50.

Moussa, a UNICEF worker who had accompanied me to the fistula clinic, had a theory about how things had started to change for the better for women in West Africa.

The local and global response to AIDS on the continent starting in the 1990s, he explained, had opened the door to talk about sex in ways that had been taboo in the past. And it included women in the conversation. Billboards and paintings on public walls illustrated how to use condoms. Sex and sexual practices were discussed during call-in radio shows aimed at preventing HIV. The frank talk also opened the door to talk about women's health and relationships.

Advocates began calling for more rights for women. International Women's Day, long ignored as a toothless declaration, began to catch on with women marching for their rights. Nations began instituting quotas for women on ballots and for civil servant jobs. Foreign NGOs offered more funding to countries that outlawed domestic abuse and put in place more rights for women. Those new laws weren't always enforced but having them on the books was a start.

At the same time that this was happening, throughout the 1990s and even earlier, an urbanization phenomenon was taking place in the region. West Africans poured out of the rural countryside, seeking better lives in the cities. There, they encountered different and often more liberal lifestyles. The flood into cities was so widespread that even people in the most rural of locales likely knew of someone who had been to a city—and had heard about their experiences and new ways of thinking. Layered onto this was the rapid spread of the Internet, allowing anyone with Wi-Fi or 3G instant access to how women were living elsewhere in the world.

Most countries in West Africa had entire ministries dedicated to women's issues. Domestic violence was still a problem. But local as well as international aid organizations supporting women's well-being were on the ground almost everywhere, helping women access better health care, get an education and run businesses. Their messaging was on posters and radio programming. Even some conservative imams were now accepting training in the Koran's support for women's rights.

Despite all the awful stories I had heard from victims, things were beginning to look up for many West African women.

Meanwhile, American women seemed to be experiencing a collective setback. The new president in the White House mocked women and opposed abortion rights. Thousands of women were rallying, some feeling so threatened that in modern-day America they needed to hold posters reminding the leader of the free world that "Women's Rights Are Human Rights."

Of course it wasn't easier to be a woman in West Africa than in America. But the future America my kids would inherit was a far different one than I had left behind.

FROM MY OFFICE in Dakar, I called Moussa at his UNICEF office in Niger to ask if he had any ideas about someone who could tell me whether more women were seeking divorce there like they were in Senegal.

"This sounds like something the Sultan might know about," he said.

"The who?" I asked.

He was, it turned out, referring to the Sultan of the Kingdom of Maradi, the Muslim religious leader for the area. The Sultan had a "kadi," or deputy who acted as a judge at an Islamic court that wasn't far away. The kadi settled scores for pretty much anyone who had any kind of dispute within a 100 mile radius of Maradi, a major trading center on the border of Niger and Nigeria. Many people went to him because his rulings were quicker and less expensive than municipal court.

The kadi handled divorce cases every day, Moussa told me. He suggested that I could talk to him about the women who came before him to ask for divorce.

I was eager to get going on the story but I was grounded in Dakar until Todd returned from Uganda. It would take a while to get the permissions for my trip, so it seemed as if, for once, we'd planned our tag-team travel just right.

I HAD SENT Jaime out to tie up some loose ends on a story we'd been working on in a town that was far in the countryside from Dakar; it was about people who risk their lives trying to get to Europe. He should know. At one point, he was one of them.

Migration was one of the biggest issues in West Africa, where unemployment soared and a rapidly growing population ensured things probably weren't going to get much better in the future.

As a teenager, Jaime had set out on his own from civil-war-torn Sierra Leone for Gambia, hundreds of miles away, with nothing more than wild determination that he could set sail from there to Europe, where he imagined he'd find a better life. He made it to Gambia but had to live on the streets, finding small jobs to earn money to pay smugglers to get him across the ocean. On three separate occasions he set sail, boarding crowded, rickety vessels that turned back because of stormy weather. He gave up and moved around the region before finding his way back to Sierra Leone.

The smugglers' route of choice had changed since Jaime's attempts, shifting along with the whims of various European countries that had locked down their borders or African countries that were blocking migrants from crossing to get to the sea. The path these days was through lawless Libya. It was grueling.

Migrants from Senegal had to climb aboard rickety buses that took them through hundreds of miles of desert, through terrain crisscrossed by terrorist groups and, even worse, bandits who lay in wait to rob the migrants of the life savings they knew was stuffed in their desperate pockets. If migrants made it unscathed past the robbers, and if the bus didn't break down or get caught in a sandstorm, leaving passengers to die of thirst, they then entered Libya, where smugglers levied another huge, surprise fee to go the rest of the way. Many migrants wound up enslaved, trying to earn enough money to pay the new fee for a boat ride across the ocean. Some smugglers took them hostage, locking them up and forcing them to call home to plead for cash wired to them to earn their freedom.

Then, once they'd assembled enough cash, came the sea crossing. Almost none of the migrants could swim. The vessels they were put on were far from seaworthy—rickety wooden pirogues or large inflatable rafts. If life jackets were distributed they were ill-fitting and so worn they were worthless. They set off like this into the open Mediterranean, a crossing that took days.

Some migrants nicknamed the trek "Temple Run," after the video game where players must navigate perilous cliffs, zip lines, mines and forests while running away from monsters and demons.

Thousands of them had drowned through the years. But the world was focused on another set of migrants: Syrians. Stories and photos of women and children on their terrible journey rightfully were landing on the front page of every newspaper in America. Unlike others who had embarked on the dangerous crossings to flee a horrible war, West Africans often were running away from daily life they had decided was so miserable they would assume the risk.

The bar was higher to get the world's attention for this continent's migrants, made up mostly of poor black African men—the bottom rung of any demographic ranking in terms of generating attention. Yet these men were the breadwinners and arguably the most important for the survival of any family, or any village. Sometimes they were rescued at sea or picked up on European shores, detained and repatriated to their home countries. But many of them never returned home, knowing how ashamed their families would be that they didn't make it. Even the ones who did, who somehow beat the astronomical odds, arrived in countries like Italy and Spain to find a weak job market and a bitter population that didn't want them there.

And yet there were success stories that served as siren calls to Europe. In one village far outside Dakar, a multicolored, tiled, two-story house made of concrete and lined by Romanesque columns loomed over a community of shabby, mud-brick homes. A motorbike was parked out front and a satellite dish poked from the rooftop. The homeowner was a migrant who landed in Europe and spent a desperate decade of sleeping on subways and wondering where his next meal would come from. Finally, he scored a job at a Parisian petting zoo. His was a kingdom built from scooping French goat poop.

Jaime had found a rural family in another Senegalese village and traveled by car, on potholed roads that gave way to narrow dirt paths that tore through barren peanut fields. The family lived in a circle of one-room homes made from mud, so small their beds were outside. They had sent son after son through the desert and across the sea, one dying after another on the dangerous journey.

"If they would have made it, it really would have changed things for us," the elderly mother told Jaime.

Two sons were left. Before they tried their luck getting to Europe, the family decided they should leave home to try to find work elsewhere in West Africa. The youngest son, just 14, boarded a bus to head for the border of Guinea, where an imam spotted him sleeping on the streets and took him in.

The other son, Adame, had been working in Gabon but it wasn't going well. When Jaime arrived, he was at the family compound and had decided to prepare for his own attempt to get to Europe. Jaime sat with Adame and his parents, talking about their options. At one point Adame started coughing violently and dropped dead,

right in front of Jaime, the final blow in a string of Job-like tragedies for the family.

Jaime was understandably upset and called me to say so.

"Come home," I said, without really knowing what else to say.
He was a 12-hour drive away. "We'll talk about it."

I KNEW I should have spent more time comforting Jaime, but at
home things were coming loose at the seams.

The generator stopped working during our neighborhood's frequent power cuts, leaving us in the pitch dark during a long spell
of blackouts. A would-be highway thief tried to distract the *Times*
office manager by throwing a boulder at our company car on a
late-night drive, to get him to stop so he could rob him. A wrought-
iron balcony on the side of the house collapsed, forming a crater of
hundreds of pounds of concrete and twisted metal in the patio. A
live wire under the backyard nearly electrocuted Luther and his
friends while they were playing on the Slip 'N Slide. ("The buzzes
are fun!" one of the boys cried out, undaunted.)

The cat was brawling with the neighborhood strays, coming
home with deep cuts in his head and a new nasty attitude. Ants
were overtaking the house, swarming any morsel of food that
dropped in the kitchen in a matter of seconds. They'd even found
their way into our upstairs bathroom, crawling into my allergy
medicine before I realized I'd snorted a handful. Luther got another parasite, a hookworm in his foot that we could see wriggling
just under the skin.

"That kid needs to make a scrapbook of his weird worms," Ash
texted, adding a baby bottle emoji for good measure.

Each incident on its own was manageable, but here it seemed
like everything always happened at once.

And then Zola, out of the blue, one night at dinner, asked for an
arranged marriage. All the little girls back home in America who

spend their childhoods dressing up as brides and princesses were bad enough. I was appalled that I now was raising a daughter who didn't want to pick her own mate. I demanded an explanation.

"It's just that I really trust you and Daddy," she said. "I know you'd find me a good husband."

I melted. In the age of hookups and Tinder, maybe she was on to something.

But this place was starting to get overwhelming. Maybe it was the stories of the women I'd met that created a constant low hum of stress. I felt like I had too much to take care of. I hadn't spent enough time talking to Jaime about what he had witnessed. I hadn't filed a story in a couple weeks. I wasn't spending enough time with the kids. I wasn't running enough in the morning or reading enough books at night. I was too tired to do either.

I hadn't had this feeling of confused helplessness since a few weeks after my girls were born and I was sleep-deprived, smarting from a C-section, with three kids under the age of two and a dog dying of cancer. I remember waking the morning after we had the vet put the dog to sleep, unable to recall if I had one less, or one more, thing to take care of. It was one or the other, I was certain, but I couldn't for the life of me figure out which for a few confusing minutes. Until I remembered my dog was dead, which made me sob.

In Dakar, my kids, meanwhile, started calling me "Daddy Mommy," a result of correcting themselves when the word "Daddy" came out naturally first when they addressed me. It was a constant reminder I was in second place now.

When my husband was the solo parent, he used the extra time we had working from home to supplement the kids' math skills. Math wasn't my thing, so I tried to engage them in extra writing. I assigned the kids timed writing exercises—imagined conversations with President Trump, a pretend marketing pitch for adopting out our mean cat or an essay on Tabaski, told from the soon-to-be-sacrificed sheep's perspective.

"Tonight, you're going to write a restaurant review of our meal at home," I announced one night after dinner. "Don't forget to evaluate the ambience."

They whined and groaned but knew they weren't wiggling out of it. I set the timer for 20 minutes and we sat in silence at the table as they scribbled in their notebooks. One by one they read aloud their finished work. Mostly the reviews assailed my skills at food preparation. Fair enough. I'm a terrible cook. Maude seemed enthusiastic about her piece. She lifted her sequined notebook and presented her audience with this:

> "There is no peace at this place. There is only one waitress and she is very grumpy and mean. She makes you eat every single bite. They only have one drink, milk. The green beans were raw and undone. The tablemats were broken and ripped. You could not pick a song. You could only plead to Dionne (the waitress) to change the song and she wouldn't listen. Maybe if you're lucky she will change it but it is not likely."

"Make your own green beans next time," I told her.

But wow. *There is no peace at this place*. That line haunted me. Were we crazy for trying to pull this off?

CHAPTER 16

Zalika

MY HUSBAND CAME home from his Uganda trip and I shipped out for divorce court in Niger.

The *Times* assigned a photographer—Laura Boushnak, who was a mom about my age—to travel with me to report on the Islamic court. It was so nice to be with someone else with sensible shoes, comfortable pants and that familiar look of exhaustion on her unmade-up face.

Almost every beat I had ever covered involved the legal system in some way. I knew my way around criminal courts and civil law and even cases at The Hague. But I had no experience with an Islamic court.

We wound through the unpaved back streets of the city of Maradi, a regional agriculture hub that sits on a flat sandy plane near the southern border with Nigeria. The car turned down a narrow road made even more narrow by cars parked on both sides. A flock of sheep crossed in front of our vehicle, and Laura and I hopped out.

We pushed back a tattered yellow curtain that was strung across an otherwise bare doorway and entered a room with dirt-smudged blue walls. Dust-covered books were scattered everywhere, in heaps on top of a desk, lined up on high shelves and piled on a side table.

Most were in Arabic. Faded portraits of a dozen male religious leaders, some with long beards and elaborate turbans, hung on the walls. I sat down on a couch and a cloud of dust rose up around me.

A barefoot man with 1980s-style aviator-shaped eyeglasses and a gray goatee entered and sat on the floor. It was the judge—or kadi, as he was called.

"How can I help you?" he asked.

"You handle divorce cases, right?"

"Yes, divorce, property disputes, theft—people come to me for everything."

"I'm wondering if you've noticed more divorce cases lately?"

His eyes widened.

"Yes, the rate of divorce has really gone up. For the past two years I have seen a drastic increase in divorce—especially women coming to me to ask for divorce."

It was exactly what I had hoped to hear. My story might just fall into place.

"So," I asked, "why do you think more women are coming to you to break up their marriages?"

"I've thought about this a lot," he said. "There are a few reasons."

The judge explained his chief theory: Men were still almost always the breadwinners of families in the farming community. Traditionally after harvest time, they locked up their stores of grain—they didn't trust their wives to be capable enough to manage the rations—and took off until planting time to look for work across the border in Nigeria, a more prosperous country than Niger.

But years of war with Boko Haram had crushed Nigeria's economy and work there had dried up. A recession in Nigeria had hurt Niger, too. Anyone who did business across the border, from farmers to money changers, were struggling. Wives wanted to work to help make ends meet. A wife suggesting she get a job was enough to enrage some husbands in this patriarchal society. The men would be ashamed if other people thought they couldn't provide for their families. But the women needed to feed their children. Some left their brooding husbands and sought a divorce.

"I want to be clear," the kadi said. "Many women ask me for divorce, but I don't always grant it."

Here comes the patriarchy, I thought.

"I'm trying to slow things down," he explained. "There are so many. Young women are aware of their rights. They don't want to suffer anymore. There is a solution to their problems and they can find it with me."

The kadi wasn't refusing to grant women divorces. He just wasn't granting divorces willy-nilly. He saw his role as marriage counselor as well as judge.

"We men are mean, that is true," the kadi said. "When a husband can't provide, he has to let his wife work."

"Islam grants women rights and they know their rights," the kadi continued. "If someone thinks her rights are violated by a situation, I'll support her."

Out in the middle of Nowheresville, Niger, where tweens get married off and have babies, where genital cutting is shunned but sometimes still practiced, where some parents still won't let their girls go to school because they worry they'll get knocked up on the walk home, I had managed to find a feminist Islamic court judge in the kadi of the Sultan of the Kingdom of Maradi. And he wielded quite a bit of power. The police sent plaintiffs to him instead of to the municipal legal system. He took up cases that local judges had flubbed. He was on call 24 hours a day, seven days a week. He was, it turned out, one of the main arbitrators of disputes for hundreds of miles around, with a jurisdiction of three million people.

"There are many reasons women are asking for divorce," the kadi went on.

"Can you give me some examples?" I asked.

"Why don't you see for yourself," he said. "Follow me."

Laura and I trailed the kadi outside. In the time we had been talking, a big crowd had collected on the sidewalk. There were more than 100 men—all of them spectators there for the show.

The men parted when the barefoot kadi approached, to let him through, and he plopped down on the sidewalk atop a double-layered sheepskin rug—his official judicial bench. His calloused feet poked from his gown. He made space for me to scoot in near him and called the first name on his handwritten list.

The first plaintiff arrived. It was a woman in a pink hijab who squeezed between all the men to sit cross-legged in front of the kadi. A man entered from the other side of the crowd and sat down not far from her.

The woman, Aishatou, launched in, as though she was picking up from an interrupted conversation. I guess she was just cutting to the chase.

"I got pregnant and I wanted my boyfriend to marry me. He wanted me to get an abortion then he changed his mind and decided we should have the baby and he would help me take care of everything.

"But now," she continued, "I had the baby and he hasn't done anything. He doesn't even come around."

Aishatou explained she had taken her boyfriend to municipal court, where the judge ordered him to pay child support. Since then he had made only one payment. She hoped the kadi could talk some sense into him.

The kadi looked at the couple sitting across from him.

"It's impossible to have a baby without two people having sex. What you have both done is immoral," the kadi said. "This baby did not choose to come into this life. You created this child and this child has rights."

"I'm not the only woman who has a man who won't pay up," Aishatou said.

"Listen," her boyfriend pleaded. "I was a truck driver but I lost my job. I'm unemployed. I live with my parents."

"You recognize this child is yours, and so you need to help out," the kadi said.

He ordered him to return with proof he had made his child support payment.

I sat alongside the kadi for the rest of the day, listening to him settle marital problems and divorce cases.

One was a woman who came before the kadi to complain that her husband had gone away to find work after harvest, and two years later he still hadn't come back. She wanted out of the marriage.

Another woman told him she had stormed out of her house, angry at her husband, only to return a few days later to find another woman's belongings in the home.

Yet another woman, her husband sitting alongside her, said she wanted a divorce because he had left her home alone, penniless, for three days.

"He locked me in the house and didn't even leave me money for breakfast. I'm a human being. I need to eat."

"I bring her food," her husband shot back. "She just doesn't want to cook."

"Let us decide together what to do," the kadi said, ordering them to cool off and return the next day for another hearing.

Abortion. Deadbeat dads. Cheating husbands. This court began to resemble a courtroom anywhere in America. The kadi was Niger's own Judge Judy. Like the horde of men who had gathered to watch the show, I was transfixed.

Day after day, in hearings over more than a week, I listened as women came to the judge to air their complaints about boyfriends and husbands. Not all of them were seeking a divorce—not all of them were even married. But they all had problems with men in their lives that transcended religion, geography and demographics.

I was taken by the case of one young woman, Zalika, a 17-year-old who wore a tiny diamond stud in her nose. She had been training to be a tailor when she was invited to a wedding. Weddings were notorious pickup scenes of matchmaking and come-ons. At the wedding, a friend introduced Zalika to a wide-faced man named Noura. He was single and looking for love.

Zalika didn't find him that attractive. It wasn't that he had bad features. He was tall enough, and his thick arms seemed strong. But she had a crush on a man who had left to find work in the capital, a 12-hour drive away. It had been months since she'd heard from him. Prodded on by her friend, she agreed to give Noura a chance.

Noura wooed her with his knowledge of the Koran, an appealing quality in this heavily Muslim area. He was sweet and gentle with Zalika's elderly mother and seemed to fit in with her family. He was a tailor, just like she wanted to be, and promised to show her the tricks of the trade.

She talked to Noura for hours, about their families and their dreams, about anything. He doted on her, bringing her new scarves and spices—little presents that she treasured. Soon they were married.

Zalika had been living in her family's compound in the middle of the city. It was a bustling mud complex made up of her entire extended family—sisters, aunts, cousins who spanned the generations. Scrawny old women sprawled out to sleep away the heat of the day on plastic mats stretched across the dirt in the central common area. Bits of hay swirled in the chalky air. Kittens and rabbits scampered in and out of the rooms and chickens pecked in the dust. Zalika and her sisters, who were all close in age, spent their days washing dishes and clothing. They plucked chicken feathers by moonlight; there was no electricity in that part of town. They gossiped and listened to religious shows, or whatever else was on their little battery-powered radios, the main source of entertainment for families. Zalika kept her red radio tucked in the folds of her gown, clenching it to her leg as she walked through the compound.

Noura lived by himself in a small apartment on the edge of town. After the wedding, Zalika moved in. When he left for work,

Zalika was alone for the rest of the day. She sat inside counting the hours until he returned home. Zalika told her husband she'd like to continue taking tailoring classes at a sewing center in town. Noura saw that as a waste of money. He could teach her what she needed to know, he said. He placated her by buying her a part of the body of a sewing machine—he couldn't afford to buy the whole thing but promised to buy the other pieces as soon as he earned more money.

Bored and lonely, Zalika stewed at home, staring at the piece of the black sewing machine in the corner and watching neighbor women walk out the door every day to meet up with friends. Maybe she could get a job, she suggested to Noura. It would curb her boredom and help out with their finances. He refused, disgusted at the idea of his wife out wandering the streets alone as she went to and from work.

One morning Zalika woke up with a cold. She sent Noura out for medicine. He didn't come back until the end of the day; he had forgotten the medicine. He didn't react when she pointed out his mistake. How could he be so uncaring about his own wife?

This wasn't how their relationship had been in the beginning. Recently, when they walked down the street together, she noticed sometimes he stared at other women.

Zalika felt like she had contributed to the household. She lined Noura's barren cupboards with cooking pots and a plastic water kettle she brought from her mother's home. She even brought a couple bags of rice. He seemed ungrateful.

Zalika turned to what seemed like her only friend, her little red pocket radio. She started listening again to her radio shows. One was a soap opera–like serial broadcast called *Light in Darkness* sponsored by the government and UNICEF. Aimed at helping women know their rights, the show featured characters tackling domestic abuse and health issues. One story line followed a woman unhappy with her husband. "Men just don't care about women," the wife on the show liked to complain.

Zalika could relate. She wanted more out of her marriage.

Soon, however, Zalika became pregnant. When she went into labor, she traveled to the local clinic and called her husband. He didn't answer. The phone rang and rang. Nothing. Finally, she got through and told him where she was. He didn't show up.

Tradition in Maradi dictated that Zalika move back in with her mother for a few weeks while she adjusted to nursing the baby. Zalika arrived home from the hospital to find her husband had already packed her bags. Everything was there, she noticed, except for the sewing machine part.

At the family compound, she was back in the company of other women, including her mother, who was a sympathetic ear for all Zalika's complaints about her husband.

"He doesn't treat you right," her mother told her. "You need to stand up to him."

Her mother didn't advocate for divorce though. She had been married when she was 14, to a stranger twice her age. Of course couples had spats, she told Zalika. She couldn't understand the fuss. She herself had stuck with her husband for five decades until he died, and was appalled that young women these days don't do the same.

Zalika detailed her situation to the kadi in a series of court hearings over several days. She knew she would have to move back into her family compound, and that she might have to give up custody rights when the boy was older. But she couldn't take it anymore. Noura sat silently across from her. One day after the hearing, I spotted him with his head down, leaning against a car.

Noura viewed Zalika's complaints as ridiculous. She had blown up at him once when she asked for yams and he brought her potatoes. Yams were too expensive, he had explained. She got angry when he gave his brother a bit of money to buy medicine for his sick children yet didn't have enough money for her. Didn't she understand that times were hard?

The wartime economy had worsened in recent years and Noura's tailoring business had started to dry up. He had to lower his prices so much that it was impractical to stay in operation. He was earning less than half the salary that he used to make. His brother offered him a salesclerk job at his small grocery store that stocked rice and pasta. It didn't pay much but at least it was a job.

Noura couldn't afford the lifestyle he had when he first met his wife, and Zalika couldn't understand this.

"I'm sick of coming here," he said, looking up at the kadi's sidewalk, where hearings were still under way. All the days in court had worn him down. Noura had made up his mind to give Zalika the divorce she wanted.

The next day, the couple sealed the deal with a thumbprint stamped in ink on a divorce decree. Zalika was thrilled.

I GOT BACK to my hotel room that afternoon and my phone rang with a FaceTime call. I looked at the screen. It was Todd's number. Maybe he missed me so much he had come to his senses and was calling to thaw the iciness that had settled between us after he passed up his CEO offer. I answered to find Luther's giant head staring into the screen.

"Dad?" he began.

"No, this is Mom. How are you doing, honey?" I said.

The kids were forbidden to use our electronic devices but it was nice to see my son's face while I was out in the middle of Niger. I was happy to cut him some slack.

"Where's Dad?" he said, flustered.

I paused.

"What do you mean, 'Where's Dad?' Isn't he with you?"

"No, he left to go surfing about an hour ago."

"He did *what*?" I fumed. Todd left the kids home alone to go . . . surfing? This was insane.

"Mom," Luther continued. "Can I go to Jonathan's house?"

"I have no idea if you can go to Jonathan's house. I'm in Niger. You need to talk to your father."

"But he's not home."

I was getting more and more angry. How could Todd leave the kids all by themselves? What if a fire broke out? What if a robber came? What if they fell down and broke a bone?

"Mom, just tell Dad I went to Jonathan's," my son said.

He hung up.

"Wait, no!" It was too late. He was gone and didn't pick up again.

How could this be happening? Todd was going to arrive home, who knows when, to find a child was missing, without any idea where to find him.

I dialed Todd's cellphone. No answer. I suppose he couldn't take his phone with him while he was acting like some teenage beach bum.

I fired off the most measured email I could, informing Todd that our 10-year-old son had contacted me here in the middle of my work assignment in rural Niger to let me know he would be going on his own to a friend's house for the afternoon.

An hour later, he replied.

"Don't judge," was all the email said.

I wanted to rage. But I took a breath. I suppose it was fair. I was going on my second week of being away, reporting a fascinating story in an interesting part of the world, completely consumed by my job, with no familial responsibilities whatsoever. I tried my best to take his advice.

Luther was fine in the end, of course. And I didn't have time to ponder how the subject matter of both my home life and my work life were colliding, chiefly because more annoyed wives were waiting for me.

———

CLOSER TO THE center of town was an organization for women called "Femmes Dynamiques." Situated off the street in a simple concrete building, it was started by a marabout—a Muslim scholar and religious leader.

I entered the gate and crossed the courtyard to get to the main office and a woman in a headscarf came out to meet me. She—and I was amazed to find she was a she—was the marabout. The photos of marabouts I had seen—plastered as icons on the sides of buildings and even taxi bumpers and on the walls of the kadi's office —were always all men. I suppose you could equate her to a Catholic nun, but still I was surprised. In my church growing up, women weren't even allowed to pass the collection plate. Men were leaders, we were taught, and women were there to serve them.

But this marabout, Rakia Modi, had been offering religious guidance to young women in Maradi for years. Her teachings had morphed into marriage counseling. She recognized a growing need in Maradi for young wives to have a place to blow off steam so she created Femmes Dynamiques.

"Women come here to complain," she said. Rakia led me through her headquarters, which fronted as a training center for women. A cake recipe was scrawled on a chalkboard on one wall where mixing bowls and spoons were stacked on the floor. Along another wall, young women sat in front of a line of sewing machines as a teacher demonstrated various stitching techniques.

But the real purpose of the place played out down an unlit hallway that led to a series of small rooms where women talked in groups and private sessions about their marital issues. In one of the larger rooms, bottles of oils and lotions for sale lined the shelves. Bikinis made only of strands of beads were tacked to the wall.

"I tried rubbing oil all over my body and sitting naked in front of him, just like you said," one young woman explained to Rakia during a counseling session, "but it didn't work. He still wasn't interested."

Many women talked about how they'd met their partners, look-

ing back at the time when their relationships still held such promise. One woman said her husband had been a security guard at a
school and flirted with her when she passed each day on her way
to the market. Another said she met her husband when he spotted
her while on his motorbike and asked if she wanted a ride. She
hopped on and he got her number as he dropped her at her house.
One woman said her husband first approached her at the airport,
in the Arrivals terminal.

"You look like a nice girl, and I'm a very religious man," he had
said. That's what passed for a pickup line in this part of Niger.

Another woman, Harouna, told me she had been having problems with her husband for months. He was a money changer, profiting off of foreign exchange for years until the economy turned
and rates dropped. He went to Libya, just a few hours' drive away,
where he thought maybe he could find better work. Things were
OK at first. They talked on the phone nearly every day, and he even
came back to take her on the Muslim pilgrimage of a lifetime, to
Mecca's Great Mosque, the holiest site in all of Islam. He bought
her a gold cap for her tooth, a local fashion statement for women
who had made this journey.

But on subsequent trips home, he had seemed distant. Harouna
had dinner waiting for him but when he arrived he told her he'd
already eaten. Sometimes he stayed out after midnight.

The money he sent her started coming less frequently. Once,
when they were talking on the phone, Harouna raised the idea of
her getting a job.

He lost his mind.

"You're an imbecile!" he screamed at her. "I'm tired of all your
shit!"

"I didn't know what to say," she said. "I felt like our love was
gone."

Harouna soon learned he had taken a second wife in Libya, a
practice that was legal and common, and so it was not unexpected.
Still, she felt betrayed.

Harouna had been considering divorce, talking her situation through with the other women at the marabout's center. She worried her husband would take custody of their children. According to religious laws in Maradi, it was his right to do so.

"I was thinking about all this in my head today," she said. "It just makes me sick to think about divorce. It really makes me want to throw up."

I trailed some of these women home, interloping in their family compounds where little lambs snuggled into the sand and guinea hens pecked about. Inside one house, three women stood around a huge vat of oil over an open fire, cooking up Frisbee-shaped discs of fried dough for a baby's naming ceremony the following day. They were carrying out tasks, and living lifestyles, that were not that different from a century or more ago. They were typical women raised in close-knit religious families in a patriarchal system. And yet they were undergoing nothing short of a societal revolution. Evidence of this was painted on the wall of one of the compounds over a small flock of ducks whose webbed feet were covered in dirt. It was a large drawing of a penis and testicles, with parts of the anatomy diagrammed and labeled.

"We're learning about the male reproductive system," one girl chirped.

Rakia was teaching all the women to stick up for themselves, to be sexy, to find happiness, even if it meant leaving their marriage. Most often she advised them to get a job.

"If a woman works, this is empowerment," she said.

"Years ago women didn't know their rights, but now more girls are going to school and they know what they deserve," Rakia said. "Before, women were just stuck in a marriage, be it good or bad."

The night before I flew home, Laura and I went to dinner at a garden restaurant known for its mojitos. For days on end we had listened to stories of disintegrating marriages. We must have internalized their complaints as our own. For two hours in the swelter-

ing evening heat we unleashed about our husbands, holding the
world's biggest gripe session.

Any wife anywhere could relate to Zalika as she complained
about her husband forgetting to bring the medicine home. How
many times had something like that happened in my own marriage? Part of me thought the anger she maintained toward him
was unsettling. But who was I to judge? I had been furious with
Todd for far more minor offenses. Like the time he went to the
pharmacy when I was sick and came home with generic medicine
instead of brand name Sudafed. I can't even remember why I possibly cared which kind he bought. It was true women had more
rights in America, but we were all trying to figure out how to
make the balance work. And for me, divorce seemed like too easy
of a way out. I didn't know how my husband and I would work
through our problems at home, but we'd find a way.

For Laura it was different.

"When I was assigned to this story," she told me, "it was like this
must be a sign."

She returned home from spending time with the divorcing girls
of Niger and separated from her husband.

CHAPTER 17

Toyin

THE KIDS IGNORED me when I walked in from Niger. That was happening more and more, as they were too engrossed in new homework, new books, and this time a new complicated board game Todd had bought them. The four of them sat on the floor playing a game that no one had the patience to pause and teach me. Shut out from their game, I chased mosquitoes around the living room with the electric bug zapper racquet. At least that seemed like a contribution to the family.

I could have stayed home and found some local stories to do. And worked on my marriage. And reconnected with my kids. Instead, I booked a trip to Nigeria.

For months the editors at the paper had been nudging me to try to get in touch with the Chibok girls. Before their abduction, most of the world had never even heard the name Boko Haram.

But by the time I arrived on the West Africa beat, the girls had been gone nearly two years. I had a duty to keep the story alive, but there were no new developments. I struggled even to mark this anniversary of the kidnapping with a story. What was there to say? They were still missing. In the back of my mind was my interview with Rahila, the suicide bomber trainee in Cameroon, who told me how the Chibok girls had been plump and treated better than the rest of Boko Haram's hostages. I thought about how not long before the girls were kidnapped, dozens of schoolboys were murdered. They were burned alive. No one created a hashtag for them.

In mid-2016, the military announced that one of the kidnapped girls, Amina Ali, had been rescued—accidentally. A patrol had come across her roaming in the forest with her baby and her Boko Haram "husband." The military threw him in jail and paraded Amina before the president. The nation celebrated the homecoming of one of its daughters from Chibok. Everyone had a million questions for Amina but the government was first in line. They took her into custody to grill her. Her own family members couldn't even visit her when they wanted.

Months later, Amina still locked away, the government had managed to secure the release of a group of more than 100 of the kidnapped girls. Nigerian officials had paid steep ransoms and even carried out a prisoner swap, exchanging incarcerated Boko Haram commanders for their freedom. The rattled captives were presented to the president and local TV cameras. They saw their parents for only a few hours before they were taken into government custody. The secret police wanted to question them and make sure none were loyal to Boko Haram. Like so many of the group's freed hostages before them, they had gone from one form of captivity to another.

I knew I would have a worthwhile story if I interviewed the students to learn more about their ordeal that had so captivated the world's attention. Yet part of me was annoyed with the assignment. Their suffering of course was valid, but from the outside it seemed like it could never compare to the people I'd reported on who had been kidnapped after seeing their own son shot or watched parents decapitated in front of them. The world had hardly batted an eye at the treatment of these other victims. And think of all the people who resisted Boko Haram and were slaughtered. I had developed a sense of loyalty to the victims whose scenarios seemed worse. It was unreasonable though. I knew I needed to try to talk to these young women from Chibok.

I empathized with the parents who didn't understand why their daughters still were being detained by the government. Surely the Chibok students must have been devastated that they couldn't go back to their village and be with their families. Maybe publishing an interview with the women—all of them were over 18 now—while in detention would expose this outrage and bring them closer to true freedom. In any event, the women appearing in the pages of the *Times* would help retrain the world's focus on the crisis—no other aspect of this entire war had seized global attention the way the Chibok girls had. That became my main motivation.

The president's advisers dodged me when I inquired about meeting with the girls. His information minister, whose name was Lai—pronounced "lie"—promised immediate access. He didn't deliver. But then a new window of opportunity emerged: Nigeria's President Muhammadu Buhari had flown to London for weeks, where he was being treated for a mystery illness he refused to disclose. By leaving the country for treatment, he wasn't exactly offering a ringing endorsement of Nigeria's health-care system. But Buhari was no different from other presidents and wealthy people in the region who fled for surgeries, scans and chemotherapy. In his absence, Nigeria's vice president was running the country. Maybe he would be more amenable to allowing me to talk to the young women.

Half of the Chibok girls were still being held captive in the forest. The government was trying to get them out, too. I knew that would complicate my attempts to convince officials to let me talk to the released hostages. I decided rather than request interviews with the women, I would ask to let us photograph them, if they were willing to pose. I thought I could make a compelling case: the world had first been introduced to these hostages through images portraying them at the lowest point of their lives, scared and under the control of militant men. Portraits of them now could show them as the adults they had become, bringing dignity to these women and reminding the world of the war that was still raging in Nigeria. They could be symbols of hope in what had become a hopeless war. And maybe I could squeeze in some questions, too.

"I'm going to have to camp out in Abuja for a while to figure out whether we can make this happen," I told my editors. They thought it was worth the effort.

The paper assigned the photographer Adam Ferguson to come with me. He rented suitcases full of lighting equipment that he hauled to Abuja in hopes this assignment panned out.

I set up a meeting with the vice president's advisers in Abuja. His staff welcomed my idea to meet with the women. But they told me I needed clearance from the minister of women's affairs. She was now in charge of the former hostages.

That so many of the students from Chibok were now free was a victory for the minister, someone who championed the success of women. I thought I might have a shot at getting her to agree to at least ask the Chibok women if they would be willing to meet with us.

The vice president's office gave me the minister's contact information. I called. I texted. I sent WhatsApp messages. I emailed. I tracked her down on social media. No response.

One morning I showed up unannounced at her office, a complex of grimy rectangular buildings in the center of the city. The interior was dark—no electricity that day. I passed one office lined with thousands of messy file folders shoved into shelves and stacked on the floor. I roamed the dim halls until I found the minister's office. But her secretary told me she was traveling outside the city and unavailable. Give her a couple days, I was told, and certainly she'll get back to me.

I knew by now that hurry up and wait was a fundamental part of my job. My colleagues always seemed to have constructive, or at least entertaining, ways to pass the time. Laura brought along a good novel. Adam had flash drives full of movies. Ash went for long runs. Tyler filled the time texting friends. Other friends loaded their phones with podcasts or a Netflix series they could binge watch.

I always forgot to download anything onto my phone. I usually forgot to even bring a book. My eyes were getting so bad I could no longer focus on the small type anyway. I had aged 1,000 years since moving to West Africa. The stress didn't help. I had new wrinkles, a new splotch of gray hair, and was grinding my teeth at night. Ash, meanwhile, told me he was shaving time off his runs—at one point he ran a four-minute-fifty-second mile. I was happy for him and admired his ability to manage work stress. But I wasn't running at all. I was a mess.

My colleagues cautioned about "self-care" while reporting grim stories. But I didn't want Netflix and a facial; I wanted a story. I thought about my promise to myself to provide balance to my war coverage. I let that lead me on my next pursuit as I waited for the minister.

While I was reporting on poor housewives in remote villages, my editor had asked about women in the polar opposite scenario. What were the challenges faced by working women in major cities in West Africa who already had made it to the top of their careers, he asked. I had been in touch with a female CEO of a big bank in Lagos who had invited me to shadow her for a day and meet other up-and-coming women bankers. I took her up on her offer and hightailed it to Lagos.

Walking through the revolving doors of the skyscraper situated on the Wall Street of Lagos reminded me of walking into Lehman Brothers, back when it existed, to meet with telecom bankers when I was a *Wall Street Journal* reporter. The bank in Lagos didn't look that different. But instead of the millions of dollars' worth of art that lined Lehman's halls, plaques commemorating deals were displayed on this bank's walls. It wasn't as pretty but it seemed more applicable.

The CEO, Toyin Sanni, was disarming. She had all the trappings of any bank executive: a spacious 12th floor, window-lined office overlooking the city, framed photos of her adult children and awards out for view on bookshelves and tables. But she wasn't like any stiff New York banker I had ever met. She was a part-time pastor at her church and had written a few books, with titles like *Get to the Top*. They were filled with Bible verses and prayers and insights for young working women that she'd picked up from her own career path and from reading Sheryl Sandberg and Oprah.

Her job in the high-rise-lined financial center of a throbbing megacity was a world away from that of her mother, who had worked as a tailor in a neighbor's home and sold tie-dye clothes in a small shop about 80 miles outside Lagos.

When she was a little girl, Toyin dreamed of being a dancer—one of the scantily clad women she saw on television rollicking alongside Fela Kuti. Her father steered her interests elsewhere, specifically toward her education. He believed all seven of his children should go to college, regardless of their gender. One of her proudest moments was being able to show her father her business card with the title "Managing Director" as he lay in the hospital before he died.

Toyin's effervescent demeanor and talk about the Lord masked a tactical shrewdness. She had always been serious about work and climbing the corporate ladder.

Her husband was also in finance. They had met at a restaurant late one night, when each had stopped in for a lonely, after-work meal. The two of them bonded over banking. At one point in their careers they worked for competing institutions. Friends called them Mr. and Mrs. Smith, like Angelina Jolie and Brad Pitt in that movie about rival assassins.

Before they had children, it had been easy for Toyin and her husband to juggle their dual careers. But she grew anxious when she got pregnant. Her husband had been raised in a polygamous family. She wasn't afraid he would take another wife; he considered polygamy barbaric. But, given that women were always hovering to take care of chores at his childhood home, he thought cooking, cleaning and childcare were women's work.

Toyin knew she couldn't work investment banker hours with a husband who did the same *and* raise a family. So she did what any smart working mom would do—she outsourced. Her husband didn't care who did the work, as long as he didn't have to. Hiring a nanny allowed Toyin to come home after a long day at the office to a clean house and dinner on the table and kids who were ready to play with their mom for a few hours before bed. As her three children grew older Toyin hired a driver and rode to school with them before being dropped at her office. It was a way for her to spend extra time with the kids as they navigated the clogged roadways.

Still, her supercharged career was difficult for her children. They were jealous of friends and cousins who had stay-at-home moms.

"I couldn't be supermom but I tried to make our time together as meaningful as possible. I was probably more like a friend than a mom," Toyin said. "I tried to make up for it by depriving myself of other things. My social life was zero. It was all built around things I could do with the children."

The way she navigated motherhood sounded very familiar.

We had hired babysitters, too, back in New York. But still it seemed that so much needed to be done around the house. Early in our parenting journey Todd had presented me with an idea.

"Let's delineate household responsibilities," he said, grabbing a pen and piece of paper.

"What?" I snapped. "That's a ridiculous idea. We're both adults. We know what needs to be done around here."

Todd sensed things were spiraling out of control at home and wanted to get a better handle on life. I worried he was preparing to assign chores by gender. I foolishly shut down the discussion, before I even could sort his intentions. The fallout was brutal. No one was in charge of anything, and everyone was in charge of everything.

Toyin's two daughters and a son were grown now, and all of them were working in the financial sector. I could only hope my kids would be as successful as hers.

That day in Toyin's office, I watched as she led almost entirely all-male meetings. She was kind and polite, listening to sales pitches and updates from her team. When it was her turn to talk, she did so softly. She was the boss, after all, and everyone had to listen to her. With her dialed-down voice, the men literally had to lean in to hear her so they wouldn't miss a word.

"That's deliberate, isn't it?" I asked her as a group of men were being shepherded out of her office.

"What's deliberate?" she said.

"Your meeting voice."

She laughed and gave me a knowing look.

In her long career in banking, Toyin had bosses who hit on her, clients who disrespected her and promotions that went to her male colleagues when it seemed obvious they should have gone to her. She endured the same kinds of problems faced by women anywhere in mostly male fields—the same issues that would soon have a spotlight glaring on them with the #MeToo movement.

"Essentially, being a woman in some places you almost feel like you are invisible," she said.

In Nigeria, that message trickled down from the highest levels of government. After his own wife made a remark that was critical of him, President Buhari had taken to Twitter to remind her she belonged in his kitchen. His tweet didn't gain international outrage, maybe because the world back then was still reeling from the news a few days earlier of a recording of Donald Trump talking about his proclivity for grabbing women by the pussy.

In Lagos, I met with young women working in one of the biggest, most modern cities on the continent, who told me they were expected to get married in their 20s and become moms. But they wanted to focus on their careers. In doing so, they were practically social outcasts. The fact that so many women were delaying marriage was causing a collective freak-out here. Local newspapers ran stories trying to explain the trend. Articles in mainstream media questioned why men didn't want to marry them. They created a nickname for single 30-something women: "old cargo."

"10 Reasons Nigerian Ladies Are Yet to Leave Spinsterhood," read one headline.

The reasons listed in the story: "Some ladies are incorrigible." "Decent men are rare." "Most eligible men are not ready to tie the knot." And my personal favorite, "Dislike for domestic chores."

Under that last heading it read:

> These days many Nigerian ladies have gone Western and forgotten entirely how proud Africans are of their cultural heritage. No matter how successful you are, you are still an African lady, so don't forget to learn how to cook and do home chores. Although gender equality is the new deal of the day, it is not enough reason to know nothing about domestic chores.

The article went on to advise single women that they still had time to latch on to a husband and shouldn't give up hope: "Remember ladies, it's better late than never."

In Lagos, one woman told me her doctor refused to prescribe her birth control without a husband present. Another told me that when she showed up for her first date with a man she met online, she arrived at his apartment to find bags of groceries and a sinkful of dirty dishes. He intended to test out her cooking and cleaning skills. Other single women said they had trouble renting an apartment on their own. Landlords didn't believe they earned enough to be able to pay rent. Sometimes women were accused of being prostitutes if they showed up to look at an apartment without a man. Many successful single women still lived with their parents—and endured regular nagging about when they would find a husband. Some women told me they were considering running away from home because their parents were so insistent they throw away their college education, leave their jobs and get married.

The women investment bankers I talked to felt trapped. Their careers were all-consuming. They didn't even have time to date. Marriage for them presented a career obstacle: their bosses might assume they soon would quit to start a family. It was hard to have anyone take them seriously.

America has cycled through this phenomenon before—and always with different advice. Have your babies early and then start your career! Have your babies later! Quit your job after you have a baby! The work world is finally accommodating mothers—with lactation rooms in the closet! We haven't managed to come up with any magic formula for having it all.

One banker in Lagos told me she dreaded her upcoming 30th birthday. She didn't mind getting older, but she knew her parents would be distraught at the fact that she would leave her 20s without a husband.

"They pray to God that for my birthday he will send me a husband to provide for me," she said. Never mind the fact that she had investment funds and could provide for herself.

Toyin had tried to create a climate at her bank to help women succeed. She was a role model, showing that women could work and raise a family. She made a point of celebrating marriages and childbirths with office parties and cakes so that the younger women would see they could be promoted regardless of their life choices.

Yet the married women in Toyin's office were navigating tricky situations at home. One of them told me she and her husband had never seen each other's paychecks. They agreed that she paid for schooling, clothing and babysitting and he paid the rent. Sometimes on her long commute home in miserable evening traffic, after she fueled up on roadside peanuts or plantain chips and tuned in to her favorite radio show, her mind wandered to the family's finances. She suspected she outearned her husband. But she remembered marriage classes she took that advised working wives never to raise such topics at home to avoid embarrassing their partners. She kept quiet, and the couple was happy.

When I asked Toyin if she earned more than her husband, she changed the subject. I didn't press her.

As I waited in the lobby for Toyin to finish work I thought about how all these women were spending so much energy managing the egos of the men in their lives. How much more real work could be done if that wasn't how we all spent half our time?

Toyin had arranged for a dinner with a few bank managers who worked under her. We hopped in her car and she told me we were stopping at an office down the street to pick up one of her children, who had just started a first banking job. The car door opened and a young man in his 20s in a pin-striped suit scooted into the backseat alongside me.

At first, I was disappointed that it was her son and not one of her daughters. Documenting a mother-daughter chat about banking would have made a nice ending to my story. I could show how Toyin was bringing along a new generation of women bankers in her family.

At dinner, inside a fancy hotel, Toyin sat next to her son. The two soon were lost in conversation. She covered his hand with hers as they parsed *Game of Thrones* plot lines, discussing family dynasties and empires to conquer. And as her son started telling his mom about his day at work and asking her advice, I realized it was just as important she was shepherding the next generation of young men.

CHAPTER 18

Balaraba

"HELLO, IT'S DIONNE from *The New York Times*." I rang the minister's secretary yet again. "Is she available?"

"Oh yes, she's back," the secretary said, "but the minister needs time to recuperate. Just a few more days and I'm certain she will meet with you."

I was frustrated, but even Shehu couldn't salvage this situation. He had exhausted his connections, and his refusal to kiss up to authority figures left me on my own.

I had more time to kill waiting for the minister, again. That meant more stories to find. The war zone was the easiest place to find them. We hopped a plane to Maiduguri, the city of a million stories.

UNICEF had just released a harrowing report that attempted to calculate the number of children and specifically girls who had been blowing themselves up in the name of Boko Haram. I'd already written about women suicide bombers, but the bombings seemed to be happening on a regular basis now in Maiduguri. If I went back there, I thought I could find a new twist to the story and draw more attention to the crisis.

By now, female suicide bombers had become so common that

most every major publication had written about the incidents. Maiduguri was practically under siege, with dozens of bombings since the start of the year. They were the ultimate Boko Haram fighters. Most stories I read had concluded that the women were brainwashed. That word bugged me. What did that even mean? I'd never seen any kind of actual explanation of why a teenage girl decided to strap on an explosives belt and walk into a market and push the detonator.

Maybe Shehu could help me find a woman who had been arrested before she could detonate, or who had considered becoming a bomber. It would shed light on all these attacks and I'd finally have an interview with a dedicated Boko Haram fighter.

The plane landed in Maiduguri. Shehu was waiting as usual. I shook his hand and my eyes were drawn to a small stain on the front of his all-white outfit. That wasn't like Shehu at all. He walked to the car slowly, and seemed more unsteady than usual as his leather sandals navigated the cracked concrete. His phone rang. He handed it to the driver to ask him who was calling.

"Shehu," I said, "are you having trouble with your vision?"

"Ah, you see, the whole thing comes down to an argument I had with a reporter at my newspaper. . . ."

Shehu started to launch into another one of his wandering stories as we drove off together. I wasn't quite clear what he and the reporter had argued over—Shehu was meandering more than usual. I kept interrupting to ask questions. Finally, Shehu paused and turned from the front seat to look at me.

"I do not think you believe in these things," he said.

"What do you mean?"

He took a breath. "He put a curse on my eyes."

"Oh," I said, and was quiet for a minute as I thought of how to respond. "That's terrible."

"I have seen his byline in your newspaper," Shehu continued.

That was true. Once, several months earlier, when I was desperate on deadline and couldn't reach Shehu, I had called this reporter to help me get a quote. I never mentioned it to Shehu but clearly he had noticed and was hurt.

"Shehu," I said, "I believe you. I really do. Listen. Anyone who puts a curse on you is dead to me. You hear me, right? He's dead to me."

"Thank you," he said. I knew he meant it.

As we drove, I teased out more health details from Shehu. He revealed he had diabetes, and it was clear he hadn't been getting proper care. We talked about his diet and the clinics where he should seek treatment. He promised he would go and I vowed to hold him to it.

But Shehu didn't want to talk about his own health; he wanted to talk about suicide bombers. He already had two of them who agreed to meet me.

We drove through town to reach the women who he said were waiting for us at our hotel. It was the usual chaos—cars and kekes and people flitting between market stalls. Along one traffic circle, I spotted a new huge billboard. It was a painting of a girl with explosives strapped to her body.

"Slow down," I said, craning my neck to get a better look.

The wild-eyed girl had a vicious look on her face, as though she was grimacing to express some kind of crazy bloodlust.

"Can we go around the traffic circle again?" I asked.

The car took another pass of the billboard. I made out the words this time. Its text urged parents not to hand over their daughters to be suicide bombers. The whole thing was just *off*. The idea that parents would be willing to sacrifice their children to Boko Haram to be used as bombers seemed ridiculous to me. What parent would want their daughter to become a human bomb? I was more determined than ever to talk to these girls.

"Shehu, let's hurry," I said. "I don't want the girls to leave."

Many people in Maiduguri by this point were crossing the street to avoid being near to any young woman, just in case she was carrying a bomb. Some women had started squatting to the ground as they approached checkpoints, a sort of macabre curtsy to let soldiers know they weren't carrying a cumbersome explosives belt that would have prevented them from bending down. Even NGO workers were scared. They were rethinking how to set up food collection points because the woman of a household typically was in charge of fetching handouts. Some Maiduguri women had started bathing more often and taking special care to comb their hair and wear nice clothes to avoid looking suspicious. Suicide bomber girls were filthy and wore tattered dresses because of their harsh conditions in Boko Haram camps. *Haggard* was how everyone described them.

The suspicion had tragic consequences. One aid group documented innocent children who had been killed at checkpoints in the region by mistaken, nervous soldiers afraid that the kids were concealing bombs.

We pulled into the hotel and Shehu handed me my room key. It was just like him to already have taken care of checking in for us. He knew we were in a hurry to do our reporting, in order to get back to Abuja. I ran to my room and unlocked the door.

My eyes adjusted to the dim light inside. A TV flickered with scenes from a nature show on killer whales. A ceiling fan churned. Dust clumps clung to its spinning blades. The bed was covered with a golden polyester duvet. In the corner, in a chair alongside my bed, there was a figure: a teenage girl in a pale yellow hijab. A would-be suicide bomber was sitting in my hotel room. I gasped. She looked as startled as I was.

I backed out of the room, searching for Shehu.

"I forgot to tell you," he called from across the parking lot, "we didn't have any other safe place for interviews so I thought we could just talk to her in your room."

I gathered my composure and fished out my notebook and pen. I introduced myself and explained why I wanted to talk to her. Her name was Maimuma and she agreed to tell me her story. She wanted everyone to know what had happened to her.

Maimuma wound up in a Boko Haram camp after fighters had invaded her village and kidnapped her. She spent a few weeks with them before one of the militants told her he had a special mission for her: he wanted her to kill some soldiers with an explosives belt that he would strap to her body.

Maimuma resisted. Her initial reaction was selfish. She didn't want to die. Don't worry, the fighter told her. The moment you hit the detonator, the bomb will hop from your body to the soldiers and you'll be safe. She wasn't stupid enough to believe that. Even if you die, the fighter told her, you'll go straight to heaven. She didn't believe that either.

Maimuma didn't want to become one of those girls she had heard so much about, the ones who blew themselves up and killed other people. Everyone knew this was happening all over the region. She didn't want to die and she didn't want to become a murderer either.

Militants grabbed her anyway and pulled up her gown to tie an explosives belt to her waist. They braided her hair to prepare her body for burial. The belt was tied behind her back, making it impossible for her to undo the complex knot. They put her on the back of a motorbike and dropped her along a rural road. Follow it to where the soldiers are, they told her. Act sexy, they said, like a woman. That will distract the soldiers. Wait until you're very close to them. Then press the button.

She tried to keep her composure until she had walked out of sight from the militants. The belt was heavy and pulling at her waist. The detonator was getting hot and almost burning her skin. She was terrified of touching it and accidentally setting it off.

Tears flowed as Maimuma walked. A few people along the road spotted her sobbing. What's wrong? they asked. She told them Boko Haram had tied a bomb under her dress. They ran away. The moments passed and she kept walking. More people approached her but they also screamed and ran away when she told them that she had a bomb.

The absurdity of watching one person after another sprint from her in sheer terror wasn't lost on Maimuma. She almost laughed when she told me this part of the story. She tried to run after everyone but people shouted that they would kill her if she followed them. She was stuck.

Soon, a group of soldiers arrived. Someone must have alerted them that a girl with a bomb was walking down the road. Put your hands in the air, they told her. One soldier approached. Gingerly, he tried to untie the device. It seemed to take forever. Maimuma's arms grew tired as she held them overhead. She almost passed out. Finally, when it felt like she couldn't hold her arms up any longer, the belt was off.

At first Maimuma told only her parents what had happened to her. She knew that many people in Maiduguri would think of her as a Boko Haram member.

But she reflected on it in the days that followed as she watched more and more people arrive in her neighborhood who had fled the war. She decided that she had nothing to feel guilty about. Having a bomb wasn't her idea. If anything, they should thank her for not blowing up anyone, and she wanted everyone to know about her bravery.

I'd never met anyone so strong and sure of themselves as this young girl. Until I met the next bomber girl Shehu had lined up to talk to me.

Hadiza was barely a teenager when Boko Haram came to her family's farm and took her. Right away, a leader of the fighters presented her with a young man he said would become her husband. The man announced he was anxious to have sex with her. Hadiza started crying. The leader pushed him away and told him to leave her alone.

"I thought he wanted to help me," she said.

He didn't want to help her at all, she soon learned. What he wanted was for Hadiza to become a suicide bomber. He and the other men tied an explosives belt to her waist. They took her to a road and pointed in the direction of a town. Press the detonator when you see a crowd, they told her.

Hadiza walked along alone and afraid. She scanned the horizon looking for anyone who might help her.

"Then," she said, "help came by itself."

A group of soldiers spotted her and called out to her. She raised her dress slowly to show them the bomb and told them she needed help.

"I'm afraid to touch it," she yelled to them.

The soldiers approached her and removed the belt, asking her if she knew how to get back to the Boko Haram camp. She got in a vehicle with the soldiers and led them in the direction of the hideout, but by the time they arrived, the site was empty.

The soldiers took Hadiza to a camp for other people fleeing the war that was just outside Maiduguri. They put her in a tent with two older women. They were strangers, but they were kind. She thought she was finally safe.

But while she was at the camp, the security agents posted there spotted her. They knew she was young and on her own. In the middle of the night one called her from her tent. Confused, she followed him to an empty part of the camp. He raped her. Each night after, a soldier came for her. Terrified that her tentmates would shame her if she told them what was happening, Hadiza went along and said nothing.

In all, Hadiza told me, she must have been raped 10 times by the men who were supposed to be protecting her.

I couldn't get Hadiza's experience out of my mind. I recalled that a year before, Human Rights Watch had published a report about rapes in the camps. I hadn't heard about any action taken to prevent this.

"Shehu, do you think we can find more girls who are rape victims?" I asked.

"There are so, so many," he said.

I began calling officials to see if the government had prosecuted anyone for the rapes. Next to nothing had happened. Shehu started asking around to his sources in a local security force to see if they knew any victims who would talk to us. Yes, women told them, they would share their stories if they could remain anonymous. Maybe they could finally have justice.

We led other women inside the hotel room and they also described horrific rapes at protected government camps where they were living after Boko Haram had invaded their villages. Some had been raped by Boko Haram, only to be raped again by soldiers in the camps.

Soldiers called for the girls in the middle of the night, telling them they would be killed if they told anyone. Other security agents made women cook and clean for them, promising food or money if they did. But once they were alone in their quarters they raped them.

It was starting to seem like every time I came to Maiduguri I uncovered new and more shocking stories than the last time. But these women's endurance, their sheer survival skills, were mind-blowing.

I had done enough reporting to cobble together stories on bombers and on rapes. I worried we needed to keep pushing in Abuja to meet with the Chibok girls. I called the minister's office to check in.

"Come back to Abuja and I am certain she will meet with you," her secretary said.

WE LANDED IN Abuja and showed up at the ministry. The secretary looked up from her work.

"Did you write a letter requesting an interview?" she asked.

"Yes, I gave that to you a week ago, remember?"

She rifled through the papers on her desk until she found our letter. She held it in front of her face.

"Oh," she said, shaking her head. "This is addressed to 'Her Excellency the Minister.'"

"Yes," I said. A lot of Nigerian government officials expect all kinds of pageantry and fawning when addressed. My letter was even stamped with an official-looking seal of *The New York Times*, another prerequisite to be taken seriously here.

"What's the problem?"

"She is 'The *Honorable* Minister,'" she said. "Only the president is *Your Excellency*. You'll need to bring another letter."

We were officially being jerked around.

Adam and I sat fuming that night at dinner. This assignment wasn't going to work out. He had hauled lots of gear halfway across the world, and I had failed to even get us near the Chibok girls so we could ask if they wanted to talk to us or be photographed.

It seemed like I had pursued every possible option. I'd already interviewed their parents. They were as anxious for us to talk to the girls as we were. Maybe they would finally learn more about their daughters. I had good relationships with activists but after years of staging protests to get the government to focus on the Chibok students' return they had only antagonized the minister and other officials, so they couldn't help us.

I thought about the victims that I had just met. In particular, I thought of Maimuma and her bravery. I was annoyed we were putting so much effort into reporting on a group of students who were now living in a secure building far from the fighting while other captives were in camps where they might be raped.

In America the #MeToo movement was really picking up steam, with stories about women suffering under powerful men who had dominated their careers and lives running on the front page every day. Yet here were girls in Maiduguri who were actual war heroes worthy of presidential praise—and they were being ignored. Imagine if one single teenage girl in America was strapped with explosives and told to blow up a group of people. What were we still doing in Abuja, trying to kiss up to a federal minister for a story that might not even pan out?

"This is so stupid," I said. "The bomber girls are the real story of this war. We should be focusing all our efforts on them. You should be taking portraits of them."

"OK, let's do it," Adam said. "But I'd need a lot of them to make it work, maybe seven or eight."

"Shehu can help," I said.

Our editors agreed to let us pursue portraits of the girls. But we had a problem: we couldn't show their faces. If anyone found out who they were, not only could Boko Haram come after them but also the girls could be met with repercussions in Maiduguri from neighbors who might stigmatize them for having spent time with terrorists.

Our editors decided they had enough faith in us to produce a portrait series of people whose faces we couldn't show. It made me love my newspaper.

"We'll make it work," the photo editor assured me.

We flew back to Maiduguri while Shehu tapped our security sources. They helped him round up more than a dozen other girls who unwillingly had been dispatched as suicide bombers and managed to surrender. There must be scores of them roaming the countryside if we already found this many.

I sat in another dark hotel room interviewing the girls one by one, this time for hours on end over several days. Their stories were similar in some ways. Most of them had been forced into carrying bombs after refusing to "marry" a Boko Haram fighter. All of them were terrified.

Fighters told Fatima she would go to straight to paradise if she detonated her bomb. "But they don't control heaven," Fatima told me.

Aisha's little brother was killed right in front of her when he protested after fighters announced she was going to be married off. Aisha still refused. So they strapped a bomb to her.

Hajja was distraught when fighters tied a bomb to her, not only because she didn't want to be a murderer but because she would never grow up to get a job in government and support her older parents. She was so relieved when soldiers helped her shed her bomb. But by the time she got back to her parents they were dead, killed by Boko Haram.

Fati said her mom told her never to tell anyone she had been forced to wear a bomb. Forget it happened, she told her. But every time she hears an explosion go off in Maiduguri she remembers.

I interviewed 18 girls in all. The hotel where we were carrying out interviews didn't have electricity during the afternoons, and the heat and body odor trapped inside the walls of the small room made me dizzy. Their stories were so grim, I had to find something positive to talk to them about.

I started asking the girls what they wanted to do with their lives. It seemed wrong to end the interview without a nod to the future, to remind them there was hope. One wanted to be a doctor. A few wanted to be lawyers. Others wanted to learn how to sew. All of them wanted to go to school.

"These women deserve medals," I said to Shehu as one was filing out of the room.

"What they need," he said, as practical as ever, "are scholarships."

I had hoped when I started this line of reporting that I would find a Boko Haram fighter who could explain the group to me. What I wound up with is a complex story about how women were surviving it all.

I finished the interviews and Adam stayed on to spend more time photographing the girls, scouting locations that would keep them safe yet allow him the lighting and setting to reflect their power and heroism. It wasn't easy. His backdrops were curtains in a Chinese restaurant, hotel hallways, a mosquito-swarmed room made of mud walls and a storage room where rats scurried.

A couple weeks later my story ran on the front page, and the paper published 18 portraits. The story got a lot of clicks and tweets and shares, not only because of the chilling accounts of these brave girls but for the haunting images of the women whose faces were a mystery. It was striking how girls covering their faces could appear so powerful. Other international magazines republished the story. But I was most proud when readers told me it changed perceptions of these young women from criminals to brave victims.

I HAD BEEN back in Dakar for only a few days when I heard from the professor of the Gender Equity class I had learned about from the couple at the Maiduguri zoo. He invited me to sit in on one of his last lectures of the year. He was central to a story I knew I needed to tell, about Maiduguri's lesser-known side—one where feminism flourished. I wanted to write a story about twerking at the Valentine's Day disco, about lovers at the zoo, about men who want to do the dishes, and about nothing to do with the war. I had to get back to Maiduguri.

But Todd also needed to be away. We were bumping up against the situation we had tried to avoid: being out of the country at the same time. Our kids would be alone only for a night, and we could hire a babysitter. But I ran through the worst-case scenarios. *What if I missed my flight home? I might not get another one for a few days, or even a week. What if there was a terrorist attack? The airport might be shut down. Cell networks might even be blocked. What if one of the kids got badly hurt? A babysitter was no substitute for a parent.*

I didn't like it.

"It's going to be fine," Todd said.

If he wanted to hang on to his job he needed to keep showing up at important meetings. If I wanted to show how women were taking control of their lives in an area where terrorists aimed to enslave them, I needed to go back to Maiduguri.

Todd counseled the babysitter on all the what-ifs, not that we

actually knew what to do in case of an emergency. It wasn't obvious. Dakar doesn't have a 911 system.

But we had lived in Dakar for nearly two years without an emergency. I decided to adopt Todd's optimism and not worry about it.

I arrived in Maiduguri and crossed into the university. Militants
had stormed the gate probably a dozen times before, unleashing
suicide bombers who had killed early-morning worshippers at the
campus mosque, among them a professor of veterinary sciences. I
made my way to a large lecture hall.

There, in the hometown of Boko Haram, a most unexpected
message was being delivered by a professor in fake crocodile loafers
with a laptop tucked under his arm.

"The idea of male oppression starts from the family setting,"
Professor Raphael Audu Adole told his rapt class. "A boy is trying
to copy a man. The man is trying to dominate, and the boy grows
up with it. It's a learning process. You develop and grow with it. Are
you following me?"

"Yes," responded a chorus of 150 young men and women.

"Society is constructed to favor the interests of men, isn't it?"

"Yes," the students chanted.

"Women are marginalized, oppressed and abused. Men have
taken the part of domination and force in relations in the family,"
he continued. "This is a big problem in society and we need to do
something about it."

During the class, female students shared their stories of being
sexually harassed at checkpoints and treated as maids by boyfriends.
One of the students, a woman named Rabi, rose to address her
classmates.

"I want a man who can make my breakfast—one who will assist
me in the kitchen and who can go shopping."

Cheers broke out from the men and women in the crowded
lecture hall.

———

WHILE I WAS in Maiduguri, I met up with some of the would-be bomber girls. Seeing them again was like seeing old friends. One told me she wanted to be a journalist, just like me. I was honored. But revisiting them was also exhausting. I knew their stories had a happy ending—They survived! Hooray!—but it still left me drained. What would become of them now?

I hoped for them it was cathartic to know the world was listening. Maiduguri lacks enough psychologists and therapists who could help heal all the emotional scars in the city. So few victims I talked to showed any emotion at all.

"Forget about it," Shehu once counseled one of the women we were interviewing who had suffered under Boko Haram. "That was in the past."

The common way of dealing with trauma in this part the country was to erase it from memory and move on.

At the hotel later that night I ran into one of the reporters who had been in Maiduguri with me a few months back. We sat outside and caught up over a beer. He complimented me on our story about the bombers. It turns out while he was in town he wanted to do the same story for his publication.

"Can I ask you something about that story?" he said.

"Sure, anything," I said.

He leaned toward me and lowered his voice. "How much did you pay the girls to say all that?"

"What?" I said. "I didn't pay anyone. You know that's unethical."

"Come on," he said. "No one in Nigeria gets anything for free. We all know you paid them."

"I didn't pay anyone anything."

So that's what my peers have been saying. I walked away from the table dejected. It didn't matter that the story drew new readers who, for the first time, realized the impact of the crisis in rural Nigeria. It didn't matter that these women were now better understood. It didn't matter that editors liked the story. My competitors were spreading rumors that I had committed the ultimate journal-istic sin and bribed the girls to say what they did.

I didn't sleep that night thinking about it. I grew more and more paranoid as the hours passed. I started thinking crazy thoughts. *Did the girls tell me the truth? Were they making up the whole thing? Did the military pay the girls to talk to me? Was I duped?*

In the morning, I was scheduled to see another of the girls. In my conversation with her I found myself becoming a prosecutor, interrogating her about every last detail of her ordeal.

"Who was it exactly that asked you to carry a bomb?" I asked her as Shehu translated.

"No one asked me to carry a bomb," she said.

"What?" I said, startled.

My stomach twisted into knots. Her words were like a slow-motion car crash. I had her interview from last time printed out verbatim right in front of me. Security sources had verified her account. Was it not true? Maybe she did make it up? But we had published her account as part of my front-page story. I thought I was going to be sick. She interrupted my building hysteria.

"I didn't *carry* the bomb," she clarified. "It was strapped to my waist."

I had never been so relieved at a translation error. She went on to retell the rest of her story, every detail of which matched what she had told me the first time. I was satisfied she wasn't making up anything. I had let that other reporter get into my head and I needed to forget about him.

WHEN WE WERE finished, I scrolled through my email, hoping to find a message from Todd that he was home and all was well. In-stead, I found an email from Maude.

"I threw up and only the babysitter is here," she wrote.

That girl could do guilt like nobody else. I called Todd, who was already driving back from the airport in Dakar. He assured me he would handle everything. I felt terrible but I was thousands of miles away. There was nothing I could do.

SHEHU HAD WANTED me to meet another young woman, named Balaraba. She also had been recruited as a suicide bomber. He thought it was a good idea for me to learn more about her even though my story already was published. I guided Shehu, whose vision seemed even worse, into a chair in a dark hotel room, and he translated as Balaraba told us her story.

Balaraba, a round-faced young woman with a childish gap between her front teeth, met the man who wanted to marry her when she was just a teenager. She wanted to finish high school but he wanted to get married right away. Her mother convinced her he was a good man with a good job—a fish trader—and Balaraba shouldn't pass up the opportunity. Weeks before her final exams, she dropped out of school and got married.

About a year later, the couple had a baby girl. Balaraba took the child to her own family's house to nurse her and care for her for a few weeks, as was customary. When Balaraba returned home, her husband told her he had a big problem—some of his friends had joined Boko Haram. He had made the mistake of telling them they were wrong. Now he was worried they were going to kill him. He was convinced he was being followed.

"You're being paranoid," Balaraba told him.

But other wives had told her they suspected their own husbands had joined the group. Privately, she worried.

Late one evening, Balaraba and her husband heard footsteps outside their door and then a knock. Her husband asked who it was. No answer. Balaraba peeked out and recognized the men—all friends of her husband.

"They've come to kill me," her husband said.

Terrified, he ran out the back door and climbed over the wall that ringed their home. The men heard the thud of him dropping to the ground and ran for him. Outside, Balaraba could hear voices saying, "There he is! Go get him!"

He pleaded with them. "Please, I have a child. I have a wife. I'm the breadwinner."

Balaraba watched through the window as the men took a machete and split open her husband's forehead. They stabbed him in the belly. They kept beating him even after his body went limp, bending his leg until it snapped. Then they left.

Balaraba was practically paralyzed with shock. She wasn't sure what to do. Her relatives decided it was best to let her stay in her own home to mourn. But two nights later the same group of fighters returned.

"There's the hypocrite," they said, pointing at Balaraba.

They knew she had been educated at a Western school and that she opposed Boko Haram. The fighters killed her husband's brother, who was living in the house, and grabbed Balaraba. They held her tight as they discussed whether they should murder her daughter. They threw the baby hard against the floor as they dragged away Balaraba. She thought it might have killed the child.

Balaraba was still weak when she got to the fighters' camp, and she remained physically sick for days. Militants were taking turns raping the women captives. The men who murdered her husband were there and one talked about "marrying" Balaraba. Seeing them made her want to kill herself. But she thought of her daughter. What if she had survived? Other girls around her were discussing suicide. Two talked openly about stealing guns and simultaneously shooting each other. Or maybe they should stab each other. They argued about which was best, so loudly that a fighter overheard. When he learned why they were arguing he grabbed them both and slit their throats.

Feigning illness, Balaraba soon realized, was a way to avoid the fate of other girls around her.

"Yes, yes, keep on killing them!" she would scream, making the fighters think she had gone mad. "Western education is forbidden, yes!"

The camp where Balaraba was being held doubled as a bomb-making factory. She watched fighters pack the bombs, stuffing sharp metal objects into a bag. They hauled in large packets of bullets, mixing them in some kind of oil that everyone in the camp thought was poison, to make them even more deadly. There was a special room where they stored all the bullets and the bombs.

One day, two of the fighters got into a raging argument. One ran into the bomb storage room and detonated explosives inside. The whole place lit up. So many people died—fighters as well as captives.

"There was nothing left of them but ashes," Balaraba said.

Later, the militants decided to round up some of the girls for a suicide mission. They gathered Balaraba and five other girls. Like Balaraba, most of them were teenagers. They handed them bombs stored inside large thermoses—the kind women use to haul food they are selling to market. They told them to go to a nearby village. Find the market crowd, push the button.

Balaraba and the other girls were terrified. They didn't want to kill anyone.

They walked along, trying to find a way out of this situation. One wanted to surrender to soldiers. But the military would never believe they were innocent, they quickly decided. Too risky. Maybe they should just kill themselves, another offered. But God opposed suicide, the others argued. They trudged in silence, not knowing what to do. They passed a well. Maybe we should throw our bombs down there, one girl suggested.

"That might end up killing all of us," Balaraba said.

But maybe it could work.

The six gathered around the well and peered inside. The outer lip was made of concrete, which might shield a blast. But it was hard to tell how deep it was. Someone suggested tying their hijabs together and lowering the smallest of the girls inside to check the water level. That was a terrible plan, Balaraba told them.

But the essence of the idea was a good one, the girls decided. They pulled their hijabs from their heads and fashioned a rope. They gathered the explosives in one thermos and tied it to the end. Carefully, they lowered the hijab rope into the well and let go, sprinting away. There was no splash, but also no explosion. It worked.

But now what should they do? They couldn't decide. If they carried on to the village, people would think they were bombers anyway and might shoot them. Or maybe they would encounter more Boko Haram members. They decided to head back to the camp and lie.

Mission accomplished, the teenagers told the fighters at the camp, they had hit their target—and had lost their hijabs as they were fleeing. The fighters rejoiced, and even threw a big celebration for the girls with a hearty meal.

"It was like they'd won the lottery," Balaraba said.

But after a few days, the militants still hadn't heard news of any kind of bombing in the town. They became suspicious. One of the girls offered to swear on a Koran that they had set off the bombs. That seemed to satisfy the militants. They were back to being thrilled with the girls.

"Do you know how to shoot to kill?" one fighter asked the young women, apparently thinking they now could be deployed in other ways, too.

They didn't. Fighters brought out guns. And live human targets— other Boko Haram members who had crossed them or girls in the camp who had annoyed them. They lined them up and began firing at them, for practice. Balaraba and the other girls from the well were sickened. One of them stood up and walked straight into the line of fire, killing herself.

Boko Haram replaced her with a new captive girl and sent her, along with Balaraba and the others, on another bombing mission, this time to a mosque in a nearby village.

The new girl immediately suggested ditching the bombs. She was from the area and knew a dam where they could stash them. But the other girls wanted to stick with their old plan. Again, they found a well, made a hijab rope and lowered the bombs down into it.

The group returned to camp expecting another happy reception. But the fighters were suspicious. How did they get there and back so quickly? The new girl said it was because she grew up in the area and knew the terrain well.

Before they could question the girls further, the camp's leaders heard some news: there had been a bombing in a nearby village. The militants cheered. The girls couldn't believe their luck. What timing! They were so relieved.

But as more details came out, the fighters realized the village that was struck was different from the one they ordered Balaraba and the girls to bomb. They called the new girl over and scolded her for bombing the wrong town. Then they shot her to death.

Balaraba was more terrified than ever. Days later, fighters told her she was going to wear a suicide belt. She faked a stomachache and got out of it. Another day, fighters shoved Balaraba into a car and drove her to the Monday Market in Maiduguri—her hometown market—where she was to detonate a bomb. This time, Balaraba really was sick and was so weak by the time they arrived at the market she couldn't move from the vehicle. She sat in the car as bombs exploded, killing numerous people.

Fighters took Balaraba back to camp, where she begged God to let her die but in a place where her body would be found so her relatives would know what had become of her.

Then one day all the fighters started scrambling. They're here, everyone was shouting. The camp was being invaded by a volunteer militia from Maiduguri that was dedicated to fighting Boko Haram. Before they arrived, Balaraba heard gunshots and explosion after explosion. Boko Haram was shooting up and bombing its own camp—and its own captives—so fighters could distract invading security forces while they made a getaway. It worked.

When help arrived, body parts were strewn across the camp. The shacks where the girls had lived were burning. Balaraba was lying on the ground near a blaze, her body on fire and bone poking from her leg where the skin was burned off. A young woman vigilante fighter about Balaraba's age pulled her to safety and took her to a hospital.

Balaraba stopped telling me about her experience and began to cry.

I realized that in all the time I had spent interviewing victims of Boko Haram, I had never learned an appropriate way to comfort anyone here. Was it OK to hug her? I didn't know. I know it's not my job as a journalist to hug anyone. I'm supposed to be an impartial observer. But that seemed callous in this case.

I walked to Balaraba and touched her arm. She lifted her gown and showed me the checkered burn scars all over her body.

Balaraba's situation was more extreme than other suicide bomber recruits I had met. But it essentially was the same. I didn't know what to do with it. My story on suicide bombers already had been published. I failed her. Balaraba's story went untold in the pages of my newspaper.

CHAPTER 19

Bring Back Our Girls

I UNPACKED MY suitcase in Dakar as Todd was waxing up his surf-board.

"I'll be back in a couple hours," he said.

While I was away, he had become addicted to this new sport.

The peninsula of Dakar exposed it to surf breaks from the north and the south, making almost every day a decent surf day. Dakar's coastline is not a celebrated surf spot, yet its waves have lured generations of surfers in the know. It was even one of the settings for the 1960s-era film *Endless Summer.* The water off Dakar was generally warm. And, sadly, years of overfishing meant that the local fishermen and Chinese industrial trawlers had vacuumed from the water almost every last shark. Minus some jagged, black rocks and prickly sea urchins, it was much safer than surfing many other places in the world.

Surf schools had popped up at a number of beaches. The teachers were wiry 20-something Senegalese men with stubby, bleached dreads. Some had grown up using fragments of fiberglass abandoned on the beach to teach themselves to surf and now flew to France for surf competitions.

Our family had taken a class with them in our first weeks in Dakar. I almost created an international incident when I came close to ramming another student, who happened to be the British ambassador. I hadn't been back on a board since. But while I was away Todd and the kids had been taking more lessons. The kids found it frightening. Predictably, Todd was pretty good at it, especially for a beginner. And he quickly improved, learning how to pop up and drop in and whatever all that new surfer terminology coming out of his mouth meant.

Now at least three times a week he was heading to beaches, where he tucked his surfboard under his arm, navigated through rowdy, sandy soccer games and plopped in the water between the kids swimming in their underwear and women in bikinis, burkinis or submerged in jeans and T-shirts.

He loved the mental challenge of getting over the fear of a giant wave and the helplessness of being tossed around like a rag doll under the water, only to surface shaken but still alive. He begged our kids to surf with him. He inhaled everything written by the surfing author William Finnegan. He bought new board shorts and rash guards and wax for his board. He started wearing his swimsuit all day long, just in case he found a break in work to hit the beach. He liked to wear one khaki-colored pair to parties. I called them his dress board shorts. He came home from the ocean with scrapes and bruises and the poisoned splinters of sea urchins stuck in his feet. He sat on our back porch for hours digging them out with tweezers and a syringe, a method the local surfers taught him.

All this helped him make peace with his situation. He was working reasonable hours. He spent time with the kids and had time for himself. He went for long runs. He read more books. He took up tennis. He joined an expat softball team. Every so often, he practiced with a Senegalese soccer team. He even got invited to join the Senegalese doctors' squash team.

He was playing Frisbee regularly and Jaime was joining him from time to time on the mostly expat team. A lot of the players worked at the U.S. embassy. I encouraged Jaime to keep playing. It was a good sourcing opportunity, I told him. In the past, some

American diplomats had refused to let me bring Jaime along for interviews there. I guess they didn't trust a West African. I was outraged. I thought if they got to know him maybe he'd earn their trust.

Jaime was strong, with defined muscles sculpted by sprinting down the corniche at 5 A.M. and doing push-ups and sit-ups and finger stretches.

"It's big in Sierra Leone," he explained.

He joined in games of soccer, a sport he had been playing since he was a kid in his village. He was young and single and getting to know Dakar through athletics. Todd was too, by doing things he never seemed to have time to do in Brooklyn as he juggled the commute, his job and the kids. His lanky arms and legs were transforming into long, defined muscles.

He wasn't finding a new community of friends who would go along with his we're-all-in-this-together plan of parenting. But that was OK, he decided. The Frisbee team gave him a weird mix of people he never would have gotten to know in New York: American missionaries, Peace Corps volunteers, Western diplomats, and Senegalese university students, one of whom doubled as a cattle herder.

The truth is that he was never really going to fit in here. Working remotely, Todd had no pool of colleagues as a base for making friends with other Senegalese men. He wasn't part of the American embassy clique or the U.N. clique. He had a working wife.

But he seemed to be in a much better mood. He was filling his spare time with his old friend, team sports, and a new one, surfing. I joked he was living a country club lifestyle.

Back in New York, many men his age were living out their midlife crises on those weird, extra-long skateboards that seemed to be everywhere.

"Skateboards Are the New Combover for Men Chasing Their Youth," a headline in the *New York Post* said. "Skateboarding Past a Midlife Crisis" was my own paper's take on the trend.

"My kids grew old, so I got a dog. My dog grew old, so I got a skateboard," our story quoted one adherent. "That was what knocked the cobwebs out of my head."

Substitute *surfboard* for *skateboard*—that was Todd's situation.

As he reveled in the extra time that he was able to find in the day, I began to try to meet him when I could.

We emerged from our separate offices on polar ends of the house to gather on the back patio to have lunch together while we watched the cat gingerly step across the broken security glass that topped our villa walls. Things were generally less chilly between us.

"What is it you like about surfing anyway?" I asked him one afternoon as he hosed off his wet suit in the backyard.

"It's terrifying," he said. "I feel so small as a human surrounded by this powerful natural world. It just reminds me I'm a pesky human with a shelf life."

I just couldn't relate. I would rather step into a conflict zone than surf a giant wave. I had a better idea of how to protect myself from bullets.

"Honey," I said another day during our lunch meet-up, trying to gently raise a sore subject. "Why did you leave the kids alone while I was in Niger?"

"They're getting older, you know," he started in. Our son was now ten, after all, and the girls were nine.

"The guard is always outside if something really bad happens," he continued.

Fair point, I thought to myself.

"And we know all the neighbors."

This was true.

"Can we try to limit this though," I said, "just in case?"

"Of course," he said. "I'm not going to do it all the time."

"You seem to be feeling better," I said, raising another sore subject.

"I am," he said. "I'm worried about my work but I'm trying to make the most of the situation. I like it here."

IT HAD BEEN weeks and the editors hadn't even taken a look at my story on women seeking divorces. Zalika's tale was stored in my laptop. My story on the investment bank CEO was holding, too. It held for so long, in fact, that Toyin left the bank before it could get published.

There was just too much news going on in America. Trump's actions had gone international, consuming most of my editors' workdays. A Russia probe was heating up and Trump was calling for immunity for his national security adviser. The courts were hashing out Trump's travel ban. Someone leaked some of Trump's tax documents. The news seemed like it had become All Trump, All the Time.

Before I started my job, one of the paper's top editors had pulled me into his office to offer advice based on his experience. He had arrived in Nairobi in his new job as East Africa bureau chief just a couple of days after the attacks of September 11. He panicked at first, he said, but eventually he found it liberating. He wrote about whatever he wanted. The paper still needed to fill the international pages. What was happening in East Africa still mattered. He just learned to let go of the idea that his stories would make the front page.

I wasn't that Zen. I felt like I was failing.

Another colleague had been more pessimistic, warning me about the stress of this beat.

"Half the time you're traveling in very difficult conditions," he told me, "and the other half of the time you're panicked about where you're going to be traveling to next."

I was careening toward panic mode. What if the editors noticed I wasn't on the road? I was being ridiculous, of course. No one was hounding me for stories. I hadn't talked to my editor in days. No one even seemed to remember I was working at the paper. But insecurity is half of what fuels most reporters' ambition.

Trump sucking the air out of everything meant my stories about women finding their way were sitting in a long queue with probably dozens of other stories from around the globe that were stacked up as Trump fired another cabinet member or tweeted another insult.

But I was personally benefitting from America's obsession with itself: our family was finding more ways to be together. Without editors hounding me at night, the five of us began taking walks after dinner. I got up early and made soft-boiled eggs and mango smoothies for breakfast. We started going away on the weekends, renting a house in the countryside along a stretch of beach, where the kids frolicked in the sand before slurping down ceviche for dinner. I started to like the taste of Nescafé. Making powdered coffee was so much simpler than grinding beans. Even the cat was more at ease, adopting weird sleeping positions, sprawling out flat on his back, paws in the air, all over the house. "Relaxation cat," Luther called him.

A CALL FROM Shehu one afternoon burst my family-life bubble. He told me the students from Chibok had been transferred to an American-themed university in Nigeria that had designed a program to catch them up with their studies and then allow them to pursue a college degree. It was a privileged outcome for this group of Boko Haram hostages.

It irritated me that we still hadn't been able to meet the young women. University officials now were controlling them and for weeks were being cagey when I asked about whether it was possible to visit them on campus. Most of the women were in their 20s but were not allowed to leave campus on their own or do much of anything for themselves. They needed to be kept safe, the university asserted. Almost every moment of their day was programmed. This was deliberate. The university thought it would keep their mind off their years of trauma with Boko Haram.

Shehu's vision was getting worse and he was spending more time on a plot of farmland he bought outside the capital. But he wanted to help me with my story. He proposed complicated scenarios to get me in the same room as the women.

"Here is what we will do," he said, his voice barely audible over a crackling phone line. "First, we enlist one of the women's relatives and have them call for a girl. They will proclaim illness and say she is needed back home. Then we will send a car to pick her up from the university and drive her to Maiduguri. There, we will meet with her. . . ."

It wasn't a terrible idea, presuming the woman and her parents agreed to it. But what if something happened to them on the road to Maiduguri? Boko Haram sometimes launched attacks there. It was too risky.

Eventually, university officials invited me to campus so the women could get familiar with me—that was their plan at least. I sat in the back of their classrooms as they practiced English. I went to debate night, where they argued over the benefits and drawbacks of social media. But I wasn't allowed to talk with them—the university assigned a minder to trail me and make sure I didn't. That time would come, they kept telling me. I flew back home.

I asked the university if we could supply the women with cameras to take their own photos. No, was the answer. Maybe I could follow them for a whole year, and write a series of stories on their development. We'll see, they said.

A couple weeks later they agreed to let me come back with Adam to photograph the women who had told officials they wanted their pictures taken.

They didn't have to hide their faces. The women's identities had never been a mystery—their names and photos had been blasted across the world in the search to find them. Even when they were rescued the government paraded the women before the cameras.

We spent the weekend with the group, going to 5 A.M. yoga class and Sunday church services. We hung out in their dorm. Yes, the women were former Boko Haram hostages, but in many ways they were also typical 20-somethings—selfie-loving millennials like any women their age anywhere in the world. They grabbed my phone and posed for photo after photo.

But I still wasn't allowed to ask them questions or have real conversations. It was awkward.

University officials had decided we would photograph as many of the women who wanted to be photographed. Anyone left out would be jealous, they said. But officials also didn't want to disrupt the students' school program so they insisted we photograph the dozens of women—more than 80 of them—in one day, for as long as it takes.

Adam set up a mini studio in a basement classroom in the dormitory. I was still under the impression I would be able to interview some of the women. I thought maybe I could talk to them in a separate room as Adam worked. I was curious to hear from them how their experiences compared to other women I'd met. But the university official, an American man, who ran their program said I was allowed to interview only a half-dozen of them.

We gathered in a conference room—the administrator insisted on sitting in on my talks with them. He warned me that if I asked them about their experiences with Boko Haram, he would have Adam and me escorted off campus.

"It's just too traumatizing for them," he said.

I had met with women who were massacre victims, suicide bomber recruits and rape victims. All of them spoke to me willingly, because they wanted me, and the world, to know what had happened to them. It infuriated me that now someone, particularly a man, was controlling what this group of former hostages would tell me. They were grown women now. Shouldn't that decision be up to them?

And I had been confident their words would offer some kind of

wisdom, maybe even some kind of closure, about all of the trauma
the war had inflicted on women. They were on the other side of it
now. What had they learned? Could they offer hope for the others?

I could have called off the whole thing. But the editors were
counting on these photos. There was no question they would draw
more attention to the war. And I did still believe the images would
be as powerful as their words. It just seemed ridiculous they were
sitting in front of me and a male university official was blocking me
from a meaningful discussion with them. But the photos would
allow the women to present themselves to the world outside of the
confines of their captors, in clothing they chose, expressing themselves how they wanted. It would give them honor and dignity, and
I hoped it would replace the only other grim image they were
known for around the globe.

I relented, settling into interviews that consisted of questions
about their coursework. Even questions about their parents were
deemed off-limits. One woman's father had recently died after
being hospitalized just miles from the campus. Because of security
concerns, officials didn't let her go to him right away. And by the
time they did organize an escort, he was already dead.

The women went to their rooms to get dressed and put on
makeup for their photos. I wandered around the dorm. A dolphin
painting marked the entrance. The classrooms displayed photos of
Spider-Man and multiplication tables. It was as if the goal was to
preserve the women in childhood so they would never face their
trauma from an adult perspective. Their therapy sessions, for the
most part, were taking place in English, a language that they all
struggled with.

On the other hand, the university was providing them air-
conditioning and Wi-Fi, movie nights and karaoke, and a better
education than they ever would have received in their village
school in Chibok. The women who probably didn't grow up with
running water even had their own tablets, which had been donated

to them by a well-wisher who had been following their journey for years.

I had pursued this story with mixed feelings. It wasn't right, I know, but I felt like these women were practically spoiled compared to other victims I'd met. So many women kidnapped at their age were dead. The Chibok girls had iPads. They were the lucky ones. But this existence, particularly because of their lack of freedom, was depressing.

Later, I sat behind my computer rereading old stories written about the girls' disappearance and the agonizing wait for their return. It became clear to me they had become international symbols for Boko Haram's victims who would forever remain anonymous and unaccounted for. Those other names never would be broadcast around the globe or hoisted on signs at the Oscars. Many of their own mothers would never even know what had happened to them.

These students from a village school had become unwitting representatives of all the dead and missing victims of a crisis that for years had upended a poor, remote spot on the globe. They became daughters of Nigeria. They were daughters of the world.

I couldn't write a proper story about the women since I wasn't allowed to have meaningful conversations with them. My editors and I decided I would write an essay on how the world sees them, as the face of victims of a heinous war. *Wouldn't it be better for the women to tell their own stories?* I kept thinking. I hoped one day one of them would write her own book.

My essay ran on the front page, and online the paper published Adam's cascading portraits of 83 of the women. Each was presented individually, strong and powerful, rather than a group of anonymous, hopeless, scared girls in a Boko Haram hideout. Some of the portraits were even short video clips, moving images that brought them to life.

They provoked strong reactions. Some readers were outraged.

"This is a serious ethical breach of these traumatized women.

The photographs offend me: you have made these women appear to be as dolls or mute puppets," one reader commented. "You are using their story to sell your newspapers: your gain, their price."

A Duke University professor publicly critiqued the portraits as evoking only "a single frozen moment in each woman's life."

We had tried to give each of the women a chance to be shown as they chose—to bring them to life, to let the world know they were more than just a hashtag. My editor disagreed with the criticism when I showed it to him and told me to brush it off. But it was hard for me to have a thick skin at this point. Had I failed the women and all the victims?

Some readers, however, understood exactly what we were trying to convey. One commented:

> Thank you, NYT, for this stunningly moving re-
> minder these survivors are offering in hopes of sav-
> ing their missing sisters. Yes, we saw the initial
> photos two months after their capture but our
> minds left them at that age as we prayed for their
> return. I was shocked at the realization that these
> girls are now women. Beautiful young women try-
> ing to recapture a life stolen from them. Renewed
> prayers for them and all still captive. God bless them
> and give them strength.

CHAPTER 20

"Halfway Between a Nightmare and a Miracle"

IT WAS ALMOST the rainy season in Dakar but the heat and humidity had yet to descend. We could still sit outside in the evenings without sweating and watch the cat romp through the trees.

We were getting braver about leaving the kids home alone for a few hours at a time. Luther was in his first year of middle school. And the bureau's new security guard—the other one had caved to his wife and moved to the village—was always around if something really went wrong. Todd and I stole away to hunt for tofu at a Chinese market deep in the city or to eat tiny clams at fish shacks on the beach at sunset.

We had, after two years, figured out how to make a bit of space for our marriage in addition to our careers and parenting. For so long, we'd been on a wild seesaw of trying to prove who had the most work or the heaviest burden or the greater needs. But there would never be a winner. We were in a nearly impossible situation if we both wanted careers. So, instead, we settled for a couple of hours here and there at a plastic table on a rocky beach, eating fresh-caught mustardy grilled grouper.

Todd had also started a passionate campaign to get back to his old job in New York. He'd taken a career hit for long enough, he argued. The organization needed him at headquarters where he felt he could make more of a difference than dialing into conference calls from his little lonely office. He argued that New York City was my paper's headquarters, too, where dozens of reporters were located. It was a city where we could both have fulfilling jobs.

He had a point. Maybe finally it's time for the suburbs, he argued. I wasn't 100 percent sold. We'd come all this way, been through so many startling, mind-expanding experiences, only to find ourselves right back where we'd started.

RAMADAN HAD JUST begun and the expats in town were organizing a big weekend Frisbee tournament. The Peace Corps volunteers and missionaries were coming in to play from their posts in the countryside and across the border in Mauritania. The regulars would show up, too. Enough players had signed up to field five or six teams.

I encouraged Jaime to sign up, and he did. The teams were chosen by lottery, and he wound up on the same team as Todd and Luther, who had inherited the athletic abilities of his dad and was allowed to play on an adult team. They were all excited.

The day of the big Frisbee tournament came and the three of them marched around like a bunch of bros, in matching yellow T-shirt uniforms. Jaime wore a black compression band around one knee to help the dull ache that sometimes crept up from "that bullet," as he called his civil war wound.

My daughters were too young to play in the tournament, and I was too uninterested, but we showed up to cheer them on. Someone had brought powdered dye to spray around the audience, the kind you throw at an Indian Holi festival. Jaime grabbed a handful and tossed it into the air, creating a cloud over the field as the wild wind whipped the powder. Everyone's skin and clothing soon were covered in pinks and purples and blues. Chasing after the disc was all the more exhausting as it bounced around in the gusts. After four hard games that day, our team earned a spot in the championship match.

The girls and I lined up on the field to watch. Todd scored a goal. Luther threw a flawless pass. And in the final minutes of the game Jaime made a pass to Luther in the end zone, or whatever you call it, scoring a point. Everyone went nuts. The game was so close.

Then someone threw a long pass to Jaime. The disc sailed through the air for what seemed like an agonizing minute. Jaime was zigzagging underneath, reaching for the disc. He dove for it. His whole body was parallel to the horizon before he crashed, hard, to the ground. He howled. He couldn't get up. His teammates gathered around him, staring at the lump protruding from where his knee should be. He was badly hurt.

Just about everyone's worst fear is getting injured in a foreign place. It wasn't only me who was abroad, but Jaime, too. Had this injury happened in Sierra Leone, I'm sure he could have told me where to take him to get the best possible care. But he didn't know anything about medical care in Dakar. And neither did I, really.

Dakar didn't have a vast emergency response system the way New York did. We were familiar with the medical service that makes house calls—the one that plucked out my son's mangoworm. But this was more serious. I called the service to send a private ambulance, the only kind of ambulance that exists in Dakar, and sat with Jaime to wait. He tried to lift his leg. The bottom half below the knee sank to the bench, attached to the rest of his limb only by the skin that surrounded it. It was nauseating.

The ambulance took forever. A little girl kept passing by and asking Jaime a million questions about what had happened. He was grimacing in pain but too polite to not answer. I shooed her away but she kept coming back.

"Who's your mommy?" I asked her, hoping I could enlist her parent in keeping her away.

"Who's *his* mommy?" she asked, pointing to Jaime, wondering why his mommy wasn't helping him with his boo-boo.

Jaime paused, uncertain what to say and temporarily overcome with sadness. His mother couldn't help him. She was a poor widow battling her own health problems, living in another country hundreds of miles away.

"I'm his mommy," I said.

The girl's eyes shifted back and forth between him and me, him and me.

"But you're not the same color."

That made even Jaime laugh. But I recognized my role. I needed to help him with what increasingly was looking like a severe injury that would take at least a few weeks of physical therapy to heal. I was his boss. I had brought him to Dakar. I had even encouraged him to play in the stupid Frisbee tournament. This was on me.

The ambulance arrived and we decided to take Jaime to a clinic downtown where friends had been treated for stomach illnesses and stitches. My husband rode along with Jaime as I raced home to get cash. I knew the health system in many countries in West Africa operated on a pay-as-you-go basis. If you didn't pay upfront, you didn't get treated.

By the time I got to the clinic, Jaime was laid out on a bed with a doctor hovering over him. Todd was sitting down, arms folded, glaring at the doctor.

"How bad is the damage?" I said to the doctor as I walked into the room.

"Who are you?" he said.

"Oh, sorry, I'm Jaime's friend."

"Under Senegalese law, I don't have tell you anything," he snapped.

I looked at Jaime. "Do you know what's going on?"

He didn't.

I looked at Todd.

"He won't tell me a thing," he said.

I took a deep breath. I was going to have to make this guy like me if we wanted information. I went to work complimenting the doctor on his amazing skills and procedures, massaging the male ego to make him share with us the most basic of information about the patient under his care.

It took only a minute to untangle the source of his hostility. Todd had mentioned to the doctor that his spouse was coming with cash to pay for the treatment. But in the stress of the moment, he messed up and used the French word for "husband" instead of "wife." Senegal is a place where gay sex is illegal and homosexuality is not socially acceptable. The doctor must have thought Jaime was part of a multiracial gay Frisbee league of foreigners. He didn't like it.

I explained I was Todd's wife and that he didn't have a husband, that Jaime was my employee, and that we really needed to know what was going on.

It worked. He couldn't tell us much though. Jaime had blown some ligaments. But the X-rays were fuzzy and the MRI machine was broken. He suggested a CAT scan, if we'd agree to pay for it, just to be totally safe there wasn't some kind of freak artery damage. We agreed, and Todd left to get even more cash.

A few minutes later the doctor wheeled Jaime out of the scan room.

"Unfortunately," he said, "your friend needs surgery. Right now."

During the fall or during the transport to the clinic—we weren't sure exactly when or how—arteries to Jaime's leg had been severed. The blood wasn't flowing to his foot. They would have to amputate if he didn't have immediate emergency surgery.

"We can't do that kind of surgery at this clinic," the doctor said. "But I've called the top vascular surgeon in Dakar who works at another hospital. He can do it right away."

I'd never heard of the hospital he suggested. I had no idea if it had a good reputation. I frantically texted friends. No one knew anything about it.

"Get him out of the country ASAP," one friend advised.

For most injuries, expats and wealthy West Africans shift into default medevac mode, flying to find care in a Western nation's hospital they are certain they can trust. It always made me cringe a little. In war-torn places or remote villages, health care was lacking. But we were in a major regional capital city with big universities and corporations. Surely Dakar offered top-notch health care if we got to the right place.

At the clinic, I tried to pay the bill for the scans and the ambulance as quickly as I could but the receptionist was insisting on a proper receipt, stamped and signed. It was taking forever. The ambulance driver was outside honking. Finally we finished up. I rushed out and hopped in the ambulance.

We arrived at a sprawling university-like hospital campus with dozens of small buildings, some of them shabby-looking. The ambulance stopped outside the cardiac unit, and the driver disappeared into a building. Five minutes passed. Ten more minutes passed. We were so close to getting Jaime his emergency surgery. The wait was agonizing.

Two orderlies emerged to take Jaime from the ambulance and wheel him up a steep concrete ramp to the second floor of a building. They moved Jaime to a stretcher lining the side of a large, empty, chairless waiting room and left him. I was alone with a man who was about to have his leg cut off if he didn't get emergency surgery.

I started frantically searching for a doctor or nurse who could help. I walked down the hall, peering into rooms filled with patients lying on the floor or on worn-out mattresses. Plenty of sick people—but no one seemed to work there. Finally a man in scrubs emerged from a stairwell. The surgeon, he told us, lived far outside of town but was in a taxi on his way here. He was pretty sure he could do the surgery but we'd need to talk to him about the risks when he arrived. What risks? I was confused.

"In the meantime," he said, "you'll need to pay for some blood work to be done at the lab."

"Yes, of course," I said.

We had to wait for the surgeon to arrive but there was nothing we could do about that. I tried not to show any fear to Jaime. He was in too much pain to notice much of anything.

A nurse arrived and drew Jaime's blood into three vials. She pushed them into my hand. The glass was warm against my palm.

"Why did you give these to me?"

"Take them to the lab," she said.

"Me?"

"Yes, you," she said. "You're paying for the tests, right?"

She gave me vague directions to the hospital lab and I sprinted to my car, worried I'd never find it and Jaime would lose his leg because of my bad navigation. It was getting dark and only a few of the streetlights on the campus were working, making it difficult to tell where I was going. I was worried I wouldn't find my way back. I was worried I'd drop the vials. I was worried about everything. Someone walking down the road guided me, and soon I was racing up the stairs to the lab. It was empty. It was Sunday evening, and I was terrified the staff had gone home for the weekend. I started yelling.

"Hello! Hello! Is anyone here?"

A sleepy technician in a white coat opened up a door down the hall. He came out and I handed him the vials of blood.

"Where's your receipt?"

"What do you mean?" I said.

"You have to pay for this first."

"Where do I pay?"

"At the cashier."

"Where's that?" I asked, my blood pressure rising.

The technician pointed me in the right direction and I ran down the stairs to find the cashier's building exactly where he said it would be. I raced inside and waited as patiently as I could while the worker took my money and wrote out a detailed, stamped receipt as the vials of blood in my hand cooled.

I raced back up to the lab with the receipt, again yelling for the technician. He looked through it. Satisfied that I had paid, he took the vials.

"Come back in an hour," he said.

"An hour?"

"Yes, that's how long it takes."

Jaime didn't have an hour to spare—but I had no choice. I raced back to Jaime to wait for the surgeon to arrive. No one there had offered him any kind of pain medicine or examination. Todd showed up with a new pile of cash. Still no surgeon. We sat in silence, swatting away mosquitoes that flew through the open door. At least the evening breeze cooled the room.

"What if the guy doesn't make it here," I whispered to Todd, starting to panic.

"It'll be fine," he said, having shifted to his steady-as-a-rock mode.

When it was time to pick up Jaime's lab results, I rushed back to the lab and shouted for the technician, and he emerged with a printout of findings.

When I got back to Jaime, Todd was outside on a phone call with friends, still trying to understand if we were at the best hospital we could be. It was starting not to matter. I didn't see how we could get Jaime settled in another institution before it was too late.

While we were outside making calls, the surgeon arrived, a Tunisian man probably in his 40s. He stared at Jaime.

"Did you do this robbing a house?" he said.

"No," Jaime said, "I have a job. I was playing sports."

The surgeon scoffed.

I knew that North Africans could sometimes be racist against dark-skinned Africans. I had once written a story about how that kind of racism plays out when poor migrants from West Africa pass through Libya and are taunted and beaten. But I didn't anticipate this from a doctor.

"You were high, weren't you?" the surgeon said, looking at the blue and pink dye stains on Jaime's shirt and head and hands.

"No," he said, "I don't even use drugs."

Todd and I walked back into the room to find the surgeon hovering over Jaime. I explained I was Jaime's boss and he was a close friend and we were managing his care.

"He's a reporter?" he said.

"Yes, he works with me. We're both journalists."

The surgeon seemed satisfied by this.

"This is a very complicated surgery and one we don't do often in Dakar," he explained. "I'm not sure I know how to do it, even. But if I don't try it, your friend is going to lose his leg. So, should we do it?"

Jaime and I looked at each other. It was not reassuring news. But I was thankful for the surgeon's honesty.

"I think we have to, Jaime," I said.

"Yes, we have to try."

"OK," the surgeon said. "We have six hours from the time the injury happened to do the surgery to ensure he'll keep his leg. What time did this happen?"

"Five hours ago," I said.

"We need to hurry," the surgeon said. "But I should warn you, if there are complications I won't be able to help you. No one in Dakar will. No one anywhere around here will. You need to get him out of the country afterward, to America or Europe."

That was going to be difficult. Jaime had a passport from Sierra Leone. As a young black African Muslim male, his profile checked every box that ensured extra scrutiny at any Western consulate office. In America, Trump was trying to build a wall to keep out immigrants, making plans to deport noncitizens and separating migrant children from families. In Europe, far right groups were gaining popularity, and numerous nations were pursuing policies that created a hostile environment for immigrants. The French president was specifically targeting West Africans with proposals to toughen immigration and asylum laws. Even South Africa wasn't an option; its visa process was laborious.

I started making calls to everyone I could think of who might be able to help us. It was late Sunday night of a three-day local holiday weekend. An embassy friend told me an American visa would take several days and was far from guaranteed. I couldn't get anyone else to pick up the phone. Consulates wouldn't even be open until Tuesday. My head was spinning as I tried to think of a solution, when the surgeon came back.

"They messed up the blood tests. We'll need to do them again."

We were less than one hour away from Jaime losing his leg. And now I needed to go get more lab results.

"And I'll need you also to buy the drugs for the surgery," the surgeon said, handing me a long list of medications and bandages.

"Sure, where do I pay for this?" I said.

"At the pharmacy where you buy them."

With the clock ticking, I had to do another lab run as well as hope the hospital pharmacy was open late on a Sunday night to buy medication for the surgery.

"Dionne! Dionne!" Jaime was calling from down the hall.

They had wheeled him into a room and placed him on a dirty rubber mattress. It was common practice here, but I didn't know until then that patients had to bring their own sheets.

Blood, drugs and now bedding. And time was running out. I was utterly overwhelmed. A rush of emotions came over me as I saw Jaime lying there alone in a bare hospital room, shoved to the side as though he were forgotten. Part of me wanted to just stand and sob.

"We can do this," Todd assured me.

He ran outside and hopped in a cab to race home and get sheets and pillows. He needed to check on our children anyway. They had been alone for most of the night at this point. I rushed to the lab, woke the technician again, requested more tests and asked for directions to the hospital pharmacy.

The building with the pharmacy sign looked like it was from the set of *M*A*S*H*. The windows were boarded and there was a padlock across the weathered door. A passerby pointed me to another building.

"Knock on that window," he said. "Hard."

I pounded and pounded until an annoyed woman slid open the window. She looked at my list of medications.

"We don't have all of that here," she said.

"My friend needs emergency surgery. Where can I get it?"

"Outside," she said.

"What do you mean, outside?"

She pointed to the gate of the hospital.

"You'll have to find a pharmacy."

My heart was pounding as I drove up and down the street lined by people still coming off their breaking-of-the-fast high; I looked for the flashing green cross that signifies a pharmacy. So many of them were darkened. It was almost midnight. Jaime was going to have to have his leg amputated because I couldn't find an open pharmacy.

In my time in West Africa reporting in some of the most severe places in the world, I had listened to so many horrible stories that I had steeled myself against any emotional response to what people were telling me or to situations I was seeing play out in front of me.

The structural forces in play—whether it was corruption, climate change, demographics or war—sometimes seemed so insurmountable and fundamentally unfixable that it was almost easier to put on a brave face and assume the journalist's role. I was an observer, not an activist; a professional, not a friend to the people I was writing about. I could share their experiences, be moved by them, tell the world about them and still keep a healthy distance.

But with Jaime it was different. As his boss, I felt responsible for him. He was a friend. I cared about him. And crossing that deeply personal threshold was terrifying. I nearly fell to pieces on the drive down that empty four-lane road under nonworking streetlamps and passing darkened shop after darkened shop.

I spotted the green glow of a cross on the other side of the street. An open pharmacy. I pulled along the sidewalk, barreling the car onto the concrete, ran inside and handed the cashier the list.

"We don't have all those drugs here," she said.

"Where can I get them at this hour?"

She mumbled something I didn't understand and turned her attention to another customer. I lost it.

"You need to help me right now or my friend is never going to walk again!" I yelled.

She wrote the name of the pharmacy on a piece of paper and pointed down the road. I tried to stay calm as I drove, passing intersection after intersection with no sign of anything. Finally, I spotted another flashing green cross. I parked the car between the waiting taxis outside.

"My friend needs emergency surgery," I said shoving the piece of paper into the clerk's hand.

"Um-hm," he said, eyeballing the paper and turning to his computer.

"Do you have the drugs?"

"Um-hm," he hummed, buried behind his screen.

"I need to know!" I said, raising my voice for the second time that night.

He flipped his computer screen around to show me he was already tallying the receipt and printing it out. His co-worker was even piling the medicine into bags. Not only did the pharmacy have everything I needed, but I was in the express lane. The pharmacist didn't ask me for an explanation about the urgency. My face said it all. He handed me the bags of drugs and bandages. I wanted to hug him.

I picked up the blood results and got back to the hospital, only to learn that the doctor had forgotten to give me the name of one of the medicines he needed. And he'd forgotten to order one of the blood tests. Other than that, the surgery was ready to happen—once the operating room technician arrived.

I was shaking as I made the lab and pharmacy rounds again and came back to the hospital. Still no operating room technician. By the time the technician showed up, the surgeon had fallen asleep and had to be awakened. They rolled Jaime into surgery at 2 A.M., 10 hours after the injury.

I was convinced Jaime, a guy who had escaped civil war with a bullet wound, was now going to have his leg amputated—and not even the same leg the bullet had entered—after an accident playing in a Frisbee game I'd encouraged him to take part in. I felt terrible for having lured him into my orbit.

As a Westerner, my existence in Dakar had been more like hovering over and around society here, as I made my rounds from beachside seafood restaurants to supermarkets with imported asparagus to hotels with bouncy castles. Reporting, and our relative wealth, had provided a barrier between my family life and the firsthand stories I had been hearing.

Now I was on the inside. And even with a savings account, the vast resources of the *Times* and a clean bed with sheets and a pillow waiting for me at home, I was helpless. It was a role I wasn't used to.

The OR technician was so tired as he wheeled Jaime down the steep ramp that he slipped and nearly lost control of the stretcher. Two of Jaime's friends—fellow refugees from Sierra Leone who were living in Dakar—showed up to stay with him during the surgery so my husband and I could get some sleep. During the operation, Jaime was numb from the waist down but otherwise he was awake for the whole thing. A nurse had to swat mosquitoes from his face because his hands were tied away from his sides, Jesus-on-the-cross style. The surgeon paused, mid-operation, to break his Ramadan fast. Another nurse kept falling asleep. The operating room itself was filled with boxes and construction material, in the process of being renovated.

After four hours, Jaime made it out of surgery.

A Frisbee teammate of Jaime's who was also a nurse practitioner joined us at the hospital. Not only was her French better than mine but her skills included fluency in medical terminology. In the middle of the night, in an operating room under construction, a sleepy, hungry, racist surgeon had carried out an arterial bypass surgery with grace. And it worked. If he hadn't saved Jaime's leg, he at least bought him some time.

Over the next five days, we had to bring Jaime all of his meals in the hospital. No one bathed him. No one changed his catheter. A nurse came once a day to check the pulse in his foot, but never compared it to the pulse in his other foot. An orthopedic surgeon arrived a day after his surgery and made Jaime try to walk on his leg. It happened while I was out of the room—Jaime followed his instructions, putting weight on his precariously repaired artery. I stayed awake all that night, terrified Jaime had inadvertently ripped open the arteries in his leg again and no one would notice until it was too late.

Everyone at the hospital seemed to operate on a parallel track. There was no "system" of health care in place. Yet Dakar is full of great doctors. It's also full of intellectuals, businesspeople and politicians who get sick and injured. Dakar's medical school trains its surgeons in the latest, most complicated techniques. But without patients, they don't get any practice. Health care doesn't improve here because the people who can't afford treatment don't get treated, and those who can afford it automatically go abroad when they are in need of medical attention.

One of Jaime's friends described health care in Dakar as "halfway between a nightmare and a miracle." I couldn't agree more.

Jaime's doctors did their job but the process was beyond stressful. What if Jaime had been alone? Who would race to the lab? What if we hadn't been able to afford the scans and the drugs? I looked at the patients in the hospital lying on bloodied rubber mattresses in the other rooms. Who was running to the lab for them?

America's health-care system was far from perfect, too. My newspaper was documenting a crisis in rural health care where people had to drive for hours to reach the nearest hospital. Hospital deserts, these hospital-less patches of the country were called.

"I keep thinking of my friend from back home," Jaime told me one day in the hospital room.

When Jaime was young, he and his friends liked to play soccer during the rainy season. His hometown had terrible drainage but the kids thought all the flooding added a new level of fun. The deep puddles and splashes of water became part of the game. One afternoon, rainwater was gushing hard across the street where the boys were trying to kick the ball. Jaime's friend stepped into a pothole and fell. He had broken his leg, or worse. The boys carried him to a friend's house and worried about what to do. The nearest hospital was 15 miles away. Public transportation didn't exist. And even if they could find a ride, there was no guarantee anyone could help; most of the doctors had fled the countryside because of the civil war erupting all around. The boy's leg was amputated. For years he used sticks as crutches, often falling to the ground. He usually resorted to crawling. His friends gave him a Pidgin nickname: "Body-Walk."

"Are my friends going to call me 'Body-Walk,' too?" Jaime asked.

We decided to take the surgeon's advice to try to get Jaime abroad to make sure complications didn't arise. But we still needed a visa.

"Why don't we try for a Spanish visa," Todd said, hatching a plan out loud.

"Spain? But I don't know anyone in the consulate," I said.

Todd was thinking of a Spanish woman he knew from the crew of moms at the school; he'd never given up trying to make friends with them. This mom was one of the nice ones.

"It's a long shot," he said, "but maybe she knows someone who can help."

Todd called his mom friend, she called someone else who called someone else and soon I was on the phone with the Spanish consular to Senegal, who assured me her country could process a medical emergency visa in a matter of hours for anyone who was in need. I was exhilarated and amazed that we were able to make this happen.

The next day a team of doctors arrived from Germany, where the medevac plane was stationed, to accompany Jaime. The guy who tried to sail to Europe in a wooden canoe was boarding a private air ambulance to Madrid, courtesy of *The New York Times*. As they were loading him onto a stretcher, one of the medevac doctors discovered his wallet was missing. He eyeballed Jaime's West African friends, and even Jaime himself, with suspicion.

"Jaime can't move," I said. "I am certain he didn't steal your wallet." I wanted to scream at him for daring to blame Jaime. But I had to be as nice as I could. We'd made it this far. We needed him to get Jaime to better treatment.

A few hours after the team left with Jaime, the doctor sent me a text that his hotel in Dakar had contacted him to tell him he dropped his wallet in a taxi. The Senegalese cabdriver had turned it in with its contents intact. Of course.

Jaime landed in Madrid and was taken to a private hospital, where a new doctor there gave him one of those if-you-can't-speak-the-language-get-out-of-the-country speeches, refusing to offer a diagnosis in a language Jaime understood. A ligament specialist was ordered but a week later still hadn't shown up.

Finally, with the help of the Spanish photographer friend who had first introduced me to Jaime, we moved Jaime to a public clinic in Barcelona where the head of the hospital was a physician who had volunteered with Doctors Without Borders during the Ebola outbreak in West Africa. He had witnessed firsthand how the disease had torn apart communities like the one Jaime was from. He was familiar with the *Times'* prize-winning work on the outbreak— and with the stories, in particular, that Jaime had helped work on.

"It is an honor to treat you," he told Jaime.

BACK IN DAKAR two months later, Jaime arrived, leg intact, to begin physical therapy. He had lost so much muscle mass that when he showed up at the office, he looked like a scrawny old man. He needed another surgery in a few months to fix his ligaments, so he was making do in the meantime maneuvering metal crutches across Dakar's sandy streets and rocky pathways. In all likelihood, with the help of a lifetime of blood thinners, he was going to be fine.

Jaime posted a photo of himself and his bandaged leg on Facebook. His friends commented, nicknaming him "Wan Foot Jumpie," in Pidgin. It means "The One Foot Jumper." That was a lot better than Body-Walk. Jaime loved it.

WITH JAIME STABLE, I wanted to fly off to spend a week camping to document a modern-day range war between farmers and migrating cattle herders in Nigeria who were being violently chased off land they had used for centuries by a booming population and a climate that was increasingly hostile to grasslands their cattle fed on.

I knew Shehu had spent several days with a group of herders for a story he wrote. He had told me he slept high in the branches of a tree at their camp to avoid being trampled by cattle roaming in the dark. I called Shehu to ask if he could tap his connections and join me.

But Shehu's tree-sleeping days were over, I learned. His vision was almost totally gone. He was in the process of permanently retiring to his farm.

"I am sure my eyes will open up," he told me. "Until then, you'll be just fine."

I wasn't sure about his eyes but he was right about me being fine. However, I decided to find a group of herders to camp with who slept safely on the ground, not in trees. I would never be as badass as Shehu.

Out in the bush, in the middle of absolutely nowhere, the herders welcomed me like I was a long-lost sister, helping set up my tent amid 300 noisy cows and cooking me bowls of baobab leaf stew.

"You'll go camping with herders and not with me?" Todd teased me when I had told him what I was doing.

"It's different," I said. "This is work."

In the camp, women were in charge of cooking, cleaning and childcare. But they maintained their independence. They slept in their own elaborate huts made of sticks and tarp. Romance happened when their husbands came for a visit. Their setup made me think of old friends of mine in Chicago. A couple, each with their own careers, who had married later in life and lived in side-by-side apartments so they could enjoy each other's company when they wanted, yet have their own space.

"It's the only way I could tolerate being married," the wife had told me.

The wives of herders had their own financial independence. They had separate herds from their husbands. They were able to hand down an inheritance of their own to their children. The lifestyle of these herders had essentially remained the same for centuries, yet from a Western perspective they had the most modern of relationships.

My favorite time with the herders was in the morning, when over bowls of fresh, warm milk and pots of rice slathered in melted homemade butter the men and women would greet one another with a long list of questions.

"How was your night? How is your tiredness? How is your body? How is the dew? How is the cold? And how is your patience?"

The last question they ask because no one ever has everything they want in life, so how is your patience with not having it all?

CHAPTER 21

Your Turn

SUMMER WAS IN full swing. School was out and the kids left the house each morning for surf camp. Jellyfish season was blooming and our young surfers had to maneuver around blobs that were invading the water. Luther got stung so many times he learned the word for "vinegar" in Wolof so he could buy a bottle at the little beach shack that sold bean and egg sandwiches. The local surfers taught him to pour it in his stings to relieve the pain.

Todd seemed content to watch the kids surf from the sidelines. He was in the water less now, focusing more on his work and hitting the road more often. He even took the kind of vacation he loves, something he hadn't done since before we had kids. He went to northern Congo with friends to hike and camp in the absolute wild, in one of the only forests that has never been logged or inhabited by humans. I was happy he had the opportunity to go.

While he was away, the kids and I learned a litter of puppies had been born in the American embassy parking lot to a stray dog that roamed there. It took very little for the kids to convince me we needed one. We picked out a sandy-colored brown puppy with a splotch of white on her chest. She vomited all over us on the car ride home.

A lot of times it seemed the days Todd and I were together in Dakar were spent pulling out a giant desk calendar after we put the kids to bed, coordinating our travel plans as best we could.

One evening Maude awakened from a bad dream and came into the kitchen to find us at the table with the calendar between us.

"Am I ever going to have two parents again?" she asked.

I tried to look for stories closer to home. I reported on runners exercising in an increasingly polluted Dakar. I wrote about Senegal losing its majestic baobab trees. They were dying of thirst from rainy seasons that were shorter than ever before, or they were being chopped and burned by developers.

I stopped the car at a farm outside the city and wandered into rows of ankle-high millet plants. The field was punctuated by a single towering baobab where an old woman was hoisting a heavy stick to knock off leaves to cook in a stew. She thought I was the landlord coming to scold her. When she found out I was a journalist, she hugged me tight, the two of us laughing and swaying in a slow dance under the tree's web of branches.

With so much going on, I didn't even realize, at that point, that Todd and I had long made it past the two-year mark here. We never did pull the rip cord.

I WAS IN my office in Dakar one afternoon when the international editor called. Would I be interested in working in the Paris bureau, he wanted to know.

"Are you kidding, yes! That's the greatest job at the paper," was what I wanted to say.

But I didn't. Instead, I hedged. I knew Todd couldn't live in France and stay in his current job. His bosses already had been sending strong signals they wanted him back in New York. Paris for me would mean . . . well, Paris! But for Todd it would mean rein-venting. And that was going to be hard.

Todd and I talked through all the scenarios of how it could work for him. We simply were unable to come up with a solution that wouldn't make him miserable. I stalled giving an answer to the paper, just in case.

"Take him to Paris for the weekend," a colleague offered. "He'll see how wonderful it is."

But Todd had been to Paris. He didn't want good wine and stinky cheese. He wanted a meaningful career and a happy balance of work and family.

"There's really no way this can happen?" I asked Todd.

"I thought moving abroad would be wonderful, and in many ways it has been. I know my kids so much better than I did before. And I know myself better, too. I really want to stay at my job. I want to move back to New York," he said. "And, you know, the last couple years has been all about you."

"And you want your turn?" I said.

"That seems fair, doesn't it?"

Couples taking turns with their career pursuits had always rubbed me the wrong way. It was a cycle of constant defeat for someone. But I didn't see any other way. And he was right, of course. It did seem fair.

And so I didn't take Todd to Paris for the weekend. Instead, I declined the job offer and took him to Nigeria.

We had been invited to the wedding of a Nigerian friend who was starting her own dual-career marriage. She was a small-town girl who had moved to Lagos, where she found a job as a video producer and got engaged to a professional basketball player.

"We're both not slowing down," the bride-to-be had told me. "That's what marriage means to us."

As Todd and I sat in the airport lounge, I sank into my chair try-ing to hide from him that I was feeling bad. I had carted him across the world and in some ways abandoned him as I turned in to my work and in to myself. It was time to be a team player again. I pulled out my phone, looking for solace.

"I just turned down the Paris job," I wrote Ash.

"I'm sorry," he replied. "That hurts."

"It does," I wrote. "But I'll get over it."

"I dunno. I wouldn't throw a baby bottle at you for crying over that one."

I looked up from my phone at the bustle of the airport. So many people heading in so many directions.

My phone beeped with a text.

"Ah fuck it," Ash's text said.

I burst out laughing. And I stopped feeling sorry for myself. He was right, of course. I was being a baby. I had a far better life than I deserved. But I did wind up with a bad case of mangoworms after that trip. Six of them, to be exact.

With all its detours, dramas and triumphs, our life in West Africa had been more frayed at the edges, filled with higher highs and lower lows, but we had figured out how to handle it, mostly. I even had learned to manage my trips and not stay away for too long. My toothpaste was my guide: when I really had to squeeze to get out the last of the toothpaste from one of those travel-sized tubes, I knew it was time to go home.

In my work I had failed to find what I was looking for in many instances. But those failures had pushed me in other directions, to find a set of truly incredible women everywhere I went.

Their frustrations didn't manifest in the testosterone-soaked dynamiting of oil pipelines in the Niger Delta or in murderous rampages to try to create a religious state. But the signs of female rebellion were everywhere, as subtle as the little birds flying from cages emblazoned on the fabric of dresses worn on the streets of Dakar and as brazen as the unexploded bombs lying at the bottom of a well in the Nigerian countryside.

My reporting had some impact. A Nigerian senator had called for an investigation into the rapes of women in camps. Nigeria's president had vowed to start a new initiative to find a way to stop the use of women as suicide bombers. People sent small donations to help some of the victims I wrote about. Balaraba, the would-be suicide bomber, got accepted to a health-worker training program, a stepping stone toward nursing school.

Victories in this job didn't come through prizes or acclaim from editors, or from the number of clicks on my stories, but in getting through to people who never before had paused to relate to this region. My high school classmates from Nebraska who shared my stories on social media. My friends who went to Ivy League schools who considered for the first time what life might be like in West Africa. Friends and relatives who came to visit us in a part of the world they never thought they'd make it to.

"Can't tell you how much I so appreciate and love your vivid glimpses into a world so far from—and yet, in some cases—so close to home. Thank you!" one reader wrote to me.

In Brooklyn, we had lived a hectic life that put each of us in survival mode. We blew it up and moved across the Atlantic. Life was hectic in Dakar, of course. I got punched in the face. Zola asked for an arranged marriage. Luther sacrificed a sheep during a playdate. Maude perfected her skills at inducing mom guilt. Todd got dissed by the stay-at-home crowd.

Yet our move had taught me that, as far as you wander from home, it is not entirely possible to reinvent your life. This is true largely because I am a 40-something mother of three and no amount of restlessness will change that.

But I came to respect the differences in how other women make their way through a dramatically unrecognizable set of circumstances—and the similarities that I found we all shared as wives, workers or mothers, regardless of privilege or poverty, wealth or wartime. Except the women I had met navigated their worlds with superhero-like aplomb.

Todd and I still didn't know exactly how this next chapter of our life would play out. If I was being honest with myself, the siren call of a more humdrum life in the suburbs was beginning to have some appeal. But we were more of a family now. It felt like together we could handle the suburbs, we could handle the city, we could go overseas again, someday. We could handle anything.

EPILOGUE

IT WAS RAINY season in New York, and some of the streets of Brooklyn were flooding. Amid the downpours and the stifling heat, power outages had darkened parts of the city. New York was dealing with disease outbreak, as cases of measles were spreading. It all seemed familiar.

My phone buzzed with a text from Shehu. He was helping me track down Balaraba. He had stayed in touch with her through the months to make sure she was OK. I had never stopped thinking about her defiance of blowing up people in the name of Boko Haram. I still wanted to find a way to tell her story. I pitched my editors on the idea of a follow-up story about the girls who refused to become bombers. They were interested. But Shehu was upset.

I wasn't quite clear what the problem was. But I was stunned when I saw the words he wrote: "I'm furious."

It didn't sound right. Shehu had never before been mad at me. I dialed his number.

"I think I'm just confused," he said in a weakened voice. "I'm so sick."

Shehu's diabetes had become much worse. For the past year I had visited his home outside Abuja whenever I passed through, sitting with him on the floor of his jasmine-scented living room, his swollen legs stretched out in front of him and his eyes nearly useless. We talked about old times we had spent reporting together, but he was looking forward to the future. His new plan: ostrich farming. He even had arranged to buy two baby ostriches for me.

"I keep thinking," he had asked me, "how are you going to get them home with you?"

Instead of plotting international ostrich trafficking, we tried to strategize a way to find better care for him. Another journalist who had worked with Shehu helped me arrange for him to see doctors in the U.S. while he was there for a visit. The news wasn't good. The disease had advanced so much it had damaged his heart. His condition only worsened over the course of the next few months when he returned home. He trudged to diabetes clinics and various doctors across Nigeria. Nothing made him feel better. He had drained his savings and even wound up selling his farm to pay his medical bills.

Now, Shehu was insisting he needed heart surgery. It was an operation I wasn't sure he could survive, but I told him I would help. I raised money from reporters and photographers across the world who had worked with him and wired him the cash. We agreed I would visit on my way to Maiduguri to meet with Balaraba later in the week.

I was getting ready for the trip when I received the worst of news. Before he could even schedule the surgery, Shehu had died. I was devastated.

Telling Balaraba's story was important, and I knew Shehu would agree. I carried on to Maiduguri. Being there without him was destabilizing, like being on a listing boat where I just couldn't seem to find my sea legs.

The city was emptier now. The government had rounded up farmers and told them to go home, sending them back to a countryside that was still crisscrossed by militants. Huge markets that used to be jam-packed had few customers. All the suicide bombings in the past had made people afraid to shop.

My car pulled up to Balaraba's house and I sploshed through mud puddles lining the walkway of a small concrete compound to get to her room. I pulled back the curtain that served as a door to find Balaraba hovering over a little girl sitting with a friend, stacking bottle caps on scraps of multicolored fabric. It was Balaraba's daughter, Hairat. Her baby had survived after all.

Balaraba's rescuer, the woman with the civilian vigilante force, had helped track down her daughter and other family. She had stayed by her side through all her treatment, from the moment she pulled Balaraba from the smoldering Boko Haram camp through the months recovering in the hospital and in a psychiatric facility after she began suffering seizures from the awful memories of her time with the militants. The woman also helped cushion the blow from even more bad news: While Balaraba was being held in the camp, her brother had dropped out of university to join the civilian vigilante force in her honor, to help fight Boko Haram. After one particularly brutal clash with the militants, he went missing.

Now that she was better, Balaraba from time to time trekked to the hospital and morgue to see if she could find news of her brother. Was he dead? Had he been kidnapped like her? So far she had turned up nothing.

At home, people in Balaraba's new neighborhood were whispering about the young woman who had returned from spending time with Boko Haram. Her own sister had kept her distance since she was rescued. Maybe Balaraba was one of *them,* they all apparently thought. One elderly neighbor even told her no one would ever trust her again and that she would be better off dead.

Balaraba didn't have the energy to defend herself, to tell them all that she had been through. She simply tried to ignore the stares and snickers when she passed.

"They can say what they want to say," Balaraba told me. "I know my conscience is clean, and I have a life to lead."

She was making a business out of selling cold drinks to passersby on her road. She used the proceeds for tuition to make sure little

Hairat got a proper education. Balaraba decided she wanted to have her own pursuit, too, to keep her mind off the awful memories and the neighbors who were saying terrible things. She enrolled in nursing school.

"When I was sick, so many people helped me," she said. "I felt like it was time for me to give back."

Balaraba loved nursing school. She had a good network of fellow students. She was learning how to deliver first aid and administer vaccinations. But taking a taxi to school was expensive. So Balaraba often walked, a trip that took about ninety minutes one way. She had already worn out one pair of shoes from all the walking. She held up the canvas pair with warped black soles. She needed to get to the Monday Market to buy a new pair.

And so, on a sunny Maiduguri afternoon, Balaraba, the woman who outsmarted one of the deadliest terrorist groups in the world, put on her hijab and marched into the very market she once was sent to blow up, where she bought a new pair of walking shoes and carried on.

ACKNOWLEDGMENTS

ALL MY LOVE and thanks go to Todd, Luther, Zola and Maude for putting up with me and my absences, and with my street animals. I owe my deepest gratitude to Shehu Abubakar, for his wisdom, guidance, friendship and good humor, and consider myself lucky to have ever existed in his orbit. Jaime Yaya Barry and Ashley Gilbertson possess unending empathy, humanity and talent that made them rock-solid partners in journalism. My editor at Ballantine, Pamela Cannon, my agent, Eric Lupfer, along with Jacqui Banaszynski and Nell Casey, offered clear-eyed guidance. A special thanks to early readers, including Jim Lynch, Michael Rothfeld (my original work husband), Rod Searcey, Emily Lynn Osborn, Christopher S. Stewart, Kim Barker, Nikita Stewart, and Laura Boushnak. I'm grateful for fellow working mom Motoko Rich, who has been an invaluable friend and colleague, and for my Brooklyn moms crew, who welcomed me on visits home. And cheers to the overseas press crews in Abuja and Dakar. Samuel Aranda and Grace Anne Turner were lead members of Team Jaime and have two of the biggest hearts in the world. Much of my work could not have happened without Moussa Yahaya, Charlotte Arnaud, Ousmane Balde, Harriet Dwyer, Adam Higazi, Abdullahi Umar Eggi, Moussa Abdoulaye, and Nana Boakye-Yiadom. I am indebted to Julia Mbaebie and Ada Afoluwake Ogunkeye for fun times in Lagos, and to Julia's family for the warm welcome in Umuisim. I can't thank Kathryn Bigelow enough for her support of Balaraba and the girls who refused to become suicide bombers. And to my New York Times bosses past and present, especially to Greg Winter, thank you for making me a better writer and a better person.

ABOUT THE AUTHOR

DIONNE SEARCEY was the West Africa bureau chief for *The New York Times* from 2015 to 2019. She won the Michael Kelly Award for courage in international reporting, the Society of Professional Journalists' Sigma Delta Chi award for international reporting for her coverage of Boko Haram, and a citation for her work by the Overseas Press Club. She and a team of *Times* journalists were nominated for an Emmy for her stories on Boko Haram. She joined the *Times* in 2014 to write about the American economy after working for ten years at *The Wall Street Journal,* where she was an investigative reporter, national legal correspondent and covered the telecom industry. She has worked as a political reporter at *Newsday* and *The Seattle Times* and was a reporting resident at the *Chicago Tribune.* She started her career as a crime reporter at the City News Bureau of Chicago. She was raised in Wymore, Nebraska, and lives with her husband and three children in Brooklyn, New York.

Facebook.com/dionnesearcey
Twitter: @dionnesearcey
Instagram: @dionnesearcey

ABOUT THE TYPE

This book was set in Bembo, a typeface based upon an old-style Roman face that was used for Cardinal Pietro Bembo's tract *De Aetna* in 1495. Bembo was cut by Francesco Griffo (1450–1518) in the early sixteenth century for Italian Renaissance printer and publisher Aldus Manutius (1449–1515). The Lanston Monotype Company of Philadelphia brought the well-proportioned letterforms of Bembo to the United States in the 1930s.